ER

D0656617

ISLANDS IN DANGER

Alan Wood and
Mary Seaton Wood

NEW ENGLISH LIBRARY

First published in Great Britain in 1955 by
Evans Brothers
New edition complete and unabridged,
published in England in 1957, and
reprinted, in 1958 and 1960, by
Streamline Publications Limited.

FIRST FOUR SQUARE EDITION 1965
Reprinted March 1966
Reprinted June 1967
New NEL edition June 1969
New edition March 1973
New edition April 1976
Reprinted June 1980
Reprinted April 1984

NEL Books are published by
New English Library,
Mill Road, Dunton Green,
Sevenoaks, Kent.
Editorial office: 47 Bedford Square, London WC1B 3DP

Made and printed in Great Britain by
Collins, Glasgow

0 450 02935 2

CONTENTS

APPENDICES

BIBLIOGRAPHICAL NOTE

Some books referring to the Occupation are mentioned on p. 12. Others are H. Wyatt's *Jersey in Jail* (Ernest Huelin, 1945), and R. C. F. Maugham's *Jersey Under the Jackboot* (W. H. Allen, 1946).

Victor Coysh's interesting booklet, *Swastika over Guernsey* (The Guernsey Press, 1955) was published too late to be mentioned in the preface.

The life of Geoffrey Appleyard was told by his father in *Geoffrey* (Blandford Press, 1948); that of Lassen in *Unge Anders Lassen*, by Fritjof Saelen (A. S. John Griegl, Bergen, 1951).

Among the few important articles, etc., dealing with the Occupation are the following:

Report of the Controlling Committee of the States of Guernsey (*Billet D'Etat*, for May 23, 1945).

Report of the Committee for the Control of Essential Commodities, Guernsey (Appendix to *Billet D'Etat*, for June 5, 1946).

C. W. Duret Aubin: Enemy Legislation and Judgments in Jersey, *Journal of Comparative Legislation and International Law, Third Series*, Vol XXXI, Parts III–IV, November, 1949, p. 8.

John Wadsworth, *In Duty Bound* (Midland Bank Ltd.).

A. L. Banks and H. E. Magee: Effects of Enemy Occupation on the State of Health and Nutrition in the Channel Islands, *Monthly Bulletin of the Ministry of Health*, September, 1945. (The Report referred to on p. 10).

PREFACE

THE Germans first set foot as conquerors on British soil on a hot sunny day in June, 1940, when Luftwaffe officers landed on the Guernsey airport and drove (some of them by taxi) to their rooms in the Royal Hotel.

The Channel Islands remained the only part of British or American territory to be occupied by the Germans during the War. For nearly five years what happened there remained a secret, with nothing but strangely conflicting rumours emerging. Tales reached England of mass deportations, of concentration camps and near-starvation; others told a different story of contented collaboration by the island authorities, joint dances and football matches with the German troops, and a black market in which both islanders and Germans were growing rich.

Even after the war, much of the mystery remained. In spite of the fascinating interest and obvious importance of the story of the only British people under Nazi rule, there seemed a strange disposition not to probe too deeply into exactly what happened. It remained one of the few untold stories of the war. The only books on it came from local writers, soon after the event, with inevitable omissions on the most important points. None could deal with more than one Bailiwick, nor check wartime rumours in the light of subsequent research in Britain and Germany. The British Official War Histories ignored the islands, owing to their lack of actual operational importance. No official history was commissioned by the island authorities themselves.

In these circumstances, our publishers asked us to make an independent inquiry into what happened during the five secret years. We were given the utmost help and co-operation in all the islands, with all the access we asked to official documents; we took our inquiries to Germany, interviewing members of the occupying German forces;

and we tracked down, through the labyrinths of different Government Departments, such captured German documents as survive.

In spite of the help we received, our task was not easy. The facts first hidden by wartime secrecy and censorship were still hard to find under a haze of faulty memories. In September 1945 an official report on the Occupation, by two Whitehall medical experts, commented that "Lapses of memory of recent events were fairly frequent," and added "the causes were probably psychological." We learnt that such effects could be lasting. Almost every incident seemed to evoke a cloud of conflicting recollections. An enemy occupation, with its bodily hunger and constant mental anxiety, with its humiliations and its temptations, can play strange tricks with the memory.

Gradually, however, the pattern of events seemed to fall into place. The detailed facts, as we think we have found them, are less lurid than the extreme versions, all black or all white, given by different sides; but they are rather more interesting. We have tried to set them out as plainly as possible, without passing any judgment: for no one who has not lived under an enemy occupation should pass judgment on those who have. It must be left to the reader to decide his own answers to these questions: If the Germans had occupied Britain or America, would they have behaved in the same way? And would the reader himself have acted any differently from the people in the Channel Islands?

*

We have many acknowledgements to make: first of all to the present Bailiffs of Jersey and Guernsey, Sir Alexander Coutanche and Sir Ambrose Sherwill, for the assistance given to us by themselves, their colleagues, and their officials.

In Jersey, Sir Alexander Coutanche gave us free access to his files during the Occupation, and we filled in various gaps in talks with himself and Lady Coutanche. We were also greatly helped by Mr. C. W. Duret Aubin, the Attorney-General during the Occupation; Mr. Edgar Dorey, who was responsible for the island finances; Mr. Cecil Harrison, the present Attorney-General; his brother Mr. Arthur Harrison, Managing Editor of the *Jersey Evening Post;* and Mr. William Troy, the *Post*'s News Editor. The facilities extended to us included the full use of the Newspaper Files Department of the *Evening Post* office.

In Guernsey, Sir Ambrose Sherwill not only gave us access to the official documents we required, but also allowed us to see some private papers of great historic interest, including the diary he kept in the Cherche Midi prison in 1940, and some notes on the Occupation written in the prison and in Laufen Internment Camp. To him, to Lady Sherwill, and to Sir John Leale we owe a great debt. Mr. Louis Guillemette, the present States Supervisor, and Secretary to the President of the Controlling Committee during the Occupation, allowed us access to the personal diary which he kept from 1942 to 1945. We received much help from Mr. Frank Carey of the States Office; Mr. W. H. Arnold, the present Attorney-General; Inspector Lamy, Head of the Island Police; and the Very Rev. E. L. Frossard, the Dean of Guernsey.

To the Editor and Proprietor of the *Guernsey Evening Press* we owe thanks for every help and facility, including access to Occupation files, and files of the German Army newspaper—the *Deutsche Guernsey Zeitung*.

In both Jersey and Guernsey we were able to see the files of the German *Feld-Kommandantur*, by courtesy of the responsible officials who now held them. Unfortunately, other files were systematically destroyed before the capitulation.

To the Dame of Sark, Mrs. Robert Hathaway, and to the present Seneschal, Mr. William Baker, we are indebted for written material and much other information. In Alderney, we were helped by Captain Charles Richards, and were able to consult Brigadier French, the leading figure in the early events.

Throughout, our attempt was to see the Occupation from the point of view of ordinary citizens as well as of officialdom. Private individuals who gave us their personal recollections are too numerous to list in detail. We have, wherever possible, obtained our information on all events at first hand from those who took part in them; and we can only express our grateful thanks to the many willing helpers we found, and the many friends we made.

We owe a special obligation, however, to those who sent us diaries which they kept secretly, often at considerable risk, throughout the Occupation. One diary, written in great detail by Mr. L. P. Sinel of the *Jersey Evening Post*, was published by that paper in book form. For unpublished diaries we wish to thank Mr. F. Barton, Mr. W. Bougourd, Mr. G. Falla, Mr. S. Grant, Mrs. Gulliver-Cradwick, Miss Margaret Smallwood, and Mr. A. Topley.

We are particularly grateful for generous assistance offered to us by fellow authors. Mr. Ralph Mollet showed us the original diary on which he based his *Jersey Under the Swastika* (Hyperion Press, 1945—a careful summary of the facts as known at the time). Major F. H. L'Amy allowed us to consult a manuscript containing much interesting information on the Occupation of Jersey. Mrs. Dorothy Higgs gave us further facts on subjects mentioned in her booklet, *Guernsey Diary* (Linden, Lewis, Ltd., 1947). Mr. Victor Coysh, the Guernsey historian, generously lent us his own compilation of Occupation material. We are also indebted to Miss Noel Streatfield and Mr. M. de Havilland Gerachty.

Among books concerned with the Occupation, other than those already referred to, we should like to mention Ralph Durand's *Guernsey Under German Rule* (The Guernsey Society, 1946), and V. V. Cortvriend's *Isolated Island* (Guernsey Evening Press, 1947).

For much courteous assistance and advice, and for facilities in consulting official records in England, we owe a great deal to Lt.-Commander B. S. Mallory and Mr. B. Rawlings, of Amphibious Warfare Headquarters; to Mr. J. C. Nerney, and Mr. M. B. Thornton of the Air Ministry Historical Section; to Admiral Bellairs and the staff of the Historical Section of the Admiralty; and to others in Whitehall.

We owe part of our description of the final German surrender on board the destroyer *Bulldog* to Frank King, who represented the combined British press on the occasion.

We have a special debt to Miss Kathleen Nowlan, who was a journalist and teacher of languages during the Occupation of Jersey, and after the war worked with the British forces occupying Western Germany. Miss Nowlan helped us in many different ways, allowing us to see her own account of the Occupation, and undertaking a long journey in Germany to act as interpreter during interviews with those who held responsible positions in the German administration of the islands.

In addition, we have derived particular benefit from the thorough research of Mr. J. D. Lawson, and his detailed knowledge of the German sources. We have also been greatly helped in translations by Miss Erna Genzmer.

We are grateful for additional assistance on special points from His Excellency Sir Thomas Elmhirst, Major-General J. M. R. Harrison, Captain Sir Gerald Curteis, Brigadier John Durnfold Slater, Captain B. H. Liddell Hart, Brigadier Desmond Young, Major Sydney Cotton, Commander M. G. Saunders, Colonel F. W. Marriette, Major Rybot, Senator Krichefski, the Baronne de Coudenhove, Princess Radziwill, and Major-General Herbert Jones of the U.S. Army Department, Washington. On the German side, for documents and other information, we may particularly thank General Graf von Schmettow, the Baron von Aufsess, Admiral Friedrich Rüge, and General Blumentritt.

We were fortunate throughout in being given access to official documents, and receiving a great deal of assistance from both official and unofficial quarters, without being asked to accept any restriction on the independence of our judgments. It must be made clear, with more than conventional emphasis, that the sole responsibility for any statements or opinions rests with the authors.

ALAN WOOD

MARY SEATON WOOD

July, 1955

BESETZUNG BRITISCHER KANALINSELN DRIN-
GEND UND WICHTIG.

The capture of the British Channel Islands is necessary
and urgent.

> —Signal from Berlin to all Operational
> Commands in the West, June 20, 1940.

Landed Guernsey 2140 hours. No opposition.

> —Telephone message from Luftflotte 3 to
> Flag Officer Northern France, 1 a.m.,
> July 1, 1940.

The permanent fortifying of the Channel Islands to convert them into an impregnable fortress must be pressed
forward at maximum speed.

> —Adolf Hitler, October 20, 1941.

We can consider it certain that our Forces will be able
to hold out in the islands beyond the year 1945.

> —Admiral Krancke, Flag Officer
> Commanding German Naval Group
> West, December 31, 1944.

TERMS OF UNCONDITIONAL SURRENDER BY
THE GERMAN COMMANDER OF THE ISLANDS
SIGNED 0715 ON THE QUARTER DECK OF BULL-
DOG . . . BRITISH TROOPS NOW LANDING.

> —Signal from H.M.S. *Bulldog* to C-in-C.
> Plymouth, May 9, 1945.

CHAPTER I

ISLANDS AND ISLANDERS

In the month of June in the year 1940, triumphant German forces reached the French coast and saw British territory within their grasp. There was Jersey, the largest and nearest of the Channel Islands, ten miles from France. There was Guernsey, the second largest, further away and to the North, and only visible on a clear day; with the tiny island of Sark, and the even tinier islands of Herm and Jethou, coming in between. Finally, further still to the North and eight miles from Cape de la Hague, was Alderney, only slightly bigger than Sark.

There were pleasant islands for any conqueror to tread, and a fine setting for any story; islands famous all over the world for two things, their cows and their romantic charm. It was a man from Jersey, Sir Philip Carteret, who gave New Jersey its name; and when early pioneers crossed the Atlantic they took with them Jersey and Guernsey cattle, which still remain two of the main dairy breeds in America. But cattle raising is now of secondary importance in the islands that the cows came from. Jersey concentrates on early potatoes and outdoor tomatoes, Guernsey on tomatos in glasshouses. For the rest, they earn their livings in two curiously diverse ways: as strongholds of mediaeval legend, and as sanctuaries for modern tax dodgers. In the first way they attract tourists. In the second way they attract millionaires.

Even to this day, a mediaeval language survives in the local forms of *patois;* which (you are told) are the kind of French used by William the Conqueror. The islands were part of the Duchy of Normandy when William conquered England in 1066; so the islanders can call England "our oldest possession." When the rest of the Duchy reverted to France, they stayed loyal to the English Crown; but their Norman origin always gave them a certain independence, and they kept many special laws, customs and names.* In particular, they remained free from the English taxation system; Jersey, for instance, had no income tax until 1928, and then only at fourpence in the pound. And so, superimposed on semi-mediaeval farming communities, came an influx of wealthy businessmen and retired professional people, bent on escaping from the British Chancellor of the Exchequer.

The islanders themselves remained much the same. When, in 1944, the British Intelligence Service was providing background information about enemy-occupied countries, an anonymous officer wrote that "The Channel Islanders are of Celtic extraction, and one of their chief characteristics is a typical Celtic reticence. As in most small, fairly isolated settlements, inter-marriage has produced a number of half-wits, and the people are exceedingly clannish . . ." Unfair and somewhat exaggerated, but with a trace of truth: and it may be wondered how such clannish people reacted to summer trippers and itinerant financiers. But, among other peasant traits, they had a keenly developed sense of the value of money; and most of them soon learnt to welcome a tourist or a millionaire with a smile.

Among those who believed in moving with the times, and deliberately attracting more of these modern sources of wealth, was Mr. Alexander Coutanche, Bailiff of Jersey at the beginning of the war, Bailiff throughout the German occupation, and still Bailiff at the time of writing. The Bailiff is a kind of combination of Lord Chief Justice, Speaker, and Prime Minister: when he presides over the States, or local Parliament, his chair is placed seven inches

* For instance the "States" (Parliament), "Deputy" (Member of the States, or M.P.). "Procureur" (Attorney-General). "Jurat" (a member of the Royal Court and—until recently—of the States as well).

higher than that of the Lieutenant-Governor, the representative of the Crown. The Bailiff, in short, is the most important person in the island: and since Alexander Coutanche plays a leading part in our story, the sooner we get to know him the better.

A remarkable man, Coutanche, able and ambitious; dark and swarthy, something of a thruster and a showman, but with a saving sense of humour. He came from a long-established Jersey family, and his Scottish mother was a descendant of Robert Bruce. During the first world War —after being rejected because of a systolic murmur of the heart—he became an executive in a Birmingham munitions factory, and later a Claims Officer in Belgium, where he edited a dictionary of Anglo-Belgian law. Appointed Bailiff of Jersey in 1935 when only forty-three, he threw all his energies into developing the island. Year by year it attracted a richer haul of finance companies, rentiers and tourists; so that it was not only the largest of the islands— with forty-five square miles to Guernsey's twenty-five—but also by far the richest.

The years of success matured the young lawyer. Still black-haired, still irritably impatient at times, Coutanche had nevertheless developed a confident command of his own domain, with an urbane charm, making him the most amusing and gestureful of raconteurs when he relaxed over the dinner table or stood before his fireplace. He was to prove a decisive man in an indecisive situation, when the tourists for whom Jersey had catered were to stay away, its resident millionaires were to go away, and the Wehrmacht were threatening to arrive instead. . . .

The Bailiff of Guernsey, the elderly and conservative Victor Carey, was a rather different type. Head of the clan of Careys who first came to Guernsey in 1340, he deplored the ugly glasshouses with which the tomato-growers littered the island, and the tourists which filled it each summer. His thoughts would turn regretfully to the old days, when Guernseymen used to make honest livings by farming, fishing and privateering.

Carey's father had won renown as a General, but he

himself was too old in 1914 to have any martial experiences. Pink-faced and chubby, somewhat highly strung and absent-minded, he had pursued a placid if undistinguished career as a lawyer, when in 1935 he had suddenly become Bailiff, on the unexpected death of his predecessor. At the time he was already sixty-four, and already elderly and vague for his years; but his gentleness and kindliness, and an innate courtesy and charm, were certain to make him a benign and popular figure. Of course no one knew, in 1935, that the new Bailiff's duties would include coping with an armed German invasion. . . .

One might imagine that the Channel Islands, left behind by a freak of history as British outposts beside a foreign shore, would have strong common interests and sentimental attachments between themselves. Unhappily, Jersey and Guernsey are divided by centuries of traditional rivalry, half a joke and half serious, derived from diverse origins, and old feuds over fishing grounds. And the best that can be said about the feeling against Jersey in Guernsey, is that it is nothing compared with the feeling against Guernsey in Sark and Alderney.

The little island of Sark has always believed in going its own way and catering for nothing and nobody; although, like Alderney, it belongs to the Bailiwick of Guernsey. Sark is Sark, self-confident in its fame, which it owes to the flowerful beauty of its bays in springtime, its curiosity value as the last feudal state in the world, and the renown of its legendary ruler, Mrs. Robert Hathaway, the Dame of Sark. She inherited her title from her grandmother, widow of a Guernsey businessman who had bought out a former Seigneur of Sark who went bankrupt. Among the gifts which she brought to her unique position at the Seigneurie were wit, intelligence, courage, charm, and a knack of making people do what she wanted.

One of the Seigneurie's most admirable edicts was the banning from the island of motor cars: so the Dame of Sark can be described as the only feudal ruler in history to ride a bicycle. Mrs. Hathaway was lame from childhood, but this never stopped her cycling, or dancing, or hunting, or doing anything else she wanted; and the determination with which she overcame her disability may well have contributed to the force of character which was to keep even German invaders severely in their places.

Mr. Robert Hathaway was the Dame's second husband. He was a lean and convivial American who came to England to fly with the R.F.C. in the First World War, became a naturalised British subject and joined the sporting firm of Spaldings. One day in the 1920's, Mrs. Hathaway—then a widow with six children by her first marriage—had gone to see Hathaway in London to ask for some introductions before a visit to America. Hathaway met her boat when she returned, and took her out to dinner eight nights running. On the eighth night he proposed. Four days afterwards they were married, and Hathaway became Seigneur of Sark, where he had only one sorrow. The thing he was keenest on was golf—he liked his job with Spaldings because it carried a perquisite of free golf balls—and Sark was too small and intensively farmed to have any sort of golf course.

Unsuspecting visitors were sometimes surprised to find the island's feudal Lord talking with a broad American accent; usually, however, Hathaway preserved his incognito when out walking, replying to any tourist's questions with "Sorry, I'm a stranger here myself."

The main leadership of Sark was still exercised by his wife. Like all strong personalities, Mrs. Hathaway aroused violent antagonism as well as loyal admiration. The six hundred inhabitants of this tiny island were all divided into pro-Hathaways or anti-Hathaways, feuding between themselves with the bitter feeling which only small communities know. These two main camps were sub-divided in turn by subsidiary feuds and counter-feuds, the members of each faction being ready to tell the most scandalous tales concerning the other. It might be said, in fact, that the main occupations of Sark society were bridge-playing, scandal, and liquor; in contrast, for instance, to Alderney, which mainly concentrated on liquor. . . .

The people of Alderney, some nineteen miles to the

North, had a common bond in their permanent grudge against Guernsey. Alderney always blames Guernsey for everything; and, since it had fallen on bad times, Guernsey was blamed plentifully.

For a hundred years Alderney had some importance as a bleak and bare garrison island, a fortified British outpost against France. But France, in the fiickle fashions of high diplomacy, had turned from an enemy to an ally. The last British troops left Alderney in 1930, and thereafter it sank into stagnant isolation. Apart from primitive subsistence farming, its only important occupations were granite quarrying, exporting young pedigree calves to Guernsey, importing alcohol, and a little smuggling on the side. All water was still drawn from wells in buckets; electric light was a little-known luxury.

At the time our story begins, the leading citizen of Alderney, known as the "Judge," was Frederick French, who had retired there after distinguished careers as a soldier in India, and as a school teacher and school inspector in Burma: his ability had soon made him head of the island administration; but Judge French was not universally popular, still having something of the schoolmaster about him. He had a habit of addressing meetings of the islanders, not with the conversational "Ladies and Gentlemen," but with the single peremptory word "People!"

Such then were the islands, and such the leading characters on them when war broke out in September, 1939. There was the go-ahead Alexander Coutanche in Jersey, the elderly Victor Carey presiding over Guernsey, the Hathaways on Sark, and Judge French in Alderney. All were to react in widely different fashion when the test came.

CHAPTER II

SMOKE ON THE HORIZON

The Channel Islands are not much interested in what goes on anywhere else. When war was declared in September 1939, there can have been few places among the belligerent countries which felt more remote from it.

The islanders who had volunteered to fight in 1914 had won great distinction and suffered grievous casualties, but the life of the islands themselves had been little affected. The only difference expected this time was that, with the threat of air raids hanging over Britain, the safety of the islands would make them a popular refuge. Anxious English parents tried to send their children over to boarding school at Victoria College in Jersey, or Elizabeth College in Guernsey. And when a new tenant was wanted for Jethou, the tiny island next to Herm in the Bailiwick of Guernsey, a London agent advertised: "A peaceful island to be let for the duration. . . ."

Among the arrivals in Jersey were a group of about two hundred young men, mostly conscientious objectors, answering an advertisement in the *Peace News* for workers to help with the potato harvest.

Meanwhile the more adventurous of the young islanders were joining up, as they had done in 1914; and the island authorities, as in 1914, broke with tradition, by introducing conscription. By the ancient rights of the islanders, they could not be called upon to serve overseas "unless it be to accompany His Majesty in person for the recovery of England, or that the person of His Majesty should be taken prisoner by the enemy." These rights were waived;

by June, 1940, a number of young men had registered in Jersey, but hardly any had been called up.

For local defence in Jersey there was the Royal Militia. The Militia in Guernsey was disbanded to let its members volunteer for more active service; but another home Militia was formed from the over-age and the unfit. Nobody had the slightest real expectation of any enemy attack: in fact, any signs of martial preparedness were treated as something of a joke. Fleet Street got some light paragraphs out of the news that Alderney, facing up to the realities of war, had repealed an Act which forbade fishing on Sundays; that the male population of Herm had been halved because one of the two men on it had joined up; and that the defence of Brecqhou, a tiny island adjoining Sark, was being undertaken by seventy-year-old John Perio, on his donkey Carabelle. John Perio patrolled the island equipped with a rifle, tartan kilt, tunic and gumboots; and he declared to a reporter: "I'm not having any Nazi planes over here. Just let Old Nasty try. I'll fix him . . . Clarabelle didn't like the uniform at first, but she's used to it now."

It was typical enough that a national newspaper should interview John Perio: if the islanders showed little prescience of what lay ahead of them, they merely reflected the fatuous vacuity of the whole Phoney War period. One can smile now at the advertisement in the British Press in March 1940, describing Jersey as "the ideal resort for war-time holidays this summer". But the Jersey tourist industry was no blinder than Sir John Anderson, His Majesty's Secretary of State for the Home Department, who made a cheerful announcement on March 14 that there would be no passports, exit permits, or any other requirements or restrictions for summer travel to the Channel Islands.

Then came the lightning German invasion of Norway, of Holland, of Belgium; then came Dunkirk; then came the swift and irresistible German advance across France.

The Channel Islands, like Britain, were shocked into action; but there was little effective that they could do

22

about preparing for invasion. German and Austrian nationals were interned indiscriminately. Signposts were taken down. In Guernsey, a machine-gun post was set up to protect the telephone exchange, and one Lewis gun was hopefully mounted on a tripod at St. Peter Port, to act as the town's anti-aircraft defences. Jersey instituted a Home Guard, the "Jersey Defence Volunteers", drawing on the many retired Army officers who had settled there; and a group of die-hard enthusiasts prepared Fort Regent, high on a hill above St. Helier, for a last-ditch defence. Water, food and ammunition were laid in for a siege, and a wireless transmitter installed to keep contact with England.

On Saturday, June 8, 1940, the Lieutenant-Governor of Jersey, Major-General J. M. R. Harrison, warned London that he was sure the Germans would come on to attack the Channel Islands if they captured France. The next day, in the islands, a pall of smoke was seen rising from the horizon till it almost eclipsed the sun. The French were burning oil storage tanks, the shadow reaching as far south as Jersey; and Harrison reported the first signs of panic there. It was decided in London to send both Jersey and Guernsey a battalion each, and to withdraw various training units in the islands.

The Island Bailiffs had hesitated to bother the British Government about their own peril at a time when Britain itself was preparing for invasion. But on Friday, June 14, after the Germans had crossed the Seine at Quillebeuf, Alexander Coutanche felt he could delay no longer. He was not a man to sit waiting while other people decided his own fate and that of his island. He went to see General Harrison, the Lieutenant-Governor, and they rang up Whitehall first thing next morning.

The Whitehall Department responsible for the Channel Islands was the Home Office. The Head of the Channel Islands Division of the Home Office was C. G. Markbreiter, a man of scholarly gifts, charm and culture, whose two passions were music and mountaineering.

Markbreiter seemed a little surprised when, on the Saturday morning, he had the telephone call from Coutanche.

The Germans, said Coutanche, had crossed the River Seine; weren't people disturbed about the danger to the Channel Islands? He gathered from Markbreiter's tone that people were not unduly worried, but Markbreiter said he would ring up the War Office and ask what they thought. Half an hour later Markbreiter rang back, a rather different sound in his voice. Would Coutanche fly to London at once for urgent talks?

Coutanche went home, packed a suitcase, put a flask of brandy in his pocket, and waited. All that day he waited, but no phone call came. Then, when he got back from Church on the Sunday morning, something else happened. He was asked to go straight away to see General Harrison at Government House.

Under pledge of secrecy, Harrison told Coutanche that the B.E.F. was being brought back from France in what was to become a second, but less publicised Dunkirk. British troops under Alanbrooke had returned to try to hold a line with French troops under General Georges, but the plan had to be abandoned because the French force disintegrated. So Coutanche was told that all the small boats in Jersey should be collected and sent to St. Malo to help get Alanbrooke's troops out.

As they left for St. Malo, British troops came into Jersey. An anti-aircraft battery and a machine-gun battalion landed and proceeded, with an encouraging amount of bustle and energy, to site guns and dig slit trenches. When two Hurricane squadrons came in to the airfield, and the arrivals even included the advance staff of an Air Force NAAFI, it looked as though the new defensive strength had come to stay.

The evacuation of St. Malo was successful, a few soldiers going to Jersey, but most to England. And the British War Cabinet, with the B.E.F. saved, had time to consider one of its next problems: what to do about the Channel Islands.

On Sunday, June 16, the Chiefs of Staff had decided to recommend to the War Cabinet that the islands should be demilitarised. General Harrison, the Lieutenant-Governor of Jersey, was an old personal friend of General Dill, the

C.I.G.S., and when Dill telephoned to ask what he thought, Harrison gave his view that, in the interests of the civilian population, the islands should not be defended.

By this time it was too late for Coutanche to join any discussions in London: he had to stay at his post. To get things moving, he sent an able deputy in Edgar Dorey, a senior member of the Jersey States, who flew off in a chartered plane on Monday, June 17, armed with special credentials signed by the Lieutenant-Governor. In London, Dorey went straight into conferences with Markbreiter and Sir Alexander Maxwell, the Permanent Under-Secretary at the Home Office. They agreed that the only real problem was how many people could be got out of this islands before the Germans came. Dorey guessed that about a third of their total population, say 30,000 out of 90,000, would want to leave: a surprisingly good guess. They rang up the Ministry of Shipping and found there were still some ships left over from those got together for Dunkirk.

War or peace, the Treasury is the Treasury: and no Whitehall discussions are complete without the Treasury having a say. It was meticulously agreed that the cost of the evacuation would be paid for by the islands, and in fact careful accounts were kept of every item, so that the Treasury could present the bill after the war.

The day afterwards—Tuesday, June 18—Dorey telephoned Coutanche from London. It was virtually decided, said Dorey, that the islands were to be demilitarised. They were now only waiting for the official decision, which, of course, could only be made by the Cabinet. When, demanded Coutanche impatiently, would the decision be made? Impossible to say, replied Dorey, there were a good many other points on the agenda before the Channel Islands came up. But he suggested that Coutanche should start plans for evacuation.

Next day, Dorey flew back in an R.A.F. Anson, landing in Guernsey before going on to Jersey. He delivered copies of this letter from the Under-Secretary to each of the Lieutenant-Governors:

                              Home Office,
                                19th June, 1940.
Sir,
   I am directed by the Secretary of State to say that, in
the event of your recall, it is desired by His Majesty's
Government that the Bailiff should discharge the duties
of Lieutenant-Governor, which would be confined to
civil duties, and that he should stay at his post and
administer the government of the Island to the best of
his abilities in the interest of the inhabitants, whether
or not he is in a position to receive instructions from His
Majesty's Government.
The Crown Officers also should remain at their posts.
                        I am, Sir,
                           Your obedient servant,
                              A. MAXWELL.

   These specific orders to the Bailiffs, Attorney-Generals
and other officials, telling them to carry on in their jobs,
were sometimes forgotten by some of their subsequent
critics.

                         CHAPTER III

                    THE DAYS OF PANIC

   In Jersey the States had held a number of secret sessions.
On Wednesday, June 19, they were addressed by the
Lieutenant-Governor, General Harrison. He announced
that the demilitarisation of the island was probable.
Coutanche then discussed plans for evacuating civilians. If
it should turn out that there was not enough room for all
who wanted to go, they should "follow the old rule of the

sea, 'Women and children first'". To these should be
added men of military age.

A few minutes after the Bailiff had finished, the
Lieutenant-Governor rose to speak again. He had been
summoned from the Chamber a few minutes earlier to take
a telephone call from the War Office. The British Government, he now announced, had decided on complete demilitarisation of the Channel Islands.

(It is believed that the only important dissentient from
this decision was Churchill himself, who argued that the
Navy could protect the islands, and that it would be most
grievous, in view of their long association with the Crown,
to give them up without a fight. The Admiralty, however,
declared that the islands were untenable with the Germans
holding Brest and Cherbourg, and Churchill had to give
way.)

The two fighter squadrons left the Jersey airfield on the
same day—only two days after they had arrived.

The news that Jersey was to be left defenceless, plus the
ominous-sounding reference to "women and children first",
produced something approaching a panic. When it was
announced that those wishing to evacuate should register
their names at the Town Hall, a long queue formed,
stretching along towards West Park. But it was completely
orderly, with only three or four policemen to marshal it;
and an enterprising ice-cream seller did good business
pedalling up and down the line.

Next day, with people coming into St. Helier from
country districts, the queue was even longer. The first
evacuation ships arrived to take off evacuees that same
morning, and the piers were thronged, with little regard for
the elaborate system of priorities. Trying to steady the
situation, Coutanche and others issued a public declaration
that they were staying at their posts and that their families
were staying in Jersey with them. It was signed by
Coutanche as Bailiff, C. W. Duret Aubin as Attorney-
General, Cecil Harrison as Solicitor-General, Edgar Dorey,
and other leading members of the States.

An even more forthright attack on the panic was made

by Dorey, just back from London, who told the States he had been filled with disgust at the "cowardice" of some of the "rats and rabbits" who were leaving. Coutanche, decrying rumours and false alarms, declared that the Union Jack would fly from Fort Regent until he pulled it down personally; so long as it flew, everything would be all right.

Such efforts at rallying public opinion had little avail.

A run on the banks continued. Withdrawals were limited to £25 each, and two special envoys brought with them £300,000 in banknotes from England to supplement cash reserves. Meanwhile the banks sent all securities in their holding to England.

There was still a chaos of people arriving in throngs on the piers, many of the wealthier driving up and abandoning their big cars on the quay. One lady presented her Rolls-Royce to a young man standing about, before boarding the dirty cargo boat which was to take her to England. Meanwhile, some of the poorer people crowding the ships were carrying all they had saved of their worldly goods in bundles done up in tablecloths.

Even in the worst of the rush there was still room for some humour. "I didn't wait to clear away the breakfast things," one housewife was heard saying. "I wonder if the Jerries will wash up for me?"

There were similar scenes at the Airport, where evacuation planes took off until stopped by a warning of high flying enemy aircraft. The Airport Controller, Mr. Charles Roche, was busily refusing gifts of cars or money or anything else for unfair priority on the passenger lists.

One of the most moving sights was the queue of men, women and children bringing their cats and dogs to the Jersey Animals' Shelter to be destroyed. Two officials and two nurses worked from seven in the morning until ten at night to kill over six thousand cats and dogs, only stopping to allow the carcases to be cleared away in lorry loads.

It was soon found hopeless trying to keep to priorities among evacuees. Finally it was announced that there were enough ships for everyone. As soon as people realised that they could leave if they wished, half of those who had registered decided that they would not go after all; and by the end of the Friday the worst of the rush was over.

Spirits were not raised, however, by the departure on the Friday of the last remaining soldiers—what was left of the troops who had come in less than a week before. (General Harrison, hearing over the telephone from Whitehall of the decision to demilitarise, had looked out of the window and seen ammunition still being unloaded in the port.) Every man in the Royal Jersey Militia volunteered for overseas service, and it left as a unit. General Harrison, as a soldier, was ordered to leave too,* and under the circumstances his departure had less than the usual Vice-Regal formality, Coutanche and Duret Aubin and others coming down in their shirt sleeves, on the sweaty summer day, to see him off. That same afternoon, Coutanche was sworn in as Lieutenant-Governor in his place.

Some sort of tranquillity now came to the island; but it was the eerie quietness of houses left suddenly empty, perhaps with the remains of a last meal still on the table; of shops with well-stocked shelves but no one behind the counter; of petrol pumps, inns and cafés left deserted in eloquent disarray.

States Departments and individuals went through their files, burning documents which might give information, or offence, to the Germans. File copies of the *Jersey Evening Post* for the previous two years were destroyed.

Workmen began to take down poles which had been put up the week before, with wires strung between them, to stop enemy planes landing on broad St. Aubins' Road.

Finally there arrived a detachment of the Royal Engineers. The young officer in charge saluted Coutanche smartly and announced, "We've come to blow you up, sir". A little taken aback, Coutanche asked mildly exactly what was to be blown up, and why. The officer waved a hand with an expansive gesture—dock installations, airport, gasworks, power stations, waterworks, anything else Coutanche cared to suggest. Anything that might be of

* His subsequent duties included responsibility for A.A. training in England.

29

value to the Germans. The young officer beamed with enthusiasm to think of the joys of demolition and destruction ahead of him.

To this, Coutanche retorted that there were about forty thousand people left on the islands, and how would they get on if essential services were destroyed? For these people Coutanche was responsible. If demolition were definitely ordered, Coutanche would obey orders: otherwise nothing was to be touched. The young officer departed in a sad state of disappointment and deflation, and Coutanche heard no more.

During the same days there had been a similar rush and panic in Guernsey, where evacuation caused even more heartbreaks—because when it was not certain whether there would be enough ships, it was decided that the children should go first. The result was the breaking up of many families: in some cases temporarily, in others for five long years.

On the Wednesday, June 19, it was arranged with Whitehall that three ships would arrive at 6 a.m. the next morning to take off school children.

Teachers were told to explain the position to parents, and report back on how many wanted their children to leave. Hurried meetings were called at all the schools.

Already explosions and the sounds of war could be heard from the direction of France as the parents were asked to decide whether their children should go or stay. Many fell into an anguish of indecision. They realised, or many of them did, the imminence of air raids on English cities, if not an actual invasion. On the other hand, there was terror at the thought of Nazi rule. In the end most parents decided to let their children go and commended them, with silent hopes and fears, to the care of their teachers and the goodness of the English who were to be their hosts.

Some parents were so successful in hiding their forebodings that most younger children took it all as a great adventure. It was harder to deceive the older ones. Mrs. Cortvriend, in her book *Isolated Island*, tells of the last meal eaten with her own pale and subdued children who

30

kept asking: "But what about you, Mummy? You and Daddy *will* come afterwards, won't you?" She writes:

"We hated telling them the wretched truth that it would probably be years before we saw them and months before we heard of them again, and said evasively: 'We will if we can, but you mustn't worry about us'.

"The small daughter of a friend, told the same thing, comfortably assured her parents that she would do her best to forget all about them."

So the sad night passed, and before dawn the children were going down to the harbour. Few in Guernsey slept in those early hours; for even people who had no children lay in bed listening to the quick little footsteps passing down the streets and lanes, and the sleepy, excited chatter.

By six in the morning nearly two thousand were waiting at the quayside. Major Sherwill, the Attorney-General, who had arranged the evacuation with the Home Office, awoke at his home, and telephoned the police. He was told that the children were all safely aboard. He had turned on the taps to have a bath when he had doubts: and telephoned the harbour to learn that the children were all down there, miserable in the cold of the early morning, but there were no ships. He jumped into his car and drove down.

Even when the Sea Transport Officer in charge of the evacuation arrived on the *Antwerp*, and two other ships followed her into port, the confusion did not end. Troops and military equipment were being embarked at the same time as the children; and crush barriers were erected in case any panic-striken people rushed the boats. It was half-past two in the afternoon before the last of the children went aboard.

Meanwhile the next batches waited in their schools for their marching orders. These hours of delay added to the indecision of some parents. They came and went throughout the day in a torment of uncertainty, taking their children home, then bringing them back to be evacuated, sometimes changing their minds as many as three or four times.

By nine o'clock on the Friday morning, however, five thousand children had been sent away. Elizabeth College, unlike Victoria College in Jersey, transferred *en bloc* to England, the masters and boys marching down through the streets to the quay. A great silence came upon the island. Major Sherwill, the Attorney-General, wrote in his diary in almost Biblical words: "No children play in the streets, and mothers mourn the loss of their children and will not be comforted."

Meanwhile adults had also been registering for evacuation; the queue packed the narrow streets of St. Peter Port, with people fainting in the heat and the crush. But, as in Jersey, the carefully compiled priority register had to be scrapped, and free sea passages promised for all who asked.

When the news spread round that the Lieutenant-Governor, General Minshull Ford, had left with the last of the Armed Forces on Thursday, frightened crowds thronged the piers. Jurat the Reverend John Leale, a former Methodist minister and a leading member of the States, appealed to them for patience. Major Sherwill saw that rifles and bayonets would be available in emergency, and criticised the "unnecessary panic". A newly appointed Information Officer placarded the town, on his own initiative, with such slogans as "NO PLACE LIKE HOME", "CHEER UP!" and so on. His efforts were supplemented by a private citizen who put up posters saying "DON'T BE YELLOW". Thanks partly to these gibes, the last two evacuation ships went back to England again almost empty.

CHAPTER IV

"TWO SUITCASES FOR EVERY NOSE"

In the final upshot, about a fifth of the people of Jersey were evacuated, and about half of Guernsey—figures which faithfully represented the way Coutanche and Dorey in Jersey had thrown their influence against evacuation, and the way Carey and Major Sherwill on Guernsey had tried to keep an even balance, saying that it was up to every man to decide for himself whether he should go or stay.

Sark and Alderney provided even more striking examples of the way in which, at a time of fear and crisis, everyone will follow automatically whatever strong lead is given. In Sark, Mrs. Hathaway set her face against evacuation, and nearly everybody decided to stay. In Alderney, Judge French favoured evacuation, and almost everybody went.

Mrs. Hathaway went over to St. Peter Port during the critical days, and was appalled at the panic. She found that the High Street was packed with winding queues of anxious people drawing money from the banks. The States offices were in confusion; and one of the few people who had any idea of what was going on was a young clerk, Louis Guillemette, who was then the Bailiff's secretary.

The Dame returned calmly to her island. She had some knowledge of the Germans, and could speak and write their language fluently. She did not believe there would be atrocities if the Sarkees went quietly about their own business. Finally—and it was a tenet of faith—you did not leave your land.

So, on Sunday night after church, Mrs. Hathaway called together all the islanders and told them, in a spirited address, that she meant to stay. Those who wished, she said, could be evacuated; but those with a stake in the land should 'stick by it. "I'm not promising you it will be easy," she said. "We may be hungry. But at least there will always be fish and rabbits." Afterwards she was to look back ruefully on these words; for fishing off the mined coast was to be severely restricted, and the guns needed to shoot the rabbits were to be handed over to the Germans.

But that evening, as her few hundred islanders gathered to hear her, her voice was confident and sure; and perhaps, from what they knew of her, some suspected that she might prove a match for the Germans. That evening William Carré the Sénéschal—chief official of Sark—went round asking the names of those who wanted to be evacuated; but the response was small. Mrs. Hathaway telephoned Louis Guillemette in Guernsey, and said that no special boat would be needed.

Some English residents, however, decided to go. Among them was Major Breen, who knew more than most people what the Second World War was about. Formerly British Press Attaché in Berlin, he resigned in 1937 as a protest against "appeasing the wrong German Government at the wrong time". He had met many Nazi leaders, remembering in particular one conversation with Himmler, when he protested against the atrocities in the concentration camps. Himmler denied nothing; he simply explained without shame that every nation had sadists and perverts, and that the Nazi policy was deliberately to use them in crushing any opposition, to secure a strong united Germany. Breen was now determined that he would never submit to Nazi rule if he could help it; so he and his wife packed their suitcases and made for England and freedom in their yacht, offering a passage to anyone else who wanted to come with them. Thirteen accepted the offer.

If events in Alderney followed a very different pattern from those in Sark, there were good reasons. Mrs. Hathaway, as an islander, felt her first obligation was to stay in her island: Judge French, as a soldier and Englishman, wanted to play some part in the war. Alderney was nearest of all the islands to the approaching Germans, and it was the most isolated. As late as 1940, it still had no telephone system, and the under-sea cable to Guernsey had fallen into disrepair. Communications inside the island depended on running messages or enlisting the service (at 2s. 6d. a round) of the Town Crier. External communications were by wireless. During the crisis the use of the wireless was discouraged for security reasons. The people of Alderney were isolated, with nothing but fears and rumours to guide them.

While England was remote and cut off from communication, the enemy was literally in sight. Only eight miles separated Alderney from France, and on a clear day you could watch the traffic on the French coastal roads.

It was on June 9 that a thick pall of smoke, the same smoke from burning oil that had been seen as far away as Jersey, literally darkened the sky in Alderney, and cast an ominous frightening shadow of approaching peril. As the Germans came nearer and nearer, the sounds of battle could be heard by day, and the flashes of gunfire and explosions could be seen by night.

Fear was spread further by the arrival of frightened refugees in fishing vessels from France. They came with crucifixes nailed to the masts, babies wrapped in shawls, and brooms and pots and bundles of clothing heaped in the bottoms of the boats.

Early in the war the British Army had set up a machine-gun training centre in Alderney. On Sunday, June 16, the men were suddenly ordered to leave at twenty-four hours' notice. Most ominous of all, next day the hurriedly departing soldiers carefully smashed up the lorries and cars they left behind them, plain enough indication that the Germans were expected to arrive soon. The people of Alderney felt themselves deserted with the enemy on top of them.

The ship *Sheringham* arrived from Guernsey to take off evacuees. At this time the official view in Guernsey was that only children could be evacuated; the orders were

35

that the *Sheringham* should only take children (and men of military age) from Alderney. But in Guernsey, when the *Sheringham* came back again almost empty, it was hastily assumed in the confusion that this meant that nobody else in Alderney wanted to come.

No other evacuation ship was sent. Moreover, even the *Staffa*, the regular supply ship between Guernsey and Alderney, did not arrive—the crew had gone on strike and refused to risk the run. Alderney now felt completely cut off, deserted and forgotten. There was only enough flour to last for fourteen days, and no yeast for baking it into bread. Judge French sent a fishing boat down to Guernsey asking urgently for yeast. In Guernsey, there was yet another misunderstanding: the request for yeast for baking was taken as confirmation that the people of Alderney had decided, like those in Sark, to stay in their island.

In fact, the more Judge French thought over the position, the more he felt that everyone should go. They seemed cut off indefinitely from supplies of basic necessities from Guernsey (though the Army had left behind some valuable food stocks). There were no reserves of money in the banks: French worried about what would happen if their cash ran out on the pay-day after next. And, as a military man, he realised that Alderney was different from Sark.

Being the nearest point to England, it was likely to be heavily fortified as a stronghold. A mere 1,400 civilians, many elderly and therefore useless as labour, would only be a problem to feed. Would it not be only natural for the Germans to shift them all to the Continent? And if the people had to leave their homes anyhow, would it not be better to leave for England and freedom before the Germans came?

Thus reasoned Judge French: but on Friday, June 21, another event made the last attempt at reasoned consideration impossible. It was learned that a Trinity House vessel, the *Vestal*, was coming to take off the keepers of all the lighthouses round the Channel Islands. This, it was felt, was the end: the lighthouses would never be abandoned unless the last moment had come, and the Germans might arrive at any minute. Judge French's car was stopped and he was almost mobbed in the streets by angry men, demanding what he was doing to save them and their families.

The captain of the *Vestal* happened to be a personal friend. Long after midnight, Judge French went down to see him in the harbour, and asked him, when he reached St. Peter Port, to send a letter and cable to the Admiralty. (Wireless messages still being forbidden for security reasons.) Both letter and cable requested that, if the Admiralty thought the Germans were certain to occupy Alderney, enough ships should be sent immediately to take off the entire civilian population.

On the Saturday morning, Judge French sent the Town Crier round the island to summon a meeting on the playing field beside the Grand Hotel, known as the Butes. Standing on a lorry he addressed his fellow islanders, over a thousand strong, and gave a grim picture. Food, he said, was running out, and the Germans were fast approaching. In his opinion, the position was "extremely dangerous", and the island was certain to be occupied: if the Admiralty sent ships, it would mean that the British Government thought the same. There would be no chance to take furniture or bulky possessions. Rich and poor, said the Judge, must be treated alike. Every man, woman and child would be allowed two suitcases each—as he put it, "two suitcases for every nose". Anything which could not go into two suitcases would have to be left behind.

A voice asked: "What about our cattle?"

There would be no possibility, said the Judge, of taking them. When they got to England he would try to get a cattle ship sent for them.

He ended: "Do we go, or do we stay? Whatever we do, let's all do the same. Let's go together or stay together."

Judge French's words were passed on to those on the outskirts who had not been able to hear everything, and they broke up into small groups and talked things over between them.

Then a voice from the back shouted out, "Let's go!"

The shout became a chorus, and the voices became a roar.

Judge French announced he would post men to watch for the rescue ships, and that the moment they were sighted, the Church bells would be rung. That would be the signal for every man to make the decision to leave his home, leave his native island, leave all his life's possessions except for what could be carried with him in two suitcases.

What if, after all, the Germans should arrive before the ships from Britain came to save them?

Judge French gave orders for the police to collect all firearms and weapons of any kind, and to lock them in the gaol. Then he could give the Germans the key, with an assurance that there would be no resistance.

Early on the Saturday afternoon, the *Vestal* returned from Guernsey. The Captain told French that he had found such confusion in St. Peter Port that he had not been able to send off the message to the Admiralty. But the *Vestal* stopped in the Channel a ship on its way into Britain, and asked her captain to 'phone the Admiralty with the message when he reached the port.

Meanwhile the *Vestal* had taken a letter from Judge French to Major Sherwill in Guernsey, complaining bitterly that no evacuation ships had been sent. It was the first time Sherwill realised that the people of Alderney, unlike Sark, wanted to leave. He spoke to the Sea Transport Officer at St. Peter Port, who refused to risk sending ships to Alderney, because it was now within range of the German guns. So Sherwill asked Louis Guillemette to telephone the Ministry of Shipping in England.

French slept that night at the Grand Hotel. It was early in the morning when one of the men posted down at the harbour ran up and greeted him breathlessly with words heard on many an historic occasion: "Sir, the Navy's here!" Six small cargo boats had arrived in the harbour, under the command of an officer of the R.N.R. And so, at twenty minutes to five on that Sunday morning, the bells of St. Anne's Church rang out to wake and warn the people of Alderney to leave their homes, some of them for ever. The order was passed round that embarkation had to be finished by eight o'clock that morning, and the rush began.

Actually it was noon before the last ship sailed, but the time was still short enough. Cattle were set free or shot, when the farmers remembered. Cats and dogs were taken to the butcher to be killed. Some people had already taken the precaution, the day before, of burying valuables and bottles of liquor in their gardens.

Judge French went to all the branches of the banks and peremptorily demanded all the money in their safes. One of the Managers, a little shocked at this departure from orthodox financial behaviour, protested "That's banditry!" But French thought he would need money when he reached England to get food and shelter for his people, and the notes, of course, were duly handed back in time.

French himself had his own thirty-ton yacht lying in the harbour. He left it behind, going on one of the cargo ships with two suitcases like everyone else, while his wife left behind her silver and other precious household goods.

The ships of the evacuation party reached Weymouth safely that afternoon and evening. Only a dozen or so people from Alderney did not join the ships. Judge French cabled Major Sherwill from Weymouth, asking that a boat should be sent up from Guernsey for them. The Guernsey lifeboat went the next day, but some of the Alderney people still refused to leave.

French reported to the British authorities that he had left about 600 head of cattle on the island; but he was told that the cattle would have to be collected from Guernsey.

On the Tuesday, Major Sherwill sent up a rescue team, including St. John Ambulance men, to Alderney. They took orders that any people remaining on the island were to be removed, "by force if necessary," to Guernsey. Their other task was to bring back all the cattle and pigs they could rescue.

They found pitiful evidence in Alderney of the exodus two days before. Cars, lorries, and a motor bus were deserted on the quay. The doors of deserted homes swung in the wind. In one house a half-packed suitcase told how someone had not even taken his permitted quota of luggage with him, presumably owing to some last-minute fear of being left behind. One meal had been interrupted with a bread knife half-way through a loaf.

Cows were desperate for milking. Some, driven crazy with pain, had to be shot: the others could only be eased with difficulty of their thick and sour milk, small quantities at a time.

Some of the cattle and pigs had been left shut up in yards and sties without water or food. Sprawled on the pavement of the main street of St. Anne's lay the body of a horse, which had broken its neck trying to jump out over a fence.

With some difficulty a shipment of cattle was sent off to Guernsey on the *Isle of Alderney*, and then another, and then a shipment of pigs. According to Alderney complaints later, there were also shipped off a number of articles which the Guernseymen helped themselves to from the houses and shops, as well as bottles of liquor from the pubs; but then, Alderney always blames Guernsey for everything.

Getting off the remaining human beings was what caused the greatest difficulty. Sometimes the Ambulance men, with their steel helmets, were mistaken for German soldiers; one woman locked herself up at the sight of them. Others declared obstinately for some time that they would never leave their homes. The most recalcitrant of all was an old soldier named Frank Oselton, with tough projecting eyebrows and a fierce expression. Having sent off his wife and family on the Sunday, he had determined to stay on his farm whatever happened. What finally moved him was not the persuasion of the St. John Ambulance men—whom he greeted by flourishing a shotgun—but the discovery that, when he had been up in town, his own cows had been rounded up and shipped off to Guernsey. He followed, in a state of fury, to demand them back; and so he was in Guernsey when the Germans finally landed.

CHAPTER V

MAJOR SHERWILL GETS READY

The preceding pages frequently mention the name of Major A. J. Sherwill, the Guernsey Procureur (or Attorney-General). He had emerged as the strongest man in the island, and was to become its most interesting figure. For, as Guernsey happened to be the first island at which the Germans arrived, it was he more than anyone else who set the pattern which the Occupation was to follow.

Sherwill—later Sir Ambrose Sherwill—was a man who would have been outstanding in any community. Tall and handsome, with great personal charm and courtesy of manner, he looked exactly what he was: an embodiment of the finest qualities of the traditional English gentleman. In the First World War he had won an M.C. by an act of reckless courage, going out into the open to send an urgent signal with an Aldis lamp to an isolated detachment, and thereby bringing on himself a flail of shot and shell which left him wounded in nine places, but still miraculously alive.

Few people, meeting him for the first time, would have guessed at the remarkable story behind his career. His family came from Devon and his father had a butcher's shop with a small dairy farm. During school holidays Sherwill drove the butcher's cart on its rounds. His childhood was not happy, and his mother had to work as a dressmaker for a wage of five shillings a week. Nevertheless, young Sherwill, with no money and no influence behind him, embarked on the long course of study necessary to become a lawyer. Even when his pertinacity and ability had carried him through to become an Advocate, even with his outstanding war record as an officer in the Buffs, the past still dogged him. Memories die hard in a small, snobbish community. In the 1920's a friend proposed him for the exclusive Grange Club, and he was turned down simply because he was his father's son.

When he was going to marry his delightful and unconventional wife May, from the old-established Carey family, her grandfather told her "You will be a social leper." May Sherwill was undaunted, and by 1935 she had seen her husband become His Majesty's Procureur, or Attorney-General. Soon afterwards the highest position in the island, that of Bailiff, fell vacant; and normally the succession passes to the Attorney-General. But Sherwill was still comparatively young for the post; and with five children to bring up and no private means, he could not have afforded to take it. The honour of appointment as leading citizen fell to the elderly Victor Carey.

When the crisis came in 1940, Guernsey turned instinctively to Sherwill for leadership. He was not ideally suited for the task, as he himself protested. Though shrewd, he sometimes had touches of the kind of political naïvety and over-trustfulness to which exceptionally brave men are often prone; and he might carry courage to the point of indiscretion. But the people of Guernsey felt quite rightly, in June 1940, that courage was the quality that counted most—particularly when, as in Sherwill's case, it was a cheerful courage which could find a jest in the grimmest situation. (Sherwill had a characteristic, unusual among lawyers, of loving to pull people's legs.)

It was Jurat the Reverend John Leale, as a senior and well-trusted Member of the States, who made a suggestion whereby Victor Carey remained Bailiff, but the Bailiff and the States fell into the background for the duration in favour of a "Controlling Committee" of eight men, each responsible for one aspect of administration. The States approved this plan on Friday, June 21, when the evacuation was still going on, and appointed Sherwill as the Committee's President, with power to select its other members.* Thus it was that Major Sherwill became the first man to receive German invaders on British soil.

The main line of policy had been settled well in advance. The Rev. John Leale, for instance, had declared in the States that "should the Germans decide to occupy this island we must accept the position. There must be no thought of any kind of resistance. Should there be any resistance, we can only expect that the more dire punishment will be meted out."

Victor Carey, as Bailiff and newly appointed Lieutenant-Governor, was emphatically of the same opinion. "The one thing I was keen about," he explained afterwards, "was that there shouldn't be any sort of resistance movement." This probably also represented the views of Coutanche in Jersey. But though the policy was decided, rightly or wrongly, it was one which could be followed with dignity, or with servility: and it remained to be seen whether the Germans would respect an attitude of non-resistance, or whether they would take advantage of it. Few people had more hopes than fears.

Apart from military occupation, there was the threat of starvation. For years Guernsey had largely earned her living by importing tourists and exporting tomatoes. From the proceeds of these activities, she paid for food and other essentials to be sent from England. How the people could stay alive, when cut off from the source of revenue and the source of supplies, was a question no one could answer.

Fears and forebodings were increased by the continual arrival of pitiful boatloads of refugees on their way from France. According to one typical story retailed, someone had seen German soldiers going down the streets of a

* Jersey also set up a "Superior Council" on similar lines, but with the difference that Coutanche, the Bailiff, was President.

French town, amusing themselves by slashing off the arms of children with their bayonets.

Major Sherwill left his office and spent some hours simply walking about St. Peter Port, talking cheerfully to everyone he met, and trying to steady their fears.

Sherwill reminded people that not only was he himself staying, but his wife and younger children were staying with him. Any qualms which the Sherwills may have felt themselves were successfully hidden. Perhaps May Sherwill's worst time was when, having made the decision to keep her children in the island, she had to listen to a family friend prophesying, for over an hour, about the horrors that awaited them. Sherwill himself was called to a meeting of all the island doctors, who demanded that Guernsey should be completely evacuated. He could only calm them by promising that one of them could put their suggestions direct to the Home Office—which agreed with Sherwill that it was out of the question.

There followed days of suspense, of waiting apprehension. A German reconnaissance plane flew backwards and forwards over the island, apparently surveying its defenceless state at leisure. Then, on Friday June 28, came a sudden murderous attack which seemed to confirm the worst fears about what was to be expected from the Germans.

On that pleasant summer evening, hundreds had gathered in the main street of St. Peter Port to hear a speech by Major Sherwill, and were just dispersing. Lorries had lined up at the port with boxes of tomatoes to be sent to England on cargo ships; also in the harbour was the *Isle of Sark,* a regular mailboat which had started running again in the lull after the previous week's evacuation. A party had just landed from Alderney with cattle and farm animals. Suddenly there came the spatter of machine guns and the shriek and explosion of falling bombs, as German planes dived over the harbour. Petrol in the tomato lorries spread sheets of flames, burning to death some of the drivers who had gone under their lorries for protection. To add to the horror, the horses and cattle from Alderney panicked and

44

plunged loose; while the pulp from the smashed tomato boxes mingled in a macabre way with blood from the dead and wounded.

Other planes went machine-gunning the island at random. Haymakers were fired at in the fields. An ambulance carrying the wounded to hospital was spattered with bullets, which killed one of the wounded and severely injured one of the attendants. The Guernsey lifeboat, with its obvious markings, was machine-gunned out at sea, and the son of the coxswain killed.

With the island demilitarised, the only defence came from light anti-aircraft guns on the *Isle of Sark*.

At the same time there was a raid on Jersey, fortunately less fierce, though just as sudden and frightening. Bombs were dropped on St. Helier harbour; other planes machine-gunned the townsfolk as they fled for shelter.

The next day, when doctors and civil defence officials drew up the list of casualties, they reported twenty-nine killed in Guernsey and nine in Jersey, in addition to many wounded in both islands. They were not impressive figures compared with the mass bombing later in the war, but small communities do not think in mass terms. Every man and women throughout the islands knew someone among the dead and wounded, and grief came like an angry cloud.

Jersey sent the Home Office a telegram reporting the raid—its last official communication. Guernsey gave an even more direct report. When the raid came, Major Sherwill was in the Controlling Committee's office—which had been set up in deserted Elizabeth College—and he was talking on the telephone to Markbreiter at the Home Office. Sherwill held up the receiver so that Markbreiter could actually hear the machine-gun fire.

In the shock caused by the bombing there was unbridled bitterness over this unprovoked attack on a defenceless people. The raid on Guernsey was sarcastically called "The Battle of Tomatoes," and the Germans afterwards were at pains to say they had mistaken the tomato lorries for lorries carrying cases of ammunition. This may have been true. The pilots officially reported the bombing of "*LKW—und*

PKW—Kolonnen"—"Columns of heavy vehicles and cars." But in any event, the raid was no more a crime than most acts of war, although just as much of a tragedy.

One cannot defend the machine-gunning of a lifeboat and an ambulance, unless they were sheer mistakes: but ships loading food for England were a perfectly legitimate military target. The wrath of the islanders was because they knew they had been demilitarised, and assumed the Germans knew it too. But, although a reconnaissance plane had flown over only the day before, without being fired upon, this was merely regarded by German Intelligence as "somewhat suspicious," and the conclusion reported that "even if Flak defences are not strong, it is certain that the islands are occupied militarily."

It seems that the British Government had been trying to get the best of both worlds by demilitarising the islands; and then not saying anything about it, in the hope that the Germans would not notice. The policy of secrecy was even carried to the extent of not publishing a message from the King which ascribed the demilitarisation to "strategic reasons," said it was in the interest of the islanders, looked forward to victory and promised that "the link between us will remain unbroken."

Though obviously meant to encourage his subjects in the islands, this Message was kept out of the papers, being simply read over a loud speaker in St. Peter Port, and posted on different notice boards in Jersey.

Local newspapers had already, in fact, announced the demilitarisation. But it appears pure coincidence that the capture of the islands was ordered from Berlin* the next day (Thursday, June 20). The Germans had no Intelligence agents in the islands, and always assumed that they would be defended. One proposal was for a German landing by six battalions (three against Jersey, two against Guernsey, one against Alderney), supported by two engineer companies and a naval assault group.

An inter-services conference was called in Paris for

* See Appendix I.

Saturday, June 29, the day after the raid, to plan the landing.

The air raid, however, had an immediate effect; and this itself might be regarded as a justification of it from the German point of view. Following an urgent suggestion by Sherwill over the telephone to Markbreiter, in their talk while the bombs were still falling, the demilitarisation was announced on the B.B.C. nine o'clock news the same Friday night.

Extraordinarily enough, the German monitoring service was so inefficient that this announcement was missed. The German Service Chiefs were actually meeting in Paris on the Saturday when they heard of the demilitarisation from a Reuter message. Next day it was officially confirmed by a note from the Foreign Office sent through the American Embassy in London.

As Whitehall had feared, this was accepted as an immediate invitation to the Germans to step in. The German Navy, responsible for taking the islands, was still suspicious of the demilitarisation report, and decided to carry on with its plans as before. But the Luftwaffe, either by chance or design, went straight ahead, and greatly mortified the Navy by getting in first.

It was generally taken for granted that the Occupation had been inevitable in any case. But, after all, the islands remained islands. German documents show that only the most rudimentary thought had been given to mounting an operation to take them; and the German High Command might well have preferred to keep all the necessary landing craft for the projected invasion of England. The main reason for saying the seizure of the islands was inevitable comes not so much from strategic logic, as from the later evidence of Hitler's personal interest in them.

The only real criticism of the surrender of the islands came from a bellicose octogenarian Jerseyman, Lord Portsea. In a series of speeches in the House of Lords, he talked of "sheer stark poltroonery", and said that the British Government had behaved worse than Pétain in leaving the Channel Islanders "in the lurch". He declared: —

"If the islands could not have been held by the islanders for more than a few weeks, those men at least could have died, and died decently, instead of being slaves. And how could they have died better? ...

"Fancy a British Government, an English Government, saying the odds were too great, a thousand to one, people would be killed! We have heard of Agincourt ..."

These gibes must have been particularly galling to Churchill. But the fact remains that any real resistance on the islands could only have been an embarrassment to him: obliging him (as happened in Greece) to send reinforcements more needed on other fronts. And as will be seen in due course, it turned out the Channel Islands could not have done more towards winning the war than they achieved by the simple process of being occupied.

CHAPTER VI

GUERNSEY: CONQUERED BY KINDNESS

In Guernsey the task of meeting the Germans, whenever they should choose to arrive, had been entrusted to Inspector Sculpher, head of the Island Police. He was furnished with a letter addressed to "The Officer Commanding, German Forces, Guernsey", which said that the island had "no armed forces of any description".

It was soon after midday on Sunday, June 30—a peaceful sunny Sunday—that Inspector Sculpher, waiting with this letter in his pocket, was told that a German plane had landed on the airport. By the time Sculpher arrived, however, the plane had disappeared again.

It appeared that the pilot had climbed from the cockpit, cautiously approached the airport buildings, found it empty, and walked in. Three British planes suddenly appeared overhead. The pilot ran out of the building in such a hurry that he left his revolver behind, climbed into his plane, and made off.

The airport was once more deserted, apart from some cows rescued from Alderney, which had been put there as the best emergency grazing available.

It was between six and seven that four German transport planes approached and—after scaring away the cows, the only obstacle—came in to land, Sherwill rang up Markbreiter at the Home Office, and said goodbye till after the war. Inspector Sculpher set off again, and was able to hand over his letter to Captain Liebe-Pieteritz, the first German officer to receive the surrender of British soil. The invading party and later reinforcements were escorted, in police cars and a commandeered taxi, to the Royal Hotel.

Meanwhile, Major Sherwill had been waiting at his home —Havelet House, near the house in St. Peter Port where Victor Hugo lived for many years. It was some time after seven when a German Luftwaffe officer, accompanied by a Guernsey policeman, came to the door.

Following the air raid on the Friday, Sherwill's children had been put to sleep in the front hall, which was thought to be the safest part of the house. So, when the German officer arrived, Sherwill tiptoed out and said, "I wonder if you would mind coming in the side door?"

"But why?"

The German obviously suspected a trap.

"My children are asleep in the hall," said Sherwill. "We thought they would be safer."

"But certainly," said the German. "I would not think of disturbing the children."

After chatting inside, the officer asked Sherwill to go with him to the Royal Hotel, where there were now some half a dozen of the invaders with only one rifle between them. They found that the Bailiff had still not arrived, so Sherwill and the German officer drove off together to Victor Carey's house to fetch him. Everything was still perfectly polite. On the way the officer turned to Sherwill and said, "Have a German cigarette?" Sherwill took one.

The first sign of the Occupation could now be seen—German soldiers tearing about at high speed on motorcycles on the wrong side of the roads.

Back in the Royal Hotel, they got down to business across a table in the lounge, with the aid of a Swiss hotel proprietor brought in as interpreter. They were joined by Inspector Sculpher, Captain Franklin the Harbour Master, and others. The Germans read out a long list of complicated orders and instructions, which no one felt in much of a condition to take in: the only one which impinged without question on at least one of those present was the final demand of all, which said simply and shortly: "The full cost of the Occupation will be borne by the Island."

A Luftwaffe officer protested at the cows being on the runway of the airport, which he half suspected was meant as an act of sabotage; it was explained they were cows from Alderney, and it was promised that they would be removed. The officer asked what stocks of aviation spirit were left at the airport. Major Sherwill replied sweetly, "About 30,000 gallons," and waited for the officer's face to light up with pleasure before he added: "But the R.A.F. did quite a good job before they left, mixing it with sand, sugar, tar, and just about anything else you could think of . . ."

The Luftwaffe officer did not allow his disappointment to ruffle the pleasantness of the proceedings. "Ah, well," he said philosophically, "it was only to be expected."

The meeting broke up after midnight, and they went out into the lovely evening. A young German officer went back with Captain Franklin to the harbour, to be shown the wireless room, and then enjoyed himself walking round smashing all the valves with his stick.

Captain Franklin had the advantage of knowing many Germans through the international camaraderie of all sailors. When he went back to the Royal Hotel next morning, he saw a naval officer sitting by himself at a table in the lounge, and could not help laughing. He went up and said,

"Captain Koch, this is very funny. Do you know I have twice sailed on your ship?" Captain Koch had been with the Hamburg-American Line, and Franklin had travelled with him on visits to Hamburg. Koch asked Franklin to sit down and have a cup of coffee with him. Koch said: "I don't like this job any more than you do, but all we can do is make the best of it."

They went off together up the town; but Franklin soon excused himself because he could not bear to watch Koch, like so many other Germans, greedily buying up everything they found in the shops. They used specially printed and worthless "Occupation Marks", sending the goods back to Germany. Franklin returned to the harbour, and found four very young Germans there who were supposed to give him orders.

He asked one of them:
"You come from Hamburg, don't you?"
"Yes."
What job?"
"Water police."

The young German explained that he worked on the part of the harbour used by ships from Grimsby and Hull, and that he had many English friends. He commented sadly: "It makes it hard for me to work up hatred against the British."

Meanwhile the people of Guernsey were studying special editions of the *Guernsey Evening Press* and the *Star*. Each carried on their front pages a signed statement by Victor Carey as Bailiff: "The public are notified that no resistance whatever is to be offered." And there, under huge headlines, were the first German orders to be issued on British soil:

ORDERS OF THE COMMANDANT OF THE GERMAN FORCES IN OCCUPATION OF THE ISLAND OF GUERNSEY

(1) All inhabitants must be indoors by 11 p.m., and must not leave their homes before 6 a.m.

(2) We will respect the population in Guernsey, but, SHOULD ANYONE ATTEMPT TO CAUSE THE LEAST TROUBLE SERIOUS MEASURES WILL BE TAKEN AND THE TOWN WILL BE BOMBED!

(3) All orders given by the military authority are to be strictly obeyed.

(4) All spirits must be locked up immediately, and no spirits may be supplied, obtained or consumed henceforth. This prohibition does not apply to stocks in private houses.

(5) No person shall enter the aerodrome.

(6) All rifles, airguns, pistols, revolvers, daggers, sporting guns and all other weapons whatsoever, except souvenirs, must, together with all ammunition, be delivered at the Royal Hotel by 12 noon to-day, July 1.

(7) All British sailors, airmen and soldiers on leave in this island must report to the police station...

(8) No boat or vessel of any description, including any fishing boat, shall leave the harbours... without an order from the military authority.

(9) The sale of motor spirit is prohibited, except for essential services... The use of cars for private purposes is forbidden.

(10) The black-out regulations already in force must be observed as before.

(11) Banks and shops will be open as usual.

The same issue of the Guernsey *Star* was full of advertisements by local firms announcing "Business as Usual." It is true that Domaille and Sons, with some pre-vision, were advertising bicycles as "Your Best Friend in the Months to Come", at prices from £4 19s. 9d. But the Old Government House Hotel, destined to become a German "Soldiers' Home", was still promising intending patrons that "We Can Give You a Comfortable Home Free From Worry": while it was announced that the next attraction at the Regal Cinema would be Tommy Trinder in "Laugh it Off".

The funeral notices of the victims of the air raid the Friday before—they included a father and his two sons, killed together and buried in the same grave—were carefully worded, to give no possible offence to the Germans. All had the same phrase: "— —, who died last Friday. . ."

On the Monday more German troops came in, and the Occupation was completed without any hostile incident of any sort. One old hotel-keeper, a member of the Guernsey Militia, stood in his doorway with a rifle, pointing it and saying "I'll shoot the first German who tries to come in." But his family took the rifle away by force.

The demand for firearms to be handed in was obeyed, a few humorists adding to the pile by buying toy pistols at Woolworths and presenting them to the Germans.

Major-Dr. Albrecht Lanz arrived on the island as German Commandant, making his Headquarters in Government House. He was a man of education and culture, being a doctor both of law and philosophy; he was also a fine soldier, in command of an infantry battalion, who had chosen to march all the way beside his men in the Flanders campaign. At their very first meeting, Major Sherwill put down on the table all his medals from the first world war, and said, "I have been a soldier. I bitterly regret that I am one no longer. But as there isn't a rifle left on the island, I realise I must obey orders."

Sherwill afterwards ascribed his gesture to "some theatrical instinct"; but there was no doubt about its effectiveness. He and Lanz, both of them tried soldiers, formed an immediate liking and respect for each other, which was soon reflected in the form taken by the Occupation.

New Orders which Lanz issued on his arrival showed marked moderation: "The population is hereby required to retain calmness, order and discipline. If this is assured, the life and property of the population will be respected and guaranteed." The Orders actually allowed prayers at

Church services "for the British Royal Family and the welfare of the British Empire." It was true that "the British National Anthem shall not be played or sung without the written permission of the German Commandant." But this order did not apply to hearing the National Anthem broadcast by the B.B.C., the use of wireless receiving sets being permitted.

For one period, the Germans even went so far as to allow the local papers to publish the B.B.C. programmes.

The most irksome of the German regulations, and the one most strictly imposed, was the 11 p.m. curfew. It caused a special problem, for instance, to Mrs. Champion of Guernsey, wife of a special policeman and mother of nine children—the largest family left in the island. (They could not get away in the evacuation, because three of the children had chicken pox.) Since the family was too big for one house, they had been provided with two adjoining "States Houses"—the equivalent of English Council houses. With the curfew, Mrs. Champion could not go outside from one house to another if any of the children started crying during the night, so a hole had to be knocked in the connecting wall between them.

One group of citizens, caught outside the Royal Hotel at two minutes past eleven were arrested and held under guard at the hotel for the night. In the morning they were summarily fined £1 each for breaking the curfew regulations, and charged 5s. for their hotel accommodation.

But these were mere pin pricks compared with all the terrors that had been expected before the Germans came. Guernsey began to feel that, after all, an occupation was not so bad. German soldiers confounded all prophecy by their exemplary behaviour: the Germans in command treated Sherwill and the Controlling Committee with the utmost consideration and courtesy. Relations were made even smoother by Dr. Maass, a former missionary, who acted as Dr. Lanz's chief of staff. Maass had taken a diploma in tropical medicine at Liverpool University in 1931, and spoke English fluently.

It was not long before Sherwill was telling the people of

Guernsey that "There is constant liaison between German Military Headquarters and the Controlling Committee. Relations are not merely on a correct basis, they are cordial and friendly. Let no one jeopardise this by unseemly or unruly conduct."

CHAPTER VII

WHITE FLAGS OVER JERSEY

The occupation of Jersey came a day later than Guernsey —on Monday July 1, 1940. In Jersey, Sunday June 30, had passed without incident. As soon as the Germans landed in Guernsey, Sherwill tried to send a message to Coutanche, but could not get to the phone himself. Later that Sunday evening, however, the telephone rang in Coutanche's home at St. Aubin.

"This is May Sherwill. Is anything happening in Jersey? We've got the Germans here. Ambrose has just gone down to the Royal Hotel to see them. He asked me to tell you."

A little later Coutanche's phone rang again. It was Sir Alexander Maxwell, of the Home Office. He had been trying to get through to Guernsey on the telephone, but there was no reply. Could Coutanche tell him what was happening there?

Coutanche could. And after that there was nothing to do but wait for his own turn. He did not have to wait long.

At half-past five next morning, a German plane flew over Jersey dropping three copies of an ultimatum. One of them was picked up on the airport by the Controller, Charles Roche, who took it up to the Bailiff's home. Inside a cotton bag, made out of an ordinary bed sheet, Coutanche found two typewritten sheets of paper which began:

Den 1. Juli, 1940.

An den
  Chef der militärischen und zivilen Dienstelle, Jersey (St. Helier).

(1) *Ich beabsichtige die militärischen Einrichtungen von Jersey durch Besetzung zu neutralisieren.*

(2) *Zum Zeichen, dass die Insel . . .*

Unhappily, neither Roche nor Coutanche knew more than a smattering of German. They puzzled over the typescript: they sent for a man supposed to know German, who puzzled in turn; and, as the minutes passed in vain guesses at the meaning of the words, the Bailiff grew more and more impatient. There was some reason for agitation. The document was obviously some form of ultimatum, and it did not need much German to understand its general import: certain phrases further down rather hit the eye. If such and such things were not done, *"ein schweres Bombardement einsetzen"*—"a heavy bombardment will take place."

Then Duret Aubin, the Attorney-General, arrived: and, as was often to happen in the days to come, he saved the situation. He rang up his friend Father Rey, of the Jesuit College at St. Helier, feeling sure that there would be someone there who could read German; and, sure enough, Father Rey found an Alsatian Father. Duret Aubin took the ultimatum up to the College, it was hastily translated in the Porter's Lodge, and then Aubin phoned the English version back to the Bailiff:

To the Chief of the Military and Civil Authorities, Jersey (St. Helier).

(1) I intend to neutralise military establishments in Jersey by occupation.

(2) As evidence that the island will surrender military and other establishments without resistance, and

56

without destroying them, a large White Cross is to be shown from 7 a.m., July 2nd, 1940.

(a) In the centre of the air port in the East* of the Island.

(b) On the highest point of the fortifications of the port.

(c) On the square to the north of the Inner Basin of the Harbour.**

Moreover all fortifications, buildings, establishments and houses are to show the White Flag.

(3) If these signs of peaceful surrender are not observed by 7 a.m., July 2nd, a heavy bombardment will take place.

(a) Against all military objects.

(b) Against all establishments and objects useful for defence.

(4) The signs of surrender must remain up to the time of the occupation of the Island by German troops.

(5) Representatives of the Authorities must stay at the airport until the Occupation.

(6) All Radio traffic and other communications with Authorities outside the Island will be considered hostile actions and will be followed by bombardment.

(7) Every hostile action against my representatives will be followed by bombardment.

(8) In the event of peaceful surrender the lives, property and liberty of peaceful inhabitants are solemnly guaranteed.

The ultimatum was signed by General Richthofen, Commanding the Luftwaffe in Normandy.

As soon as Coutanche heard the translation, he immediately summoned a meeting of the Royal Court, and then of

* Another example of the sketchiness of the German's knowledge. The airport is in the *West* of the island. There is a golf course in the East.

** It was not sure whether this meant Royal Square or the Weighbridge car park; white crosses were painted on both.

the States. Copies of the ultimatum were printed and put up with an endorsement ordering the population to offer no resistance whatever to the occupation of the island. White flags began to appear on houses, and silent spectators watched workmen painting a huge white cross on the paving stones of Royal Square.

Others crowded into pubs for a final drink, word having got round that the States were passing a *règlement* forbidding the sale of intoxicating liquor.

The Germans did not wait for the ultimatum to expire at 7 a.m. on Tuesday. At about eleven o'clock on the same Monday morning, a Luftwaffe officer, Oberleutnant Kern, was circling the island when he decided, on his own initiative, to land on Jersey Airport. Charles Roche, the Airport Controller, watched his plane taxi to within a hundred yards of the control building. Oberleutnant Kern stepped out, revolver in hand, followed by his crew carrying Tommy guns. They advanced on the airport building with every one of their weapons pointing at Roche.

Fortunately, Roche was a man whose quiet manner and soft voice concealed great reserves of coolness and determination. (Before he was eighteen, in the First World War, he was flying in France for the R.F.C.) When, five minutes later, the telephone bell rang in the Bailiff's Chambers, Coutanche lifted the receiver and heard Roche's voice reporting in the most matter-of-fact way possible: "There's a German officer at the airport, sir." The German, said Roche, wanted the "Herr Governor" to meet senior officers who would be arriving later.

Coutanche went down and made a speech to the crowd in Royal Square. He read the ultimatum and raised a little laugh with a joke about the reference to an Airport in the East—"I presume they mean the West." He emphasised the last paragraph, with it guarantee to respect life, liberty and property. He said they had no option except to surrender, since they had nothing left to fight with. (An intransigent voice called out "We've got men! We've got our fists! "; it was promptly shushed.) Coutanche appealed to everyone to keep calm, to obey German orders, and to

58

go home and hang out a sheet or a pillowcase or something to serve as a white flag. He ended by saying: "I do not know when I shall have the opportunity of speaking to you again, but until then I pray God's blessing upon you all."

Coutanche remembered what he had promised in an earlier speech: that everything would be all right so long as the Union Jack was flying at Fort Regent, and that nobody but he would ever strike the flag. He felt that the time had now come, and drove through the streets to the Fort. He was at the flagstaff when he was summoned to take another telephone call. He was told: "There are hundreds of Germans arriving at the Airport."

The flag came down.

As the Germans flew in across the island they had a unique sight—looking closely from the air they could see that almost every house had its tiny speck of something white, hanging from a window or flying over the roof.

Coutanche, as Lieutenant-Governor and Bailiff, and Duret Aubin, as Attorney-General, both drove to the Airport to meet the new arrivals. "Hundreds" was an exaggeration; there were still only half a dozen planes round the perimeter. When Duret Aubin got there he was somewhat disconcerted when none of the Germans took the slightest notice of him. Eventually, however, somebody asked him what his business was; Coutanche arrived too, and they all introduced themselves and shook hands after the formal Continental fashion.

A German officer got in beside Duret Aubin in the front of his car, airmen bristling with guns piled in the back, and they drove into St. Helier. The Germans went to the Post Office to check that the cables with England had been cut; and to the Town Hall, which they made a Military Headquarters, with a swastika flying outside.

As for Coutanche, he tried to relieve his feelings by going home, changing into his oldest clothes, and working furiously in his garden. He had gone inside to help himself to a drink in the dining-room, when his butler suddenly appeared and said: "The drive is full of Jerries, sir."

A party of German officers, Duret Aubin in their wake,

marched into the drawing-room. Duret Aubin went to find Coutanche, brought him along, flung the drawing-room open, and announced: "His Excellency the Governor!"

Coutanche, in his oldest clothes, muddy from the garden, and with a hole in one knee, went in.

The German officers surveyed him through monocles. Coutanche, not to be outdone, found his own monocle, and surveyed them back. Out of the corner of his eyes, looking out of the drawing-room window and into the window of the dining-room—the two were at an angle—he could see that Duret Aubin had retired there and was fortifying himself with a large whisky and soda.

After talking for a while, they arranged a meeting for ten o'clock the following day, and Duret Aubin went round fixing up billets for the Germans at different hotels.

There was a slight hitch next morning, because everyone had forgotten that Central European Time was ahead of British time. When the German Commander in Jersey, Captain Gussek, arrived at the Royal Court House to keep the appointment, the building was locked up and no one was there. The first person to arrive was Ralph Mollet, the Bailiff's secretary, and a well-known Jersey historian. He let Captain Gussek in, and they chatted in the Bailiff's Chambers. Gussek asked how long ago the islands had been annexed by Britain. "On the contrary," explained Mollet, "*we* conquered Britain, in 1066."

Gussek asked for maps of Jersey, and Mollet sent the doorman out to buy some. Gussek made a point of saying that he would pay for them.

Then Coutanche, Duret Aubin, and Edgar Dorey arrived. The Occupation arrangements were worked out just as smoothly as in Guernsey, and on the same lines: a curfew, the sale of spirits prohibited, weapons to be handed in. The German orders also provided, as had been done in Guernsey, that the Civil Government, States and Courts were to carry on as before; but instead of new laws depending on the Royal Assent, they would need the Assent of the German Commandant. The Post Office still functioned, for instance, and the Royal Mail vans had G.R. on them throughout the occupation.

Such able lawyers as Coutanche and Duret Aubin soon had their minds much exercised by the curious position in which they were placed. Coutanche explained to Captain Gussek that, in carrying on the civil government and administration of justice, all his powers were derived from His Majesty the King. Captain Gussek replied that this did not matter in the slightest: Germany had no quarrel with the King, but only with "that warmonger, Churchill . . ." Duret Aubin felt he should point out to Gussek that, as Attorney-General, he prosecuted in the name of the Crown: did Gussek mind?" "Not in the least," replied Gussek with some humour, "unless you would prefer to prosecute in the name of the German Reich."

Nevertheless, the Crown Officers were often sorely puzzled as a result of being asked by the Germans to carry on their duties, and having previously been directed to carry on by the British Government. Within a day or so, Duret Aubin was paradoxically prosecuting an Irishman, in the name of the King, for the offence of striking one of the King's enemies. The defendant, James Colgan, had punched a German soldier on the nose after a quarrel in a café.

Duret Aubin was a very conscientious man whose massive frame and judicial manner concealed a sensitive nature and a considerable capacity for worrying. (One of the most endearing mannerisms was a habit of repeating words two or three times—"It was a terrible, terrible, terrible position.") He was much exercised at being called upon to prosecute Colgan; but, when he protested, Gussek said that otherwise Colgan would be tried by German court martial, and have a much more severe sentence. "I will guarantee that my forces behave themselves," Gussek added. "Your responsibility is to keep the civil population in order."

It had already been decided by the island authorities, as in Guernsey, that they would try to "act as a buffer" between invaders and islanders, keeping as much power as possible in their own hands to deal with their own people.

Colgan was sentenced to a month's imprisonment, after Duret Aubin had told the court:

"The Occupation has been carried out by the German Forces with the utmost consideration for and courtesy towards the civil population of the island. It is therefore intolerable that any member of these forces should be treated with less consideration or courtesy."

Duret Aubin was speaking no less than the truth in praising the conduct of the German troops: while Captain Gussek himself won nothing but respect and praise. In Jersey, as in Guernsey, people began to decide that their worst fears of the Occupation had been foolish. And, in any case, it was not going to last for long. Captain Gussek himself said so: "This is only a temporary Occupation, only a matter of weeks. You must realize that the war is virtually over."

CHAPTER VIII

"IT'S GOING TO BE ALL RIGHT"

Sark had to wait two days after Jersey for her turn. It was not till Wednesday July 3, 1940, that Dr. Lanz and Dr. Maass set off in the Guernsey lifeboat to make the eight mile crossing from St. Peter Port. Mrs. Hathaway saw them coming from the turreted tower of the Seigneurie. She rang up William Carré, the Sénéschal, asking him to meet the Germans at the landing stage and act as guide. (Throughout, she made a point of making the Germans come to see her, and never went to them.) And she instructed her servants, when Lanz and Maass arrived, to show them in with as little concern "as if I'm used to receiving enemy officers every day of my life."

William Carré had been digging in his garden when Mrs. Hathaway telephoned him. Like everyone else in Sark, he did not believe in hurrying; and he called at the pub for a couple of drinks on his way down to the harbour. It was about noon when Lanz and Maass arrived. Carré explained that he was to conduct them to the Dame, and that no motor cars were allowed in Sark; so they set off walking up the hill that so many toiling tourists have climbed. It was half an hour or so before they reach the Seigneurie, where the Dame was waiting with Bob Hathaway at the far end of the big drawing-room—so that their visitors would have to walk across the room to her.

The tense silence was broken by the sound of footsteps outside. Then Mrs. Hathaway turned to her husband and said: "It's going to be all right." She had heard the Germans stop to wipe their feet on the mat.

Lanz and Maass were shown in, and saluted. To their surprise, Mrs. Hathaway not only greeted them with complete composure, but started talking to them fluently in German. After a while Maass said to her: "So you are not afraid?" Mrs. Hathaway replied sweetly: "Is there any need to be afraid of German officers?"

They all had a pleasant lunch together.

Lanz and Maass went back the same afternoon, and the Occupation was formally started by the arrival of a German sergeant and ten men the next day—July 4th, American Independence Day. "This," remarked Bob Hathaway in his American drawl, "is one hell of a date on which to be captured."

The same sort of rules and regulations were issued in Sark as in the other islands—a curfew, a ban on the sale of wines and spirits, and so on. The formalities, however, did not last long

It was hard to keep up a rigid barrier between the small Sark community and the eleven fellow human beings in German uniforms who had become, for an enforced period, their fellow islanders. At first the Germans were very much on their guard. Like many other visitors they found something eerie and weird about Sark, particularly at night, and on their night patrols they would deliberately stamp and shout and sing, making as much noise as possible to keep up their spirits. But soon they began to relax, and took advantage of the hot summer days to go about in their shirt sleeves, without carrying any weapons. As was only to be expected in Sark, the ban on the sale of spirits and liquor had a very short life indeed; and it was not long before the Germans and the Sarkees were buying each other drinks in the pubs, while some islanders were inviting the Germans to visit their homes.

There were no complications about occupying Alderney, for it had been left entirely deserted. There were no eye-witnesses when two Fieseler Storcks landed on the little air-field on Tuesday, July 2, to be followed by seaborne soldiers brought from Cherbourg. But after the German troops were established they were joined by farmer Frank Oselton—who, it may be remembered, had chased down to Guernsey when the Guernseymen came and took away his cows from Alderney before the Occupation. He had lost no time in seeking an interview with Dr. Lanz, and got permission to go back to his farm on Alderney, being given some more cows to replace those of his own which could not be found.

Frank Oselton was a man who asked only two things of life; the right to keep his own cattle, and an occasional dose of Epsom salts. His toughness was a good advertisement for this medicine; he would boast of never having a day's illness. Oselton got his cows together, had fifty packets of Epsom salts sent up from Guernsey, and faced the Occupation ready for anything.

By some accounts the five years that followed involved little hardship. The Germans wanted milk and were ready to pay for it, in money or in kind. Oselton—known to the Germans as "Poppa"—might drop into their cookhouse and be pressed to take away presents of sugar or meat or butter; he was invited into their canteen in Victoria Street, where three bars were set up for the thirsty. Oselton acquired a plentiful stock of cognac and cigarettes, given by soldiers in return for milk; he explained after the war that he had given up smoking because he smoked so much during the Occupation that he grew tired of it.

It may be, however, that life was not always so pleasant. He could also describe how he had been pushed around and moved from place to place by the Germans, though tenaciously keeping his cattle the whole time.

One other Englishman who spent most of the war on Alderney was George Pope. He was always something of a mystery, and remains so to this day. He had arrived the year before, with his wife and children, in a converted lifeboat, which he moored in the Harbour. His wife had a baby in the Alderney hospital; then the family sailed off again, but returned during the Occupation, in the course of which Mrs. Pope had two more children—the only births recorded on Alderney during these years. George Pope acted as pilot for the Germans in taking relief ships out to the Casquets lighthouse, and took up farming in a small way.

In addition to Oselton and Pope, a number of other British people were to come and go during the Occupation of Alderney. Within three weeks a salvage party arrived from Guernsey to clear up some of the debris still left after the panic withdrawal, and collect stocks from the shops. They were followed by an agricultural party to get in the harvest, and to arrange for sowing seed again the following season.

The salvage party began by disposing of the decaying carcasses of the animals which had been shot and left unburied. Other animals were running loose in the deserted houses; a pig had farrowed in the Post Office. Litter from shops, offices and houses lay everywhere in the streets. The main street of St. Anne's was strewn by thousands of cancelled cheques from one of the banks, blown like leaves in the wind. The salvage party went through the houses, stored what seemed worth keeping, and dumped the debris in the quarry.

In the circumstances, some looting was inevitable. The Germans protested that it was not their soldiers, but the salvage parties from Guernsey, who were to blame: and with this opinion the people of Alderney, always ready to blame Guernsey, seemed to concur. Visiting Alderney in later years, one's first impression was that any dislike expressed of Germans was nothing compared to what was said about Guernseymen. "The Germans," said Oselton, "treated us much better than our own people." At any event, some of the men who had come up from Guernsey were given prison sentences for looting and pilfering. According to the evidence at the trial, one man had taken back to Guernsey 77 carpets, 76 curtains, 13 clocks, 69 shirts, a tailor's dummy, and large quantities of food and cigarettes. The culprits may well have felt, however, that anything they left would merely get into German hands.

Meanwhile the agricultural party, established in the Belle Vue Hotel, was engaged in the more humdrum tasks of working in the fields and learning to get on with the Germans. Food was poor and life was rough—apart from Mrs. Pope, Alderney was for a time an island without any women at all—but, as in Sark, it was impossible for small groups of people in a small place, though officially enemies, to avoid living together in some sort of harmony.

Among those who went with the salvage party to Alderney, for instance, was a builder and handyman named Clifford Bichard. He eventually became a foreman mason for the Germans, building them a pay-office, bakehouse and other buildings; and he reported afterwards that "as bosses, they were fair; I've found worse among my own countrymen." He would make suitcases at night from bits of plywood, and sell them to the Germans for cigarettes. He was never let down over these transactions. Once a German who was going on leave wanted a suitcase, had not enough cigarettes to pay, but promised them on return. He never came back, and Bichard wrote it off as a bad debt. Weeks later another German arrived with cigarettes, explaining that his friend had been posted elsewhere, and had arranged specially for the cigarettes to be delivered by proxy.

CHAPTER IX

SPIES AND COMMANDOS

It is time to turn back to the story of Guernsey, the first island to be occupied, and the main centre of events during the first year.

No sooner were the Germans in the Channel Islands, than Churchill suggested that Guernsey would be well suited for a raid by the newly formed Commandos.

On Friday, July 5—the Friday after the Germans landed —twenty-year-old Hubert Nicolle, a tough little quiet-spoken Guernseyman serving with The Hampshires, received a mysterious summons to go to London and report to Room 73 at the Admiralty. There he was introduced in turn to Major Warren of the Marines, and to Colonel Cantan—a fellow Guernseyman and son-in-law of the Dame of Sark. Nicolle learnt that a volunteer was needed to go into Guernsey in civilian clothes, landing by canoe from a submarine, and to collect all possible information on the German defences. The same submarine would pick him up again three nights later. Nicolle was asked if he was ready to take on the assignment. He said he was.

He was asked if he realised that, if caught, he would be shot as a spy.

He said he did.

These were the early amateurish days of the Commandos. It was eleven o'clock on the Saturday morning—he had to catch the one o'clock train from Paddington to Plymouth—before somebody remembered that Nicolle had not yet been provided with a canoe. A messenger was sent hastily to Gamages to buy one, and struggled back with it in a long brown-paper parcel to Major Warren's room. They asked an Admiralty porter to carry it downstairs for them, but the porter refused owing to some point of trade union etiquette. "It's a labourer's job," he said. So Major Warren turned to Nicolle and said, "Come on, let's be labourers"; and they carried it down the three flights of stairs between them.

Complete with his lengthy and mysterious-looking brown-paper parcel, Nicolle took a taxi to Paddington and a train to Plymouth. It was not till the submarine set off, at nine the same night, that he had his first chance to unwrap the brown paper and look at the canoe. It was then discovered that the beam was too wide to get through the hatchway, and the carpenter had to put hinges in the struts so that the canoe could be partly folded.

They submerged soon after midnight. At eleven o'clock the following night—Sunday, July 7—they surfaced about six miles south of Guernsey, and cruised quietly three miles nearer shore on electric motors. Nicolle had chosen as landing place Le Jaonnet, a tiny little-frequented bay on the south coast, with steep cliffs which he had scrambled down when he went swimming as a boy.

With a young naval officer he got into the canoe, made for the shore, and landed. The officer paddled back. Nicolle climbed the cliffs and spent the night hiding among some bushes in his wet clothes, alert to every sound. He was alarmed by what seemed to be somebody moving about in a cautious and sinister way: when daylight came he saw that it was a cow.

Next, a farmer arrived to milk the cow. Nicolle recognised him as a man named Thoume—a former member of the Guernsey Militia—and Thoume recognised Nicolle. This was one of the greatest dangers: Nicolle was bound to be recognised by many people, and if word went round that he was on the island it would not be long before German ears heard of it. He told Thoume urgently of his mission, and got in reply such valuable information as that there was a curfew. Then he told Thoume: "Forget you've seen me," and made for the airfield.

Nearby he dropped in for breakfast with a farmer friend, Tom Mansell. He asked Mansell to watch the airfield for the next three days and report everything he saw; then, borrowing a bicycle and a pair of dark glasses, he rode to his own home in St. Peter Port, went round the back, and took his mother by surprise. She promptly rang up his father, Emile Nicolle, a leading States official—Secretary to the Controlling Committee—and said he was to come home at once. She would not say any more. Emile came rushing back in some alarm. His wife had recently got a new electric washing machine, and Emile thought she must have had some accident, like catching her hand in the mangle.

In the kitchen he found his son.

"What on earth are you doing here?"

"I'm a spy," said Hubert.

Emile insisted that Hubert stayed at home and had information brought to him, instead of risking being seen outside. A next-door neighbour and friend was H. H. Collins, manager of Le Riche's stores, which had been given the job of supplying rations for the Germans; so Collins had exact figures of German ration strength—469 in Guernsey, plus 11 on Sark—and details of troop locations. Nicolle's uncle, Captain Frank Nicolle, was Assistant Harbour Master, and told of shipping movements. Tom Mansell reported on planes at the airfield—during the days in question, only two troop carriers and a reconnaissance machine. And so, when the third evening came, Nicolle was able to set off with his head full of information.

His only problem was the curfew. He made for Le Jaonnet while it was still light, and jumped over a hedge when no one was looking. He lay hidden until dark, when he made his way down to keep the rendezvous, timed for 2.30 a.m. At last Nicolle saw a dinghy with three men in it. Two were coming ashore for a purpose which he did not hear about till later. The third he recognised as the young officer from the submarine who had landed him. Nicolle jumped in the dinghy, and they made off. The only remaining risk was overshooting the submarine in the dark; but at five-minute intervals they shone a torch southwards, and the submarine saw and intercepted them.

Arriving at Plymouth, Nicolle was promptly flown to London to make his report and receive all the congratulations he deserved.

The two men who came ashore by the dinghy which took Nicolle away were Philip Martel of The Hampshire Regiment, and Desmond Mulholland of The Duke of Cornwall's Light Infantry. They were both, like Nicolle, subalterns from the Guernsey Militia, and both had received the same sort of mysterious summons to London. They were told that a Commando raid on Guernsey was being planned for the following Friday night, July 12, and they were asked if they would go ashore in civilian clothes two nights earlier, to spy out the land and guide the Commandos when they arrived.

It was impressed upon them, as with Nicolle, that if caught they would be shot. But both promptly volunteered for the job, and they went off on their mission with the scantiest of preparation and equipment consisting of torches, flasks of brandy, some Horlicks tablets, chocolate and biscuits. With their torches they were to signal D in Morse (— . .) if they had found no Germans near the agreed landing points; or a succession of quick flashes (. . . . .) to warn if the enemy were about.

Mulholland's instructions were to welcome ashore a party of Commandos who were to land near Moye Point, on the South coast, and attack the airport. Martel was to perform a similar service for a party landing, with the same object, further along the coast at Petit Bôt. A third party, still further along, was to create a diversion and build a road block to stop German reinforcements reaching the airfield. Yet another group was to land at Vazon Bay on the other side of the island.

Two nights later, Friday, July 12, saw Martel and Mulholland both in their places. Nothing happened.

They had been told, if anything stopped the raid, that they were to go on subsequent nights to Le Jaonnet, and a submarine would try to take them off. So on the next night, and the night after, they proceeded hopefully to Le Jaonnet and flashed a torch southwards.

What had happened, though Martel and Mulholland had no way of knowing, was that the Commando raid had been postponed for forty-eight hours. There was also a last-minute change in the plan of operations; and what with the confusion caused by this changed plan, and the mishaps in carrying it out, the true story of the raid is still hard to discover.

The one thing certain is that the Commandos who were supposed to be attacking the airport never reached Guernsey at all. They set off from the destroyer *Saladin* in three R.A.F. "crash boats" (or Air-Sea rescue launches) and a whaler. The first boat, supposed to be making for Le Jaonnet, lost its direction completely owing to a faulty compass. One account says it arrived at Sark, another that it reached Herm; probably the truth is that, to this day, none of the men on board know exactly where they went to. Fortunately, however, they were able to find their way back to the *Saladin*.

Meanwhile the whaler and the two other crash boats were making for Moye Point, when the whaler started leaking. The men in it were transferred to the crash boats, and one of them took the whaler in tow. This caused a lot of delay; and then, coming in sight of shore, they saw a mysterious light flashing. It was, in fact, Martel and Mulholland signalling for a submarine to take them off. But the Commandos knew nothing of what Martel and Mulholland were doing, just as Martel and Mulholland knew nothing of the changed plans of the Commandos. It was feared that the light meant some German was signalling that they were discovered; and, as it was already too late to do anything worth while, the party turned back.

The only actual landing was made by a third party, commanded by Lt.-Colonel John Durnford Slater—later Brigadier Durnford Slater, D.S.O. He had originally been scheduled to land at Vazon Bay, but in the last-minute change of plan his destination was transferred to Petit Port in the South, just beside Jerbourg Peninsular.

Slater's force landed successfully at 1 a.m. in the morning, taken ashore by two crash boats from the destroyer *Scimitar*, which had orders to wait two hours—till 3 a.m.—for them to return, but to wait no longer. Slater led his men up the seemingly endless flight of steps up the cliff, and they advanced to their objectives, rousing a chorus of barking dogs behind them, but discovering nothing in the way of Germans. They surrounded a machine-gun post and found it empty; then had the same experience at Jerbourg barracks. They found one old man in a cottage, but he was too frightened to give any useful information. All they could do was to make a road block (wrecking somebody's rock garden to get the stones to make it), and cut some telephone wires.

By then it was more than time to return. At the bottom of the steps going down, Durnford Slater tripped. His revolver went off, the sound of the shot echoing hideously against the cliffs. This, at last, seemed to wake some Germans up, a searchlight shone out to sea for a few moments, and a machine-gun fired some tracer bullets. The waiting boats, deciding it was too rough to come right in shore, sent a dinghy to pick up a few men at a time, and their weapons. After several trips it sank, and those still left ashore had to swim for it.

Three of the men then confessed to Durnford Slater that they could not swim. They could only be left behind to be taken prisoner. The others stripped and swam to the boat. It was now half-past three, but Slater's torch signal was seen by the destroyer on its last sweep before going home.

The Germans still did not realise what had happened. Next morning they complained to Sherwill of a grave act of sabotage by the islanders—the building of a stone road block. Nearby they had also found a magazine from a Bren gun. They threatened to arrest some local residents as a reprisal. Next came complaints from sixteen angry telephone subscribers, who reported that their wires had been cut mysteriously during the night. Sherwill, guessing that there had been a raid, pacified the Germans by officially instructing the police to look for any sign of a landing; and, guessing that some raiders might have been left behind, and would need time to go into concealment, also instructed the police unofficially not to be too quick about finding anything. After an appropriate interval the discovery was reported, on the beach at Petit Port, of the smashed dinghy, some Bren guns washed ashore with it, and the uniforms discarded by the men when they stripped to swim.

By the next day the men left behind had also been rounded up.

Slater described the raid afterwards as "a ridiculous—almost a comic—failure . . . Everything was faulty, from the higher direction in London down to the landing craft and our own training." Churchill called it (in private) a "silly fiasco". Its main use was that later Commando raids —those led by Durnford Slater included*—learnt much from the mistakes made.

For those in Guernsey, however, it was naturally a major talking point for weeks. Victor Carey the Bailiff felt some concern; his home was not far from the landing point, and the Germans might well have suspected him of knowing something about it. But there was pleasurable excitement too; and soon all in Guernsey were cheering themselves up by passing on the most fantastic stories and rumours about what the Commandos had accomplished. Mrs. Frank Higgs, a housewife of St. Sampsons', noted in her diary that she had heard how a British force had landed, taken five prisoners, and left behind two Scots soldiers "doing a Highland Fling all along the Jerbourg Road, laughing and singing, 'We've done it, we've done what we came to do!' "

* See John Durnford Slater: *Commando* (William Kimber, 1953).

CHAPTER X

MEN IN HIDING

It would seem that almost the only people in the island who heard nothing about the raid were Martel and Mulholland, the men who had been sent to prepare the way for it. On the night in question they had gone as usual, with their torch, to Le Jaonnet, in hopes of signalling a submarine to take them off; with the only effect, as mentioned, of mystifying one group of Commandos. Once again, Martel and Mulholland saw no submarines; but they *did* see and hear some of the German reactions to the raid—a searchlight, and a machine-gun firing. They also heard a plane circling overhead—which was in fact a British plane sent at the last minute to drown the noise of the Commandos' boat engines. It was natural enough for Martel and Mulholland to assume that the Germans must have spotted them, and were on the look-out for them.

They lay very low, and decided not to go back to Le Jaonnet again.

From now on they were on the run, with the strain of expecting detection every day. Philip Martel began to regret the haphazard haste and lack of planning with which he had been sent into the venture. Mulholland had a pair of rubber-soled shoes, but Martel had not. The only way he could get about undetected after the curfew was to go barefoot, and his feet were soon sore and bleeding. Another problem was the state of his clothes and the growth of his beard; he was beginning to look so disreputable as to be conspicuous. Earlier he had been to his sister's home in Queen's Road, but he refused to endanger her by going there again. Accordingly he broke into a house in St. Martin's, which seemed empty, to steal a suit of clothes and a razor. For all he knew, the house might have been one requisitioned for German officers, and he was listening the whole time for the sound of any occupant returning. But he was so completely exhausted that he could not resist resting for a moment in an easy chair, and before he knew what had happened he was fast asleep. He was woken by the sound of someone moving about in a shed in the garden. By now his nerves were in such a state that he bolted upstairs and hid under a bed until the other visitor —probably another Guernseyman also on the scrounge— had gone away.

Martel and Mulholland made many attempts to get back to England, hampered by the strict watch which was being kept on fishing boats. Once they managed to steal a boat in Perelle Bay. But neither knew much about sailing; they nearly went on the rocks, and felt themselves lucky even to get back to shore.

They made a trip to Sark, mingling unsuspected with German officers on the boat, but they found it was equally impossible to get away from there; the Germans had all the fishing boats concentrated at the harbour, and to the harbour at Sark there was only one way of approach—a guarded tunnel through the side of a rock.

Back in Guernsey they moved from hiding place to hiding place. They spent some nights in the house evacuated by Colonel and Mrs. Cantan, son-in-law and daughter of the Dame of Sark. They ended up in a barn next to a house at Vazon. But even here they could not escape attention: one morning the lady of the house spotted them and recognised them.

They felt that it could not go on. Apart from the endless strain on their own nerves—they were now understandably jumpy—there was the danger to their families, and the fact that they were rendering more and more people liable to punishment for knowing of their presence but saying nothing. They decided that the only thing was to give themselves up.

One morning Major Sherwill had gone down early, about six o'clock, to stoke up the boiler at his home, Havelet

House. He heard somebody knocking and wondered, with some irritation, why the milkman could not just leave the milk on the door-step. He opened the back door, and found himself confronted by Desmond Mulholland, whom he knew well already as a friend of his daughter, and who introduced Philip Martel.

Quickly they told him their story. Sherwill asked if they were quite determined to give themselves up: they said they were. By now they were done in: their nerves had had as much as they could stand. Sherwill learnt they had landed in civilian clothes, thus making them liable to be shot as spies. He promptly determined on a course of action which made him liable to be shot himself. For he decided that the only way of saving their lives was to find uniforms for them.

First of all, however, he felt he should ask his wife if she was prepared to run the risk of letting the boys stay in the house. May Sherwill brushed aside his warnings of the grim penalties for helping spies, making one characteristic and practical reply: "I'd better get them some breakfast." Drawing the curtains of the dining-room, in case any German should happen to glance in, Mrs. Sherwill set the boys down to a dish of eggs which they ate ravenously. Next, Sherwill sent them up to a room at the top of the house to rest and sleep. He then took his wife's baby Fiat car, and set out to see his friend Dion Bisset, who had a pub at the Vale Road. Bisset was a builder, and Sherwill reckoned that in such a trade he must have keys to fit almost any lock in the island.

"Don," said Sherwill, "put all your keys in your pocket —we're going burgling."

He then confided, to the astonished Bisset, that he had to get two British uniforms, and that he thought they might find some in the house of a Guernsey Militia officer who had gone to England. Bisset, a Captain in the Militia, pointed out instead that there was still a stock of uniforms at the Town Arsenal; and to the Arsenal they went, driving past a German soldier who took no notice of them.

They found a chest full of service dress, and hastily

76

selected two uniforms that they thought would fit. One, which Sherwill recognised as belonging to Major Jack Falla, who had commanded the Militia, had a number of first world war ribbons. Sherwill cut them off, and then saw that the place behind them, protected by the ribbons, was cleaner and less faded than the rest of the cloth. He rubbed it with his thumb to try to make the tell-tale patch the same colour as the rest, having first rubbed his thumb on the floor to make it grimy. Next, he spotted that the uniforms had Royal Militia buttons; and Mrs. Dawes, wife of the caretaker of the Arsenal, did a heroic high-speed job of snipping them off and sewing on British Army buttons instead. Finally, Sherwill piled the uniforms in his car, dropped off Bisset, and drove home—suddenly terrified that a German might stop him and ask for a lift. Fortunately nothing of the sort happened. He got back to Havelet House, woke up Martel and Mulholland, gave them dinner and started the job of dressing them up. A last-minute snag occurred when they found they were a pair of braces short: Sherwill had to sacrifice his own.

Then came the critical moment.

Sherwill went to the telephone, asked to speak to Dr. Maass, and said: "Two British officers have surrendered to me."

"Two British officers?"
"Yes."
"When?"
"I won't lie," said Sherwill. "It was two or three hours ago. They were in a pretty bad way, so I gave them a chance of some food and a rest before telephoning you."

Sherwill knew that, by admitting delay in handing them over, he was admitting he was guilty of an offence. He calculated that an appearance of frankness was his only defence. For, of course, he had had to lie: it had taken about eight hours to carry out his plan.

"Are they in uniform?" asked Maass.
"Yes."
"At your house?"

"Yes."

"You mean they were able to walk through the streets to you in British uniform without being seen?"

Sherwill saw the trap in a flash. He had already said that they had only been at his house for two or three hours: if he altered his story, and said they had arrived before daylight, he would never be able to explain what had happened in the interval.

"Of course not," he said quickly. "Do you think they're mad? They landed in uniform, but they got some civilian clothes to come here. I've kept the clothes to show you."

The civilian clothes were made into two brown-paper parcels, and they set off for the German headquarters, then in the Channel Islands Hotel. On the way, Sherwill impressed on the two men that they must tell nothing but Name, Rank and Number—"Otherwise you'll get shot, and I'll get shot too."

The sentries outside the hotel seized their weapons in a panic at the sight of two British officers. Sherwill waved them aside, asked for Dr. Maass, and they went into the lounge to wait.

Maass was at his most smooth and charming when he arrived. He shook hands with all three of them; and in the pleasantest way possible, with the air of one merely making agreeable conversation, asked Martel and Mulholland when they had arrived. To Sherwill's horror, one of them told him. Sherwill had enough experience to know that unexpected friendliness can be a more effective means of extracting information than torture. At this rate, he thought, the whole story may soon come out. After the men had been led away he decided he must make another attempt to put them on their guard.

"Do you mind?" he asked Maass. "I meant to give them cigarettes, and forgot." He went into the guardroom, and handed round some cigarettes with a cheery smile and a whispered mutter of "You bloody fools, nothing but Name, Rank and Number."

That was the last Sherwill saw of them, and he could only guess at what might come out at their subsequent interrogations. When he could not stand the suspense any more, he asked Maass as casually as he could manage: "By the way, have you heard anything about how those two young officers are getting on?" To which Maass replied enigmatically: "They'll be all right, if their story holds."

Martel and Mulholland were flown to France, and interrogated separately at Dinard for hours at a time. Their trousers were taken away every night to make sure they could not escape. Shortly afterwards Sherwill was alarmed to hear that they had been playing Russian pool with two Germans; it seemed like the technique of extracting information by friendly relations. But the explanation was quite simple. An interpreter, who was anxious to improve his English, had produced another German and challenged Martel and Mulholland: "Now we play a game—Germany against England." And England won.

During the match they talked about nothing but politics, foreign travel, and the habits of tourists; while Mulholland amused the Germans by reciting some choice English limericks.

Martel and Mulholland must have kept their end up with some skill, for the official German report accepted their story that they had landed in uniform and got civilian clothes from an empty house. They were treated as prisoners of war, and Sherwill heard nothing more.

Strangely enough, they were never asked why they landed, not in battle dress, but in service dress: extraordinary garb to wear into action in 1940. The Germans mostly asked questions about the relics the Commandos had left behind—the wrecked dinghy, the weapons, the uniforms—and wanted to know what they meant. As mentioned, Martel and Mulholland had not even realised that the Commando raid had taken place: their bewilderment at the questions was obviously genuine, and their very ignorance may have been their salvation.

The ironic thing was that the whole ordeal was unnecessary. Martel and Mulholland had no way of knowing that, on the morning when they gave themselves up, their rescue was already arranged.

C.Q.M.S. Stanley Ferbrache, another Guernseyman serving in The Hampshires, had volunteered to go in by motor torpedo boat, find the two men, and bring them back by the same means. He landed at Le Jaonnet, and spent the night on the cliffs. In the morning he set out, doing his best to look like an ordinary civilian, and feeling uncomfortably conspicuous in a smart check cap which he had borrowed from an English pub keeper.

The first person he met was a friend who greeted him, naturally but disconcertingly, with: "Hullo, Ferby, I thought you were in the Army!" Ferbrache replied in a swift and urgent whisper: "So I am." Ferbrache called on his uncle, Albert Callighan, who gave him a good meal and sent out for two bottles of beer from the pub, and then went to his own home to change into some of his own clothes. That night he made cautiously for the bungalow owned by Mulholland's mother, tapped on the door, and told her that he had come to collect Desmond Mulholland.

She confirmed the rumours he had already heard, that two British officers had just given themselves up. He was too late, by less than a week

He made what use he could of his visit by collecting information, including a bundle of copies of the *Guernsey Evening Press*; then went back to the cliffs where he had first landed, to keep his rendezvous with the M.T.B. But fog came down soon after midnight, and it could not see the three dots he signalled from his torch. Determined not to wast his time waiting, he made a visit next day—August Bank Holiday—to the airport, where he ran into a party of eight Germans walking along a lane.

He managed to look casual and unconcerned, and they only glanced casually at him. At 2.30 a.m. that night the M.T.B. arrived to take Ferbrache safely back to England.

CHAPTER XI

"A MODEL OCCUPATION"

The episode had been, at best, a lucky escape for Sherwill; but it only began to cause him anger and apprehension when, in time, he learnt of Hubert Nicolle's earlier visit. The islands had, after all, been left by the British Army to get on with the Germans as best they could; and so far things had gone better than the island authorities could ever have expected. But it hardly made their position easier now to have Britain, instead of getting out and staying out, deciding to send in spies; particularly as one of them was the son of a leading States official.

Sherwill had a special anxiety. Like Coutanche in Jersey, he had a son in the Navy. Young John Sherwill knew the Guernsey coast by heart, and seemed a likely enough choice for the next visitor.

If Whitehall wanted information about the islands, there might be simpler methods than espionage. Sherwill had often wondered how to reassure Channel Island evacuees in England about the fate of their families. He wanted them to know that the most fearful predictions about German behaviour had not been fulfilled.

Any direct communication with England, of course, was cut off. Sherwill asked a visiting official from the German Foreign Office to arrange a Red Cross message system, but was told that the war would be over before it could be started. Sherwill then gave the official a letter which he asked should be dropped over England by parachute. We have found no evidence that this was done; and no copy of the letter seems to have survived. (Among other points, it made a somewhat impractical request for a ship to be sent from England with essential supplies.) Next, Sherwill recorded a speech which was broadcast over Bremen Radio, and which was criticised by some people as lending itself to German propaganda:

"This is His Britannic Majesty's Procureur* in Guernsey, Channel Islands, speaking. . . .

"I imagine that many of you must be greatly worried as to how we are getting on. Well, let me tell you.

"Some will fear, I imagine, that I am making this record with a revolver pointed at my head and speaking from a typescript thrust into my hand by a German officer. The actual case is very different. The Lieutenant-Governor and Bailiff, Mr. Victor Carey, and every other island official has been, and is being, treated with every consideration and with the greatest courtesy by the German military authorities. . . .

"The conduct of the German troops is exemplary. . . .

"I am proud of the way my fellow-islanders have behaved and grateful for the correct and kindly attitude towards them of the German soldiers.

"We have always been and we remain intensely loyal subjects of His Majesty, and this has been made clear to and is respected by the German Commandant and his staff. . . .

"Will the B.B.C. please re-transmit this message and will the daily papers publish it."

The B.B.C. and the national papers did not comply, for obvious reasons. At that time the Battle of Britain—maybe invasion—was just ahead; the whole country was nerved to its finest hour, in the certainty that conquest by Hitler's Germany was a terrible fate which could never be borne. It would undoubtedly have been disconcerting in this mood to be assured, on first hand testimony, that Occupation by the Germans was not at all bad after all; just as, in the Channel Islands themselves, the good behaviour of the Germans had been a shock from which Sherwill and others had still not fully recovered.

But if one can understand why the broadcast caused

* i.e. Attorney-General.

some anger in Whitehall, one can also understand Sherwill's point of view. He had done no more than speak the truth as he saw it, without the qualifications which would have occurred to a trained politician. He believed that the survival of the islands depended on keeping good relations with the Germans, and any policy he embarked on he was likely to follow whole-heartedly. And his immediate concern was simply to relieve Channel Islanders in England of needless anxiety.

On August 8, 1940, came the first meeting of the Guernsey States since the Occupation. Victor Carey, the Bailiff, presided; and everything was as usual, except that the chair reserved for the Lieutenant-Governor was occupied by the German Commandant, Dr. Lanz. He sat with the Royal Coat of Arms behind him, and facing a huge portrait of King George V, which remained in the Chamber throughout the Occupation. The States heard a long address from Major Sherwill, ending with a passage from which was coined the phrase, "A Model Occupation": —

> "We are, let us remember, in enemy Occupation, and are treated with consideration. So long as we comport ourselves as we have during the past five weeks, refraining from provocative behaviour and going quietly about our task, there is no reason to fear harm to anyone.
>
> "May this occupation be a model to the world—on the one hand tolerance on the part of the military authority and courtesy and correctness on the part of the occupying forces, and, on the other, dignity and courtesy and exemplary behaviour on the part of the civilian population; conformity—the strictest conformity—with orders and regulations issued by the German Commandant and the civil authorities."

After the Occupation, Sherwill ended, they should be able to say that "We were civilians and we behaved as such in the strictest sense in accordance with the usages of war."

The speech was greatly applauded by the States; and that night, Dr. Maass did an extempore translation for senior officers in the German mess. On the whole, it also had a good reception from most people in Guernsey; though there were some mutterings.

There had been real anger when the Royal Court, on July 31, suddenly passed an Act making any talk criticising the Germans an offence liable to imprisonment of up to a year; and H. H. Collins, the manager of Le Riche's stores, was tried the same day on this charge. The public could not know the story behind this, which was as follows. Sherwill had found two of the Germans at the *Feldkommandantur* buckling on ther revolvers and preparing to arrest Collins, who had reproved a shop assistant for leaving a local customer and giving prior service to a German. Collins was a sick man, and Sherwill feared he could never survive imprisonment. He suggested that Collins should be tried, not by the Germans, but by the Royal Court; and he offered (against all the canons of criminal justice) to pass a retrospective Act under which the trial could be staged. The Germans agreed. Collins was elaborately tried and elaborately acquitted, everyone was satisfied, and the Act was never invoked again.

Some actions by the authorities were harder to defend. Anti-Semitic edicts, emanating from the German command in France, were registered by the Royal Courts both in Jersey and Guernsey. It was felt that the number of Jews was so small—less than ten in each island—that it was not worth asking for trouble by making an issue of the matter. In Guernsey there was one dissentient vote. It was that of Sir Abraham Lainé, a retired Indian civil servant who distinguished himself during the Occupation by his administration of the Essential Commodities Committee.

The edicts against Jews were, at first, mild. All Jews had to enter their names on a special register; and any business owned by a Jew had to have a placard as a "Jewish undertaking". Later came an Order for the sale of Jewish businesses, which only affected three concerns in Jersey. (In the case of one of these at least, Krichefski's draper's shop, it was evaded by the Manager acquiring the business and returning it after the war to the owner, who had gone to England.) Coutanche successfully resisted a proposal for making Jews wear yellow stars on their backs. In the end some Jews were deported to the Continent.*

With the German occupiers came secret police, referred to loosely as "the Gestapo". In fact they did not belong to the real Gestapo (*Geheime Staatspolizei*) but to the *Geheime Feldpolizei*, secret military police. In addition there were the *Feldpolizei*, or ordinary military police. The *Geheime Feldpolizei* sometimes wore plain clothes, but as they were soon all known by sight, this did not serve as much disguise. It may be that some of them, to impress the islanders—and even more the German soldiers themselves—pretended to belong to the Gestapo: but it seems that the Gestapo was never really represented on the islands. The secret police Headquarters, at "Silvertide" in Jersey, were to get a bad enough name; but the islanders were spared anything worse.

The methods of the Germans also had a certain unimaginative ponderousness which gave the quick-witted islanders some protection. The chief of the *Geheime Feldpolizei*, for instance, was easily recognised because he always travelled in the same maroon-coloured car: and to give added warning of his arrival he had a habit of slamming the door violently whenever he got out of it.

Once Arthur Harrison, of the *Jersey Evening Post*, was discussing some point with a German official, who asked Harrison to telephone him about it.

"Isn't that rather dangerous?" asked Harrison slyly. "Somebody might be listening."

"You needn't worry," the German said in all seriousness. "*I'm* the one who does the listening to telephone conversations."

Among the first acts of the *Geheime Feldpolizei* was to go round the libraries removing anti-Nazi books. They were particularly shocked by some Penguins in the Book Department of Boots at St. Peter Port, with David Low's cartoons of Hitler and Mussolini. After they had finished their inspection, and confiscated some four hundred books,

* We were surprised to be unable to obtain any reliable information as to their ultimate fate, even from present members of Jewish communities.

the Boots librarian, Miss Marion Key, turned to them innocently and said: "Perhaps you should have a look at this one too; it's by a man called Dr. Goebbels."

"That one will be all right," they replied gravely.

This visit had an important sequel. The German who came as interpreter got talking with Arthur Butterworth, the Manager of Boots, and mentioned that in civilian life he worked for a chemist's wholesalers in Hamburg. Butterworth was already worried about essential drugs for the islanders, now supplies from England were cut off; so he asked this man whether he could get through an order to his firm. Eventually a reply came that if Butterworth could send the money, the firm would send the goods. So an obliging German Corporal, going on leave, took the order and £700 in *Reichskreditkassen* notes to Hamburg; and, finding these Occupation Marks useless in Germany, made a special trip back to Belgium to change them. Thanks to this Corporal, a trade connection was established which allowed Boots—with the approval of the States—to import some £50,000 worth of first-class medical supplies, which they distributed in turn to all the chemists in all the islands. German soldiers were sometimes irritated to see German drugs on sale to civilians of a better quality than they could get themselves.

It was a happy outcome, for the islanders, of the decision by the *Geheime Feldpolizei* to ban some books in Boots.

The Germans also suppressed the Salvation Army and the island Free Masons, masonic relics being pillaged and sent to Europe to be featured in anti-Semitic displays. The Churches on the islands were respected—except for deserted Alderney, where they were despoiled and turned into Army stores. German padres used the local churches for their own Army services, with a swastika over the altar; and the Reverend E. L. Frossard of St. Sampson's, later Dean of Guernsey, was one of those who used to be present at services in his Church, although not in any official capacity.

Sometimes he would argue afterwards with the German padres about how they reconciled Nazism with Christianity. They would use such phrases as "We're Christians up to a point", or even "We're post-Christians."

On the whole the Germans made little attempt to interfere with teaching in schools, although there was compulsory German, and German songs at prize-givings. The local papers even hopefully ran German lessons for adults. They were compiled by Pierre Hollard, an accomplished linguist living in Guernsey who tried to enliven instruction with humour.*

The island newspapers—the *Jersey Evening Post*, the *Guernsey Evening Press*, and the Guernsey *Star*—were throughout under the stringent control of the Germans, giving the war news as laid down by Goebbels, and with every item subject to censorship. Arthur Harrison, however, the editor of the *Jersey Evening Post*, scored some points from time to time, like insisting that Churchill and Roosevelt should always be referred to as "Mr.", and resisting efforts to introduce German propaganda into the local news. He risked allowing some queer forms of English, which left no doubts about their Germanic origin, to creep into news items, including a speech by Victor Emmanuel:

* For example, German lesson No. 271:—

Have you been abroad?	*Sind Sie im Ausland gewesen?* (*Zint Zee im Owslahnt gevayzen?*)
Yes, once.	*Ja einmal.* (*Yah, ynemarl.*)
Did you manage to make yourself understood?	*Geland es Ihnen, sich verständlich zu machen?* (*Gelang es Eenen zish ferstendlish tsoo makhen?*)
Once I wanted to buy an egg . . .	*Einmal wollte ich ein Ei kaufen . . .* (*Ynemarl vollter ish yne Eye kowfen . . .*)
Of course you clucked like a hen.	*Natürlich gluckten Sie wie ein Huhn.* (*Naturlish gloockten Zee vee yne Hoon.*)
Yes, but they brought me a motor cycle.	*Ja aber man brachte mir ein Motorrad.* (*Yah, arber mahn brakhte meer yne Mot ohrraht.*)

87

"I have unshakable unbelief in the final victory of the Axis Powers."

The *Jersey Evening Post* was also called upon to print a daily paper in German for the troops, the *Deutsche Inselzeitung*, proudly described as the first German newspaper, "for the time being", to be published on British soil.

The behaviour of the German troops themselves continued to be almost irreproachable. One of the early fears, of course, had been for the womenfolk, and early in the Occupation there was one particularly unpleasant case of rape. The soldier responsible was drunk, and the woman concerned was very elderly. Sherwill told the German Commandant as soon as he heard of it. A Court of Inquiry was held first thing the following morning—Miss Riderer, a German lady living in Guernsey being brought from her home before breakfast to act as interpreter. The Germans did everything possible to spare the feelings of the woman who had been the victim; she did not have the ordeal of appearing in court, being allowed to wait in an ante-room while questions were put to her through Miss Riderer.

The soldier responsible was convicted, taken to France, and reported to have been shot. There was only one other case of rape in all the islands during the whole Occupation; and the two Germans concerned in this were port officials, and not soldiers. It is doubtful whether many armies in the world could boast as good a record; even including armies stationed on Allied, and not Enemy, territory.

Many attempts were made by the Germans, and sometimes by the islanders, to pass beyond correct behaviour to fraternisation.

The Luftwaffe was challenged to a few football matches by local teams, and beaten 5—1 by one Jersey side; such matches were given up for lack of any particular keenness on either side, rather than because of any strong feeling against them.

The Germans made a feature of band concerts, and to conduct them there arrived Obermusikmeister Gerhard Anders; who, as the *Guernsey Evening Press* put it, "has

bright eyes that flash with the genius of music in them."
Some joint dances were also held in the early days. But
there was not enough public response for them to continue,
even though one in Guernsey was attended by Dr. Lanz
himself, and a local paper—under the headline: "Commandant's happy gesture"—reported that as the curfew
hour drew near, and "it was obvious that everyone present
was enjoying themselves to the hilt", the Commandant
allowed the dance to go on for another quarter of an hour.

From the start there were a small minority of girls who
were willing to treat the Germans on more than friendly
terms. They were soon given the name of "Jerrybags" or
simply "Bags". It must be remembered that, in the early
months, the German conquerors represented the finest
manhood of their race, while the finest young men of the
islands had gone off to fight. It must also be remembered
that the Occupation was to last nearly five years: and that,
by the end, girls were growing up who were too young to
know or understand or remember how the war began.
Sometimes there were genuine love matches, though for
the German soldiers marriages were forbidden. What
roused more indignation was the conduct of some older
married women whose husbands were away fighting with
the British forces. But on a subject like this it is perhaps
best to avoid either condoning or condemning, and to keep
to such definite facts as can be found.

Statistics for illegitimate births during the Occupation
can be found in Appendix IV. They are obviously not
entirely reliable, and obviously not all illegitimate children
had German fathers. (As Dr. McKinstry, the Jersey Medical Officer, put it later: "After all, the Jerseymen didn't
abdicate completely.") Nor should any contrasts be drawn
between Jersey and Guernsey; in the case of a married
woman, the Jersey law requires the registration of the
husband's name as the father, however improbable his
paternity may be.

The figures, however, at least make it clear that some
British newspaper estimates after the war—1,000 German

babies in Jersey, 250 in Guernsey—were greatly exaggerated. The most reliable estimate made in Jersey gave a figure of about 100 born in the main maternity hospital.

There were many cases when German overtures to girls were rebuffed. Among those most sought after were the assistants at Boots, whose branches have the reputation of being staffed by the prettiest girls in the islands. The Germans used to sunbathe on the roof of a building overlooked by Boots' shop in St. Peter Port, and tried to make the most of their opportunities, but without avail. They had more success in St. Helier, and the Manager there dismissed a girl whose conduct had become well known. He was threatened with a court-martial unless the girl was reinstated and—on the advice of Cecil Harrison, the Solicitor-General—gave way. But such incidents were usually reckoned as inevitable in the circumstances.

It was also inevitable that very young children on the islands—those who had not been evacuated—should be incorrigible fraternisers. With the admiration of any children for any soldiers, they would cluster round sentries and rush out excitedly, armed with toy guns, to join in mock exercises. The Germans, with their usual fondness for children, liked to encourage them, and would give them cigarettes to take back to their fathers.

Some parents tried to discourage such friendships and told their children, if the Germans talked to them, to pretend to be simple-minded. Since there was a certain amount of genuine simple-mindedness in the islands, owing to interbreeding, this ruse could be very successful, and the Germans were left shaking their heads sadly at coming across such large-scale lunacy.

Finding billets for soldiers naturally caused hardships and unhappiness, though some Germans proved considerate and obliging guests. The three officers who were billeted on one Guernsey housewife were made to come in the back door and change into house slippers to save the carpets: whereupon her husband promptly started coming in the front door and keeping his boots on, to show who was in command of this portion of the islands.

All in all, most islanders began to feel that the phrase "A model Occupation" might not turn out to be too far off the mark. But they would not go quite so far as the *Völkischer Beobachter*, which reported to its readers that:

"The Channel Islanders, as appears natural to the German public, are almost mad with joy at having German soldiers on the islands . . . The population is extremely happy. Everybody is learning German."

CHAPTER XII

THE COUNT FROM SILESIA

The first German troops in the islands brought maps of England with them: and it was not long before the Jersey and Guernsey airfields were being used for the mass air assault on Britain that was believed to be a prelude to invasion. Day after day, during the Battle of Britain, the islanders would count the planes going north—60 one day, 68 the next, and so on. Sometimes bombers from bases in France would circle overhead till they were joined by escorting fighters from the islands.

Fortunately the islanders still had their wirelesses. They were heartened each evening by the B.B.C. news on the day's raids, to counteract the stories of German triumphs in the island papers. (A German report in the *Jersey Evening Post* said the air raid damage was so great that the King had been "unable to open Parliament in his golden cab.") Sometimes there were bits of local gossip to confirm B.B.C. accounts of the R.A.F.'s success: word went round that Luftwaffe pilots had arranged a celebration dinner for the night of August 15, but the casualties were so great that it was hurriedly cancelled. It was said that one German soldier, watching a mass raid depart, was heard to remark: "They're going over for lunch." To which a Guernseyman replied: "Yes, but they won't be back for tea."

Final confirmation came after the Battle of Briain, when British planes came over the islands dropping leaflets headed "News from Britain—Distributed by the R.A.F." They gave facts about Luftwaffe losses, and the first item was a message from the King;

> The Queen and I desire to convey to you our heartfelt sympathy in the trials which you are enduring. We earnestly pray for your speedy liberation, knowing that it will surely come.

> GEORGE, R.I.

German soldiers were sent scouring the countryside to collect these leaflets, even climbing trees to get those caught in branches, and chasing and searching civilians on Vazon racecourse who had picked them up first. Major Sherwill felt he should issue a warning—which was much criticised —emphasising that the German ban on having British propaganda material carried a fifteen year sentence, and saying the leaflets should be handed in to the German authorities. Whereupon, it is said,* one Guernsey lady promptly wrote a letter of some spirit to the Germans, saying that if she had a leaflet she would not surrender it, as it had been sent to her by His Majesty the King. She signed her name —Collas, a common one in Guernsey—but gave no address. To catch the culprit a German official, armed with a directory, made a tour of the Collas's of Guernsey, making them write specimen signatures for comparison with the letter. The guilty Miss Collas was then discovered to be a lady of over eighty, was was let off with a reprimand.

Though the Battle of Britain might be won, heartsick personal anxieties remained. Parents who had sent away their children had no way of knowing whether they were in areas being bombed. It was not till January 1941 that

* Ralph Durand: *Guernsey under German Rule*, p. 58.

divided families had their first news of each other, when a Red Cross message system was started.

During the Battle of Britain, the islanders who saw the German planes setting off could only watch helplessly—though it is said that the vicar of one church in Guernsey, as the bombers went over, could be seen on his knees in his study, praying for their destruction. Another idea occurred to Charles Roche, the Airport Controller in Jersey, who had been an airman in the First World War.

He told his Chief Groundsman, Joe Quémard, to adjust the cutters of the mowers so as to make the grass as smooth as a lawn, instead of the usual four inches. He thought that, with rain and dew, and pilots not touching down soon enough, this might encourage planes to run on into the fence which used to surround the airfield. Twenty-eight planes were damaged in this way before the end of the year, including a record occasion when one slid into three others parked along the fence. Eventually even the Germans commented on how short the grass was cut. "We *have* to cut it like that," said Roche blandly. "It grows faster in Jersey than anywhere else." But the Germans later took to cutting the grass themselves.

In later years, a German soldier from the first occupying force told the present authors of the things about the islands which had particularly struck him and his companions. They marvelled at the goods in the shops, and the general cleanliness compared with France. But most striking of all was the complete absence of any sabotage or resistance. The Germans were always expecting to be ambushed or attacked, and always surprised that nothing of the sort happened. When they proceeded, soon after their arrival, to requisition motor cars, they would refuse two-door saloons because of the difficulty of getting out of them quickly if attacked. And at first they would drive the requisitioned cars slowly and gingerly, fully expecting them to have been tampered with so that a vital part would give way at a crucial moment. They were amazed when nothing of the sort ever happened.

The surprise felt by the Germans at the conduct of the

islanders was more than equalled, of course, by the surprise of the islanders at the unimpeachable conduct of the Germans. Once Sherwill was bold enough to tackle Maass directly on the subject, and asked why the German behaviour was so markedly different from that reported elsewhere. To which Dr. Maass replied that British people could not conceive the bitterness of the feelings in Europe —in Poland, for instance, where any German soldier was likely to get a knife in his back after dark; or even in France.

It is certainly something of a curiosity that the Channel Islands, the only British territories among all the countries occupied by Germans, were also almost the only ones where there was no resistance movement. Perhaps the main reason was that men of fighting age in the islands had been urged to leave before the Occupation and join the forces. Those who did so were just the men who might have led resistance. They were to win glory for their islands on many fields, led by Major Le Patourel, the V.C. of North Africa. The position was quite different from France, where young men were caught at home. Added to this are the facts that the islands had no worthwhile railways or factories to sabotage, and that the concentration of German troops was to be far greater. At one time there were more Germans per square mile in Guernsey than in Germany itself.

Yet another difference was the inherent respect of the Germans for the British, and for Sherwill in particular. To a large extent this was reciprocated. Sherwill described Lanz as "absolutely straight and kindly". The first of the German invaders were the finest type of soldiers, who marched the islands singing as they went—singing interminably, till the islanders grew sick of hearing them.

About the middle of August, however, came the first stage of a process of steady deterioration. The improvised military rule, under Lanz in Guernsey and Gussek in Jersey, was ended. Both went on to fighting commands: Lanz was to be killed on the Russian Front, Gussek in North Africa. Dr. Maass also left. Instead, there was introduced a much more complicated system, the military command of the islands being separated from *Feldkommandantur 515*, responsible for civilian administration. The *Feldkommandantur* was mostly staffed by peace-time clerks, lawyers, etc., who arrived in vast numbers.

The only consolation felt by the islanders, as they watched this cumbrous organisation establishing itself, was that it meant a German admission that the Occupation —and therefore the war—was going to last a long time.

Captain Gussek, going to say goodbye to Coutanche in Jersey, remarked sarcastically of his bureaucratic successors: *"Jetzt geht der Papierkrieg los!"*—"the paper war is going to begin." Gussek was reminded of his early prophecy that the Occupation would only last six weeks. "It's more than six weeks since you came here," he was told, "but you haven't won the war yet."

Gussek took it in good part, with the philosophy of a regular soldier. *"C'est la guerre,"* he said.

The Germans who came and went during the following years were so numerous, and the division of responsibility between them so complicated, that few made much impression. One of those most praised was Dr. Casper, of the *Feldkommandantur* in Jersey. Another popular figure was Prince von Oettingen, of the Guernsey *Feldkommandantur* —a wealthy Bavarian landowner, a cultured internationalist, and a devout Catholic who saw that German soldiers went to Church. But the one outstanding figure was a Silesian aristocrat, Colonel Graf von Schmettow, who arrived towards the end of September 1940 as military Commander-in-Chief of all the islands. He set up his headquarters in Jersey, with a Major Bandelow as the military Commandant in Guernsey.

Count von Schmettow, a nephew of von Rundstedt, was a German aristocrat and hereditary soldier of the old school. His father was a personal friend of the Kaiser and visited him each year in exile at Doorn. Schmettow himself, joining the cavalry in 1909, had served continuously in the German Army for over thirty years. He was wounded on the Eastern Front during the First World War, and later lost a lung when gassed on the Western Front, where he commanded an infantry regiment. In bearing he was tall and erect, with parabolic eyebrows, and he had a dour look which concealed a dry sense of humour and unusually wide interests for a soldier. He was fond of classical literature and of country life, and at his happiest on horseback.

When he was appointed to the Channel Islands, Schemttow was given only one directive by Count Brockdorf, his superior officer: "Remember that it is English territory you are going to, not defeated France." Schmettow was determined to avoid repressive measures, believing that if English people were treated fairly there would be no trouble.

The civil administration of the islands, however, did not come directly under Count von Schmettow, but under *Feldkommandantur 515*, which had its headquarters at Victoria College House, Jersey, and a branch of the Grange Lodge Hotel in Guernsey. The *Feldkommandantur* commanded by Colonel Schumacher and later by Colonel Knackfuss, took its instructions from General Schreiber, head of "Section A" at St. Germain: "Section A" being itself one subdivision of the German administration of France. For administrative purposes, including food rationing, the Channel Islands were put under the Department de la Manche. This, explained the Germans, was "rectifying the map of Europe".*

Schmettow and Schumacher, however, protested against automatically applying all measures for Occupied France to the Channel Islands, like reproducing the grim notices in the newspapers about Frenchmen who had been "fusilated" for sabotage. They had continual battles with the Germans in St. Germain and Paris, who hated to admit that the islands were not part of their bureaucratic Empire. To create a better understanding of the islands, and their

* The German propaganda, of course, was that the Channel Islands should not feel themselves bound by any loyalty to Britain, since they were French islands which had been stolen.

Dr. Brosch, of the Guernsey branch of the *Feldkommandantur*, even asked Sherwill's legal advice on whether it was possible that Guernsey was not really at war with Germany. Sherwill stoutly retorted that there was no doubt whatever about it.

unique position, Schmettow asked for an historian to write a book on them, and this assignment was duly carried out by Dr. Hans Auerbach.

Soon after Count von Schmettow arrived, he was able to get permission for himself and Colonel Schumacher to reject or modify, on their own responsibility, the regulations which came from St. Germain, so as to allow for the special circumstances in the Channel Islands. Their continual pleas for favoured treatment for the islanders became something of a joke. When General Oberst Hase, commanding the German 16th Army, was on a visit, he opened their talks by saying, "Don't tell me now—we're going to hear more about your 'special circumstances'." To which Count von Schmettow was able to retort that the circumstances certainly *were* special, in comparison with all the sabotage, resistance, and trouble which General Oberst Hase was having in France.

The Occupation, in fact, still kept something of an informal flavour about it. Once Dr. Brosch of the *Feldkommandantur* in Guernsey, calling at Major Sherwill's home, took off his belt and revolver and hung them up in the hall. Sherwill remonstrated with him, saying he was afraid his children might get hold of the revolver and start playing with it. "Don't worry," said Brosch. "It's not loaded."

CHAPTER XIII

SHORTADES AND A MISSION

For the time being at any rate, and politics apart, there was no doubt that the future of the Channel Islands lay with France. Cut off from England, they must get supplies from France or else starve and shiver. Their highly speci-

I.I.D.—D

alised forms of agriculture could not feed everyone: even their famous cattle did not make them self-sufficient for milk and milk products. Guernsey, for instance, was in normal times an *importer* of butter.

Of the two main islands, Jersey was always more favoured than Guernsey. The lie of the land in Jersey is tilted south to catch the sun, whereas Guernsey slopes in the opposite direction, with high cliffs in the south and flat country in the north. Under the vigorous leadership of Coutanche, Jersey quickly transformed itself from a potato island to a wheat island, and the old water mills were brought into working order again for making flour. But Guernsey was handicapped, not only by the lie of the land, but also by its glasshouses. They stood in the way of arable farming; they were a drain on fuel for heating; they also needed plentiful water supplies, and that meant more fuel for the Water Board's pumping stations.

At the time of the Occupation, about half the season's tomato crops had been sent to England; the rest was fed to cattle and pigs, given away, or eventually thrown away. The glasshouses were taken over by a public board which made the best use of them it could. Some tomatoes were still grown, with a view to exporting them to France, and other crops tried. But most experiments were unsuccessful. Glasshouse wheat, for instance, rose to a magnificent height, but failed to form any ears. The best crop turned out to be sweetcorn, which could be ground for flour.

(In one other respect the glasshouses also put Guernsey at a disadvantage. Whereas Jersey had plenty of trees for emergency firewood, in Guernsey many trees had been cut down because they put the glasshouses in the shade.)

On both islands, of course, the problem was not only to grow more food, but to stop the Germans requisitioning it for their troops, by pretending that there was even less food than there was. Here again, generation after generation of Jersey farmers, versed in every traditional trick of the weighbridge—the earth with the potatoes, the dog that jumps on the cart—had a great advantage over the upstart glasshouse growers of Guernsey. The typical Jersey farmer, wealthy and canny and secretive, often still keeping his money in a cupboard rather than letting any bank have it, too shrewd to appear anything but simple, was something far beyond the ken of most of the German administrators.

They would be baffled by a strange lack of comprehension, a kind of good-natured inability to grasp the point at issue. And the Jersey farmers were well served by one of their number, Touzel Bree, as President of the Department of Agriculture.

Bree was a small man, with a perpetual twinkle in his eye. The eldest son of a big family, he had left school early when his father died, and built up the family farm by the hard work and shrewdness typical of the Breton peasant stock from which he came. Now he used the same craftiness against the Germans.

The German in charge of agriculture had no chance against him. Throughout, Bree systematically hid food stocks and falsified returns; but however much his adversary might fuss and fume, he could never catch Bree out. Bree remained the same: always imperturbable, walking slowly with a shuffling gait, speaking slowly and softly. Nothing could ever make him speak faster or raise his voice.

"My dear boy, my dear boy," he would remark gently to the enraged German, "you don't know what you're talking about." Touzel Bree made a point, however, of keeping on friendly terms with the Germans, and aroused hostility among some Jerseymen by giving them presents of fruit and vegetables.

Guernseymen never enjoyed deceiving the Germans, and trying to lead them a dance, as much as the Jerseymen. (As far back as the Civil War, when Jerseymen had been Royalists, Guernseymen had been Roundheads and Puritans.) Grey-haired Ernest de Garis, head of one of the three agricultural boards in Guernsey, and known everywhere as a man of the highest honour, said sorrowfully after the Occupation that "It's a terrible thing to live a life of lying."

However successfully both islands might grow food, and

keep it from the Germans, it was plain that many basic foodstuffs would have to come from Europe. All the islands also needed to import essentials like coal, petrol, paraffin, manufactured goods, clothes, medicines and drugs. Nobody knew what the chances were of getting supplies; the B.B.C. announced that Europe itself was threatened with famine.

But one Sunday afternoon, soon after the Occupation began, Major Sherwill was looking out of his window over the Russel, when he saw the smoke of a steamer. To his delight, it was making for St. Peter Port. It turned out to be the s.s. *Holland*, which had come to start up a new service between the Channel Islands and the Continent. This was taken as a harbinger of possible hope for the future. It was decided that Jersey and Guernsey would send over a purchasing commission to Granville, on the French mainland, to see what could be done about buying supplies.

A man for such a mission would need an ability to get on with both French and German people; a fluent command of French; some knowledge of French businessmen and their methods; abundant energy; and enough native shrewdness to be able to buy wheat or wireless batteries or coal or drugs or children's shoes or meat or anything else, without being diddled too badly. Where in Guernsey, asked Sherwill, was such a man to be found? His colleagues agreed that there was only one man: Raymond Falla, the Chief Guernsey Agricultural Officer, and opposite number to Touzel Bree of Jersey.

Falla was dark and tough and tirelessly energetic, with fluent French and a flow of talk amusing enough to beguile even the Germans and the French black marketeers.

On August 16, 1940, with an assistant and £7,000 in Occupation marks in his suitcase, he left for Granville and was joined by Jersey's enterprising representative, John Louis Jouault. They travelled all over France hunting down supplies. Throughout this period Falla rarely wrote a letter, and never wrote a cheque, all his dealings—frequently in the Black Market—being carried out by personal contact in some strangely unconventional places, and with cash.

He could not open a banking account in France in the

name of the States, for this would have counted as a British-owned asset and therefore been liable for confiscation. His only bank was a rickety wardrobe in his hotel bedroom in Granville. Whenever he needed more money, Louis Guillemette's, the Bailiff's, secretary in Guernsey, or some other official would bring over £75,000 or so in franc and mark notes, packed into Tate and Lyle sugar boxes or whatever else they could find. As Falla had to deal so much in the Black Market, he kept two sets of books—one giving the real figures, and a second to show the Vichy authorities. For the first set he always collected receipts for every payment—even "commissions."

Once, when he paid £3,000 to a dealer for agricultural seds, it took both men two hours to count out and check the notes stacked upon his bed in a small top-floor Paris hotel room.

Though Falla went back to Guernsey to keep on his work as Chief Agricultural Officer, he continued making frequent visits to France.

Since the French themselves were hungry and short of everything the Channel Islands wanted, it needed more than bribery to get supplies. But Falla could speak the dialects of the different districts, and would often spend a couple of hours chatting with a man before bringing up business. Then, in his soft, droll way, he would talk of his native islands and of the plight of *"les cousins normands"*, until the Frenchman felt he had known Falla and the Channel Islands all his life.

The supplies from France, of course, were often imperfect stopgaps: shoddy goods which were a poor replacement for the stocks bought out of the shops in the early days by the Germans, paid for by paper money, and sent back to Germany as booty in the form of gifts to soldiers' families. Falla and Jouault and the others in France had to take what was going when they could get it, and the most surprising consignments arrived—including ten thousand pounds' worth of false teeth, some of them coloured. Basic necessities remained scarce, and got scarcer and scarcer as the Occupation proceeded.

When salt grew short, attempts were made in Guernsey to get it by evaporation from the sea in the Model Yacht pond; and salt water was used for cooking. One of the many curious sights of the Occupation was to see two nuns from Les Côtils nursing home driving a horse-drawn carriage down to the Longstore. On the van was an ordinary bath. Arriving by the sea, the nuns got down with buckets, proceeded to fill the bath with seawater, and then drove back again.

With scarcities came the inevitable Black Markets, supplied with food from local farms, and with luxuries brought in by sailors on the ships from France, or by German soldiers returning from leave. Some Germans used their positions to make friendly arrangements with local Black Market operators. The Black Market in Jersey was flagrant and unashamed among those who could afford the prices; after the war, one man in Jersey boasted to the present writers that he had never lacked a Sunday joint. (His butcher's bill had come to about £60 a quarter.) Defeating rationing and price regulations was usually looked on as a kind of game. In Guernsey, characteristically, the attitude was not quite so lighthearted; partly because of the noncomformist conscience derived from Huguenot and Methodist tradition, and partly because the scarcities were so much greater that even the Black Market would run out of supplies.

As the shops found most of their usual stocks exhausted, many could only keep going by turning themselves into "barter shops", where one sort of article was handed in to be exchanged for another, either over or under the counter.

They said in Guernsey, after the Occupation, that the only two things which never ran short were fresh air and toilet paper. The latter necessity was met by the huge stocks of different-coloured paper used for packing tomatoes. This was cut up in sheets and sold in packets: and some housewives remarked that it represented a rare refinement of luxury to be able to choose a toilet paper to match the colour scheme of their bathrooms.

CHAPTER XIV

BRITISH AGENTS RETURN

Hubert Nicolle, after his secret visit to Guernsey just after the Occupation, had gone back to his regiment. Towards the end of August 1940 he was summoned to London again and asked to take on a second plain-clothes fact-finding mission, this time in company with another young Guernseyman from The Hampshire Regiment, Jim Symes.

The high-ups were still experimenting in different ways and means of sending in agents. This time they travelled by motor torpedo boat from Portland, and were landed at Petit Port at about 3 a.m. on September 4, 1940. They avoided the steps, climbing a path up the cliff. Allowing for pauses when they heard rabbits moving which they thought might be Germans, it took them about an hour to get up.

Each had exactly 5s. 4d. in cash, and a flask of brandy. By the time they got to the top Symes' flask was empty.

They went to the Ville au Roi, to the home of Nicolle's uncle—Captain Frank Nicolle, the Assistant Harbourmaster. They had breakfast, and a sleep: Symes slept so soundly that they had difficulty in waking him. Afterwards he remarked that he had been so frightened that first night that he would never be frightened again.

Symes wanted to be able to watch the airfield; and also, if possible, to avoid implicating his parents by letting them know of his presence. His girl friend, Mary Bird, was living with her parents in a house near the airfield, and Symes decided to make it his headquarters. Frank Nicolle and Mary's father, Wilfred Bird, had a common interest in stamp collecting; so Nicolle rang him up, said he had come on a rare specimen, and asked if he could see him about it. Bird was then working in an office at Elizabeth College: they talked outside in Frank Nicolle's car, and Wilfred Bird agreed to shelter Jim Symes.

So Symes went off to the house, Mrs. Bird being so taken aback by his sudden appearance there that she fainted.

Hubert Nicolle stayed on with his uncle, all went well, and the two men got all the information they wanted. It had been pre-arranged that the M.T.B. was to pick them up again three nights later. They went to Petit Port on the appointed night, climbed down to the beach, and then, with their specially hooded torch, flashed the letter 'R' in morse out to sea at intervals of twenty minutes. They went on doing this from one in the morning till four, reducing the interval to ten minutes, but nothing happened. They tried again the following night; the arrangement was that, if either side missed the rendezvous, it was to be repeated. Again there was no result. They tried a third time, just to make sure; then they gave up and stayed at their homes. It was useless going on frequenting the mined cliffs of Petit Port on the increasingly remote chance of an M.T.B. putting in an appearance.

Another way of escape was planned. A retired sea captain, Captain Noyon, who was to become one of the heroes of the Occupation, had a fishing boat. He agreed to slip in to Bordeaux Harbour, so that Symes and Nicolle could pick up the boat there and set sail for England. But there was a setback.

On Friday, September 6, a party of eight men had escaped in a boat from Guernsey to England. Like all escape stories, their exploit appealed to the imagination, and they were welcomed as heroes in Britain. But the Germans soon after decided to ban all fishing from harbours round the Guernsey coast; and ordered boats to be concentrated, under strict control, at St. Peter Port. This made any chance of Symes and Nicolle getting away very much more difficult, though the escapees could not possibly have foreseen it. The restriction also meant a blow to the fishermen's livelihoods, and a further deprivation of food suplies for the islanders. Major Sherwill was moved to issue a strong condemnation of the escapees, which caused some controversy. He described them as "running away", and added:

> "In the event of a repetition of any such incident there is a grave possibility that, by way of reprisal, the male population of this island will be evacuated to France."

Sherwill followed up this notice by ordering the police to keep a special watch on all bays, to stop anyone else escaping. He did not know at the time, of course, that there were two British officers on Guernsey who were trying to get away.

It happened, however, that Hubert Nicolle's father, Emile Nicolle, the Secretary to the Controlling Committee, had been sent on sick leave by the States a little before, and was now with his wife at Grandes Rocques. They wanted to be able to come back and see their son without rousing suspicion, so Emile Nicolle asked to be recalled to work. Major Sherwill was consulted about it, and was thus implicated in knowing of the presence of two agents in the island.

It cannot be denied that there were some strong feelings on the part of the Guernsey authorities. If Sherwill had angered Whitehall by his broadcasts from Bremen, he himself was now thoroughly angry with Whitehall. For the second time they had chosen to send in, as a secret agent, the son of a prominent States official. Sherwill thought again of his son John, in the Navy, another possible arrival. Louis Guillemette, the Bailiff's secretary, learnt that his brother was actually next on the list to come in; and for weeks he was always listening for the faint tap on door or window that would mean that his brother had arrived.

Meanwhile the problem of finding some way of saving Nicolle and Symes was becoming increasingly urgent. More and more people were learning of their presence, and becoming liable to drastic penalties—Sherwill and different

States officials; Nicolle's father and mother, his uncle the Assistant Harbour Master; his girl friend Jessie Marriette, her parents; Symes' father and mother, his friend Mary Bird, her parents, and so on.

To try and save their families from possible punishment, Symes and Nicolle kept away from them and spent three nights in the cricket pavilion of their old school, Elizabeth College, sheltered by Bill Allen the groundsman. In the evenings they would stroll across the playing field and climb over the back wall into Bill Allen's cottage, where they would listen to the wireless and drink Bovril made by Mrs. Allen, and where Jessie Marriette would come in to see Nicolle. In the morning Bill Allen would take them over a jug of tea to the pavilion.

They were determined to hold on as long as possible. They did not want, like Martel and Mulholland, to surrender too soon. And in fact an attempt to rescue them was made, towards the end of September, by a special volunteer—Captain John Parker, a regular soldier, who had been brought up on the island and whose father still lived there.

One escapee from the island had reported in England that all men of military age had been removed from Guernsey. This was quite untrue; but it was a fortunate mistake for Parker. For he decided that, if any young man still on the island would attract attention anyhow, he might just as well go in uniform. His plan was to move only under cover of night—get ashore and hide the first night, contact Symes and Nicolle the second, and get away the third.

He arrived in an M.T.B., which came in for the last five miles on electric motors to cut out noise. It was a black night, with a new moon, when he landed near Corbière. He proceeded to try and work his way up the cliff by crawling forward on his elbows in the approved manner; but unfortunately the people who write training manuals had not reckoned on gorse. His arms bleeding, Parker had to proceed on foot, to the alarming sound of the popping of gorse pods. He trod as lightly as he could—"like a ballet dancer" as he put it afterwards—and managed to reach the top of the cliff before, in the groping darkness, he plunged with an appalling clatter into a trench which had an ammunition box at the bottom of it. He had tip-toed straight into a German A.A. gun battery.

He lay still, hoping that German regulations against showing any sort of light in the blackout might be as strict as in Britain, and that after the first alarm he would be able to creep away. Unfortunately these hopes were dashed: there immediately appeared from one side a sentry armed with a torch, and from the other side eight men armed with Tommy guns. They gazed down upon him.

"For you," one of them remarked, "the war is over."

He was sent over to prison at Cherbourg, where throughout repeated interrogations he succeeded in hiding the real object of his mission; stoutly maintaining, in spite of obvious German suspicions, that he had been sent to watch the airfield.

Some of the efforts to trap him into talking were not very subtle. He was told he was to have a fellow prisoner, who had been caught with a wireless transmitter in Jersey. The new prisoner started chatting to him in what seemed rather a stilted form of English. Parker was not encouraged to answer his questions by the fact that, warming his hands round the hot-water pipe in the cell, he had found behind it a pair of wires running to a microphone hidden in the ceiling. . . .

Parker's fellow prisoner ended by making clumsy attempts to scare him. He had come back to the cell, as though from an interrogation, to remark gloomily, "They're talking of hanging now." Early next morning guards came into the cell, ostentatiously handcuffed him, and led him away. Any doubts Parker might have had about his genuineness were removed by his final words, delivered with a rather un-English air of melodrama. He had turned to Parker and said: "Well farewell, Captain!"

Parker, still suspected of something irregular and still not talking, was moved on to the Cherche Midi prison in Paris: and eventually the Germans decided to treat him as an ordinary prisoner of war.

The Germans also interrogated Parker's father in Guernsey, but he of course knew nothing. Extraordinary rumours spread about the affair. Just after Parker had been taken prisoner, the Germans had heard the M.T.B. which had brought him in starting up its engines, having travelled the first few miles out on its electric motors. The Germans mistook the sound for an aeroplane's engines, and guessed that Parker had landed by parachute. The more he insisted that he had come in by boat, the more certain they were that he was lying. The story of his arrival by parachute became so firmly established that it was not long before his father was being presented, as a souvenir, with "a piece of the actual parachute" with which he had landed.

CHAPTER XV

MAJOR BANDELOW'S PROMISE

Whatever the Germans may have thought or suspected, the purpose of Parker's mission could be guessed easily enough by Sherwill, Symes and Nicolle. Thereafter their position was almost hopeless; for they knew that another four weeks must elapse before the moon would be right for another landing.

They went on planning more ways of escape. Symes was a good enough linguist to speak passable German, and their most daring idea was to get hold of the motor boat used by Major Bandelow, the Guernsey Commandant— Symes posing as Bandelow—and then make a run for it through the harbour entrance, between the guns on the north and south breakwaters. The difficulty was to get someone to come with them to work the engine; they had protracted bargaining in which they offered successively £100, then £1,000, plus the proceeds of selling the boat when they got to England, plus the proceeds of selling copies of Occupation newspapers—the rumour had come back of escapees selling information about the Occupation for big sums in Fleet Street. But in the end they could not persuade the man they were dealing with that any possible reward was worth the risks.

It was certain, sooner or later, that the Germans would hear the spreading whispers about British officers being on the island. They realised how easy it was for men who knew the coastline to slip ashore on dark nights. They also suspected, wrongly, that there were still soldiers left behind after the July commando raid. So Major Bandelow, the Commandant in Guernsey, rang up Colonel Graf von Schmettow in Jersey, his newly arrived Commander-in-Chief.

Bandelow said that he proposed to take a whole battalion and comb the island. Schmettow retorted that it was ridiculuous to think of searching every house, every field, every cart, every milk lorry. Most German soldiers could not speak English, and the islanders could not speak German, so there would be no way of interrogating civilians. And, since there was no identity card system, nobody could tell if a man really *was* a British officer, or a local inhabitant, even if they caught him.

Schmettow suggested, as an alternative, that an amnesty should be promised to any British officers in hiding, provided they surrendered. In the meanwhile he ordered the introduction of identity cards.

And so, early in October, Major Sherwill was sent for by Major Bandelow, who chatted to him about how he had been shooting rabbits on Herm. Sherwill remarked cheerfully that one day a Spitfire would be coming to shoot up Bandelow in his Headquarters at the Channel Island Hotel. Bandelow laughed, and they got down to business.

Bandelow said that he believed British soldiers were in hiding in the island. Sherwill expressed great surprise at hearing any such suggestion, and thought quickly. Once again, there might be nothing but his wit and skill in playing a dangerous game to save two young men from being shot.

109

Bandelow said that any British soldiers who gave themselves up would be treated as prisoners of war. Sherwill accepted this proposal, and had the promise confirmed by an interchange of letters which, at his suggestion, was published in the *Guernsey Evening Press* of October 12, 1940. Both letters were drafted by Sherwill himself.

Bandelow, after a friendly reference to the "pleasant relations" existing on the islands, went on to make his promise of an amnesty. Sherwill replied:

Dear Herr Commandant,

I have the honour to acknowledge the receipt of your letter of to-day's date.

In the first place I welcome your kind message to the effect that, having acquainted yourself with conditions on the island, you can assure me of the continuance of the pleasant relations which have hitherto existed between the Army of Occupation and the population. ...

I have noted that you intend to arrange with me a time limit within which any personnel of the British Armed Forces in hiding in this island (if such there be) must surrender, and that, if this direction is complied with, such personnel will be treated as prisoners of war and no measures will be taken against any of their relatives.

This, Herr Commandant, is a generous gesture on your part. . . .

It gives me ground for confidence that, at a period when the nations to which we respectively belong are locked in a combat, the consequences of which will be momentous to Europe and the whole world, it is possible—though only in the Channel Islands—for a German officer and a British official to enter into friendly correspondence, to engage in full and frank discussions and to exchange courtesies.

I beg that you will acquaint me of any happening to which you may take exception, and I ask that, with that humanity of which you have consistently shown yourself to be possessed, you will permit me to intercede on behalf of anyone who, unwittingly or without appreciation of the consequences, may offend against the German Military Code.

A. J. SHERWILL.

Sherwill himself was to remark in later years that some phrases in this letter were "a bit too smarmy", and they came in for considerable criticism in Guernsey, where, of course, few people had any idea what lay behind them. The crucial words were those in brackets: "(if such there be) . . ." Sherwill was warned that they might afford evidence against him of deliberately misleading the Germans. But he refused to take them out.

And in this, as it turned out later, he was right: Bandelow, in suggesting he knew that there were British soldiers on the island, had not really been certain.

As in the case of Martel and Mulholland, Symes and Nicolle had to be found uniforms before they surrendered. This time the problem was solved by Nicolle's uncle, Captain Frank Nicolle, the Assistant Harbourmaster. He learned from Gerald Hamon, the Harbourmaster's clerk, that in one of the harbour sheds there was a stock of battle-dresses brought back from Alderney when its machine-gun training unit was evacuated before the Occupation. Captain Nicolle had the use of a car, and a free pass in and out of the port area; so it was fairly easy for him one lunchtime to drive up to the shed, let himself in with Hamon's key, stow two uniforms in a sack, put it in the boot of the car, and drive away.

The final Notice calling for the surrender of British servicemen, with its promise of an amnesty, was signed by Dr. Brosch of the *Feldkommandantur* and dated October 18, 1940. Sherwill had contrived to have the date for surrendering delayed till October 21, so that Symes and Nicolle had over a week's respite to try other ways of escape. A chance of getting away with a party escaping from Grand Havre was lost because the Germans got wind of it and put on extra guards. Symes and Nicolle then planned to steal a boat themselves; they even contem-

111

plated trying to cross the Channel in a canoe; but every scheme came to nothing. All the same, they still hesitated about what to do until Symes went to consult a retired officer from the Hampshire Regiment, Major-General Williams, who was emphatic that, for the sake of their relatives and the people in the island, they should give themselves up.

Emile Nicolle also consulted Sherwill, who gave the same advice.

"Will the Germans keep their word about treating them as prisoners of war?" asked Emile.

"Yes," said Sherwill, "they will keep their word."

Symes and Nicolle had a farewell party in Nicolle's home, and some bottles of champagne were even found for the occasion. Then, just before the last appointed hour, they surrendered to the police, wearing uniforms and carrying civilian clothes in a parcel.

Sherwill happened to be at a meeting of parish Constables when he got a telephone message that two British officers had just given themselves up. His simulation of surprise was such an excellent piece of acting that everyone present was taken in by it.

Count von Schmettow had agreed with Colonel Schumacher, the *Feldkommandantur*, that they would say nothing to their respective superior officers unless the promise of an amnesty brought any results. Once Symes and Nicolle surrendered, Schmettow reported this to Count Brockdorf, and Schumacher reported it to General Schreiber at St. Germain. Brockdorf agreed with Schmettow that, since an amnesty had been promised, there was nothing more to be said. But Schreiber became obsessed with the idea that Symes and Nicolle had been landed to organise a resistance movement; he demanded that an example should be made of them and their helpers, severe enough to discourage anything else of the sort in future—not only in the Channel Islands, but also in France. The German Counter Intelligence service immediately took the matter up, and arrived in strength in the islands.

Symes and Nicolle were taken separately to Fort George

and questioned from nine in the morning to twelve; then from two to six in the evening; the same thing the next day and the next. The same questions were asked over and over again: "Where did you land?", "When did you land?" One day, Nicolle's interrogations lasted for fourteen hours.

At the same time the Germans called in their fathers and mothers; their friends, Jessie Marriette and Mary Bird, and the girls' fathers and mothers; even Bill Allen, the Elizabeth College Groundsman who had sheltered them. It must be said that the German secret police who made the arrests sometimes showed themselves sympathetic. The plain clothes man who picked up Emile Nicolle, Hubert's father, was a pre-war schoolmaster named Schröder. He sighed heavily as they went off in the car, and asked, "When will this war be over?" And after the German police arrived to arrest Bill Allen, his wife made some remark which gave away that she also had something to do with looking after Symes and Nicolle. One German quickly silenced her: "Don't say anything more about it."

Bit by bit the Germans pieced together the story of what had happened. It was, in fact, quite impossible for as many people as were questioned to agree in telling the same story, without detailed rehearsal beforehand about what story they would tell. Captain Nicolle, for instance, was asked about his nephew's civilian clothes. He discovered that Hubert had told the Germans that he had got his grey flannel trousers from his uncle, and of course Captain Nicolle confirmed that the trousers were his. Then he was asked questions about them: were they new or old? Patched or not patched? Where were the patches? Captain Nicolle, of course, was hopelessly caught out.

The main interrogator was a fat little German judge whose legs were so short that he had an upturned wastepaper basket in front of his chair to rest them on. Whenever he caught out someone telling a particularly obvious lie, he would shout with anger and kick the wastepaper basket across the room; whereupon the Orderly standing

113

behind him would solemnly march forward, retrieve it, and put it in front of his chair again.

At the beginning of his last interrogation, Hubert Nicolle was greeted with "Why didn't you tell us about your earlier visit to the island?" and he knew the game was up. At the end the German spat out: "You are a common or dirty garden spy. You will be shot."

CHAPTER XVI

"A FEW DAYS IN PARIS"

German Security Police came round to Havelet House to place Major Sherwill under house arrest. He received them with his usual good manners; and, it being a cold day, called out to his wife to put a match to the drawing-room fire. In a flash, two of the Germans dashed off to see if he was burning any incriminating documents.

Sherwill was questioned, and said nothing; but it was soon obvious that the Germans knew that he had known of Symes and Nicolle being on the island. "We never expected this of you," said one of his interrogators. "We thought you were our man." For the first time Sherwill realised that the conciliatory tone of his letters and speeches could be misinterpreted. "That's not true," he retorted hotly. "I was never your man, and you know it."

Meanwhile, as they talked, his wife waited helplessly outside. She could not even telephone to the Controlling Committee to let them know what was happning, as there was a guard on the telephone in the hall. But nothing could daunt May Sherwill. When at last she could get in the room she upbraided Sherwill's interrogators so savagely that the Germans appealed to him to protect them.

"Please—tell her that we haven't been treating you unfairly," they said.

Nothing could stop her.

"Your husband did not tell us the truth," they pleaded. "We've got it down in black and white."

"I don't mind if you've got it down in blue and purple," she retorted. "I know my husband. He never told a lie in his life."

That night, May Sherwill lay awake upstairs till dawn, wondering miserably what she could do, and whether she should risk trying to use the telephone extension in the bedroom. Sherwill spent the night—which he fully expected to be one of his last on earth—sitting up before the fire with two German guards. They had begun the evening by retiring to a corner and ostentatiously loading their revolvers with noisy clicks. But they began to relax in the early hours of the morning, and it ended by them all having a pleasant discussion—in French, their only common language—on world politics.

One of the two Germans was a professional soldier; he explained that a war meant casualties, and casualties meant promotion. The other was a peace-time architect from Cologne, who hated being in the Army. "Ah," said Sherwill, turning from one to the other with a smile, "*Monsieur Destruction—et Monsieur Construction.*"

In the morning more German officers arrived. "I suppose," Sherwill asked one of them, "I am going to be shot?" He was told: "No, we don't shoot people as easily as that. You will be tried first."

Sherwill asked if he could clean his son's shoes. It was something he did every morning. One of the Germans went down with him to the basement and watched till he had finished.

The Controlling Committee of the States of Guernsey, in the absence of their President, met that morning in agitated session at Elizabeth College—having first looked behind all the pictures on the walls to see if there were any concealed microphones. The Germans had already acted swiftly. All wireless sets had been confiscated, on the other islands as well as Guernsey, as a punishment to the populations as a whole for harbouring spies. Jurat John Leale had been told that, if all those responsible were not discovered, twenty leading citizens would be seized as hostages and shot.

"I suppose that includes me?" asked Leale.

"Yes, but you mustn't take it like that," was the reply. The German seemed quite upset. "It's not a personal matter."

To the astonishment of the Controlling Committee, their meeting was ended by the sudden appearance in their midst of Major Sherwill. Soon after midday, a German officer had arrived at his house and inexplicably announced that he was to be set free. But Nicolle, Symes, their relatives and girl friends and other helpers—a party of seventeen in all—were taken to France and put into solitary confinement at the Cherche Midi prison, Paris.

Despite protests from Schmettow, General Schreiber had determined to stage a big trial there, to strike terror into anyone in France should British agents arrive to start resistance movements.

Sherwill tenaciously protested, taking his stand throughout on the fact that the Germans had promised an amnesty. The Germans, in reply, agreed that a promise was a promise; but said the final decision now would have to be made in Berlin. And they could claim that the promise had been won by a trick, because Sherwill, trying to save Symes and Nicolle, had pretended not to know they were on the island. In this the Germans had some justice on their side; and Sherwill felt certain he would be shot.

He had no illusions when, one afternoon, he was told that he also was being taken to Paris "for a few days."

He arrived at Guernsey airport to find a Junkers transport plane awaiting him. He joked with the Germans that he was always airsick: they took him literally, and put a fire bucket on the plane beside him. Next he professed great fear that the Junkers might be shot down by a Spitfire; they solemnly explained that this was most unlikely.

"All the same," said Sherwill, "I wish I could have a

little Union Jack to wave out of the window if a Spitfire comes. Then I would be safe, and you would be safe, and I would be given the Iron Cross."

Sherwill spent the night in a luxury suite at the Hotel des Ambassadeurs in Paris. At ten o'clock the following night, however, he was abruptly transferred to prison at Versailles, and shown into a cell with a straw palliasse on the floor, no blankets, a table, a bench, a water tap, a leaky water jug, and a filthy lavatory in one corner.

In the days of solitary confinement that followed he found himself, for the first time, understanding the meaning of the phrase, "the balance of his mind was disturbed." He was alarmed to realise that he was alternating between light-headed optimism and deep depression, and deliberately tried to counter-balance each mood. Whenever he felt too cheerful, he would remind himself, "You know, you're for the High Jump"; when he became depressed, he would assure himself that things weren't so bad. To occupy his mind, and save himself from going mad, he set about cleaning his cell. As implements he had a nailbrush and a razor blade. First he cleaned the lavatory bowl, and scraped and scrubbed the seat till it was spotless. Then he polished the water tap till it shone brightly. Next he turned his attentions to the walls, covered with obscene drawings, and scraped them clean, inch by inch. German guards came peering into the cell to watch the mad Englishman.

Allowed out in the yard for exercise, he picked up three sycamore leaves, and brought them back to his cell—two as plates for his bread and butter, and a multi-coloured one for ornament.

He remembered that he had promised one of his boys a bicycle, and wrote a letter to his wife enclosing £5 in notes. He was not allowed to send it.

Sherwill had started scraping his table clean when, after four days, he was transferred to join the others from Guernsey in the notorious Cherche Midi prison.

Here each of the prisoners was confined in a cell measuring ten feet by five, dimly lit from a tiny window high up in one wall. There was a little round inspection hole in every door, and from time to time the fishlike eye of a guard could be seen watching silently; some of the prisoners began to feel an almost irresistible desire to poke the eye with a finger. Only once a day were a favoured few allowed out of the cell—to empty their sanitary buckets in a cesspool in the yard. Soon Captain Nicolle was denied even this privilege, after he had been caught giving part of his bread ration to an R.A.F. prisoner in the cell opposite him. Thereafter, when the time to empty the buckets came, Captain Nicolle would put his table on his bed, his chair on the table, and climb up to look through the window, from which he could at least get a daily glimpse of fellow human beings—Sherwill and the others emptying their buckets in turn into the cesspool. But the danger was that any German guard in the yard below, looking up and seeing a prisoner's face at a window, was liable to take a potshot at him: Hubert Nicolle had a bullet flattened on the wall beside his head when he had climbed up on his chair and table to have a look out.

Each of the prisoners found his own way of filling in the hours and saving his reason.

Captain Nicolle, a Mason, went through the Masonic ritual in his head, tried different memory tests, and cleaned the walls of his cell with the handle of a spoon. Wilfred Bird did physical exercises, and walked a mile every morning—650 times up and down his cell—and a mile every afternoon. Bill Allen, who had learnt a trick or two as a soldier in the Manchester Regiment, had the diversion of surreptitiously smoking six packets of cigarettes which he had brought with him, and had hidden under a bench while he was being searched. Sherwill spent most of his time writing.

He was lucky in that one evening, having washed a sock, he had pulled it over the electric light bulb to dry. It hid the light so effectively that the guard, when he came round at Lights Out, did not notice it was on. So Sherwill always repeated the trick, and could have his light on all night if he wanted.

He wrote a long statement on the whole Symes-Nicolle affair, and sent it to the authorities as the case for their defence. He wrote a lot of notes on his experiences so far during the Occupation. And he wrote, scribbling endlessly with a pencil on whatever paper he could find, a diary of his days in Cherche Midi which was preserved afterwards.

He recorded the cold, the gloom, the meagre sustenance —a cup of ersatz coffee for breakfast, soup for lunch, perhaps bread and cheese for supper. (If there was any talking, soup was stopped for three days as a punishment.) Sundays were worst; there was nothing to eat at all after a slice of bread and margarine at midday.

"Cell very cold and dull," wrote Sherwill.

"No sun ever enters. Lack of sun and solitude tend to get one down, but one must not let that happen."

"We live almost like animals and yet, pathetically, we all try to preserve our dignity, courtesy, and humour. Never have I been in touch with so much misery at the same time."

"There must be a great deal of human misery per cubic foot of Cherche Midi, but there is also much kindness and gentleness and goodness. I pin my faith on these to save the world."

"Had my hair cut. How terrible and demoralising it is to have nothing to do or see. Difficult to sleep at night."

"Nothing happened. Of good courage."

"Nothing happened. Cell very cold."

On many days the entry was simply: "Nothing happened." But sometimes there were gleams of pleasure: "Visited by American Quaker who is going to have my washing done and give me a clean towel." And many times, as he closed his entries for the day, his thoughts would turn to his wife and children. "Good-night to all my darlings and God bless and protect you."

They had been in prison for nearly six weeks when, two days before Christmas, Symes' father was found dead in his cell, under circumstances never definitely established.

The Germans said it was suicide; but those who knew Louis Symes best, and knew his courage and toughness, were certain that he had been killed and an apparent suicide staged afterwards.

The prisoners had learnt that if a cell door in the Cherche Midi was opened, that they could never know what it might mean—another interrogation, a transfer to another prison, perhaps a firing squad. On Christmas Eve, Captain Nicolle, who was on a floor below most of the others, heard the sound of doors being opened all down the passage, and then his own turn came. He was led out, and saw that a Christmas tree with coloured lights had been put at the intersection of two corridors. The German guards sang a carol in German. Then they called on French guards to oblige in turn. Next they demanded a British carol. The only British people on the floor were Captain Nicolle and the R.A.F. prisoner. But they felt they should keep their end up, and produced a sturdy version of "Good King Wenceslas".

Next night Sherwill wrote in his diary:

"The first Christmas that the family has not spent together. May God bless each of my darlings and protect them from harm and may I soon have definite news concerning myself. I pray that all is well with dear little Guernsey."

All this time, May Sherwill and other relatives back in Guernsey had no news from the prisoners, and no clue except anxious gossip as to what their fate may be. Then towards the end of December, the people of Guernsey began reading with anxious foreboding a proclamation by Colonel Schumacher. It announced that Second-Lieutenant Nicolle and Second-Lieutenant Symes had been found guilty of espionage, and the others guilty of high treason and having lent assistance to espionage. It solemnly recounted the penalties provided by International Law. Nevertheless the pledge of an amnesty would be honoured.

Nicolle and Symes would be sent to a camp as prisoners of war, and the others allowed to return home.

At the time, nobody knew quite what argument within the German camp produced this final leniency. It seems plain, however, that the chief credit must go to Count von Schmettow, who insisted throughout that keeping a promise was a matter of honour on which there could be no compromise. He refused to believe General Schreiber's argument that Symes and Nicolle had landed to start a resistance movement, pointing out to his German superiors that there was no evidence of such a movement, or of any desire for one, in the islands. He insisted that breaking a promise would stop any good relations with the civil population in future; he asked to be relieved of his post in such an event, and Colonel Schumacher and Major Bandelow associated themselves with this threat to resign. Colonel von Schmettow was obviously running some risk in going against an officer of higher rank, General Schreiber. But Schmettow appealed direct to his own superior officer, Count Brockdorf, flying to see Brockdorf personally. Brockdorf thereupon sent a member of his own staff to Berlin to see Admiral Canaris, Chief of Counter Intelligence. Canaris agreed with Schmettow, and the projected trial in Paris was thereupon cancelled.

It was argued by some people in Guernsey afterwards that the weeks of solitary confinement in the Cherche Midi prison, with their ordeal of suspense, was itself a breach of the promise that there would be no punishment. But in the circumstances, few felt disposed to complain: and the party from the Cherche Midi came back to a joyous welcome. Food and drink were already running short in Guernsey. But the Sherwills gave a party with their last bottle of French wine, and with some stale black bread brought back from the Cherche Midi as a souvenir, cut up into squares to serve as savouries. Emile Nicolle had a visit from Schröder, the man from the *Geheime Feldpolizei* who had arrested him, and who called to welcome him home with a present of a bunch of chrysanthemums.

*　*　*　*　*

For one man, the story of Symes and Nicolle was still not over. Before Jim Symes gave himself up, he passed on the information he had collected to his cousin in Guernsey, Bill Symes, and asked him to try to get it back to England. Bill Symes ran a pub in Fountain Street known as "The Dive," much frequented by sailors from the ships bringing supplies from France. Through Maquis among them he was able to smuggle out messages to a British agent in Spain—first the facts collected by his cousin, then a map of German fortifications and other information. He became known to the Maquis as "Sandeman Bill," owing to the Sandeman sign hanging outside his pub.

He took the precaution of seeing that his messages were never signed, and when eventually the Gestapo intercepted one of them, and he was arrested, he denied any knowledge of it. Nevertheless he was taken to the Cherche Midi. He still refused, through continual interrogation and maltreatment, to admit that he had been sending out messages, or to give the names of the Maquis who had carried them for him. But he was sentenced to imprisonment for the rest of the war—first at Compiègne and then at Roumainville, the "hostage prison" from which men were selected for shooting as reprisals. From there, as we shall tell later, he was sent to Buchenwald, and so he was among the first Channel Islanders to reach a Nazi concentration camp.

CHAPTER XVII

JOHN LEALE TAKES OVER

Because of his part in the Symes-Nicolle affair, the Germans made Major Sherwill retire into private life, "as further co-operation is no longer possible." It is a curious commentary on human nature that some people in Guernsey, instead of applauding Sherwill and the others for the risks they had taken in helping Symes and Nicolle, reproved them for having jeopardised good relations with the Germans by doing so. A leading Churchman actually gave a severe lecture to Bill Allen; and a prominent member of the States was heard to say that he never wanted to see Sherwill again. It was left to a German, Dr. Brosch of the *Feldkommandantur*, to ask how Sherwill could manage to live and support his family without his salary as Attorney-General, and to express the hope that the States would not cut him off without a penny.

Sherwill was not a man to lapse into bitterness, and he set himself to do what he could in his state of enforced idleness—which was to last until July, 1942, when the Germans allowed him to become Attorney-General again, but not President of the Controlling Committee. He devoted himself energetically to growing vegetables and keeping goats, and might be seen pushing a handcart through the streets of St. Peter Port, loaded with produce from his garden which he was equally ready to sell or to give away. May Sherwill also became one of the best-loved figures of the Occupation; in the grimmest days, her unconventional liking for colourful clothes was a constant pledge of her own courage and cheerfulness; and her talents as an actress made her the mainstay of the amateur dramatic shows which did so much to lighten the monotony and gloom. Once she even persuaded her husband to take part in one too. He was a great success as the Judge in "Night Must Fall".

Sherwill's position as President of the Controlling Committee was taken by a close friend, Jurat the Rev. John Leale, whom we have already mentioned at different times. A man of completely different type, he was as successful as Sherwill in his own way; and the story of his emergence as an outstanding figure during the Occupation is something of a romance.

John Leale's father was head of Leale Ltd., one of the biggest and richest merchant firms on the island. John was always the quiet one of the family, sometimes regarded as something of a failure, with none of the genial gifts and widespread popularity of his brother Roy, who died when only twenty-five after fighting in the First World War. Quiet, studious and ascetic, John's own brief and undistinguished military career had ended when he was invalided out of the Royal Guernsey Militia: subsequently he became a Methodist Minister at Wesley Hall, Great Ancoat Street, Manchester. (Afterwards bombed.) He only returned to the island when his father died in 1928.

In the early days after his return, he had sometimes been known as "the dreamy Leale". He might be seen sitting and reading a book on a rock by the sea, or perhaps just sitting. Though a very rich man, he was simple in his tastes, caring nothing for food or drink or conventional pleasures. He had only one human vanity: a liking for clean and well-fitting clothes. He confessed to a weakness for the feel of fresh linen and of a crisply pressed suit. It was a weakness which was to have less and less gratification as the Occupation proceeded, and he was soon as shabby as everyone else.

When Sherwill appointed his Controlling Committee, he made Leale the member responsible for economics and finance. Leale's clear-headedness, and his serenity in any crisis, soon made him outstanding; and he had taken the lead by obvious choice from the time when Sherwill was first arrested.

As President of the Controlling Committee, Leale kept absolute integrity, in days when even the female relative of a leading official was overheard innocently enquiring of a policeman: "Can you tell me the way to the Black Market?" He did not even claim privileges to which his position clearly entitled him, like the use of a car. Every morning he walked the two miles from his home at St. Sampsons' to his office at St. Peter Port, and every evening he walked the two miles back again. If Sherwill had the virtues of a soldier, John Leale had some of the virtues of an ascetic, and he proved that the Germans could have respect for both.

One other name must be mentioned again here: that of

Louis Guillemette, a young clerk with spectacles and curly dark hair, who became Leale's secretary throughout the Occupation. He had previously been secretary to the Bailiff; he was the same young clerk whom Mrs. Hathaway had noted, in the panic days before the German arrival, as one of the few who kept level-headed. In his new position he had to bear the brunt of most of the day-to-day dealings with the Germans; rather like Duret Aubin in Jersey, though in a far more junior position, and without the opprobrium of being forced to sign his own name to unpopular measures. Guillemette's contacts with the Germans were so close that he could expect little but blame and unpopularity. So it is a great tribute that many accounts praise him for the work he did for the island, following the example of Sherwill and Leale in never giving offence to the Germans unnecessarily, but never yielding a point without a fight.

Though John Leale was not without the occasional Christian guile whereby Methodists are sometimes characterised, his main strength was always in his equally characteristic singlemindedness. In his dealing with the Germans, he practised the policy which Sherwill had always preached —unlimited patience. (Sherwill once told Guillemette that "we must out-Job Job.") Leale always took his stand on the letter of what the Hague Convention said about Occupied Countries—a document which had been drawn up in conveniently vague terms, giving endless room for argument. Leale secured a German translation of it which became a kind of Bible. He protested at anything the Germans did which went beyond their legal rights. But he recognised that they could do anything for which they could find authority under the Convention, and he recognised the Convention as ruling out resistance or sabotage.

For instance, Leale was sometimes asked by growers and fishermen whether they should obey orders to grow crops and catch fish for the Germans. And he told them that the Hague Convention did in fact give an occupying power the right to requisition labour in this way.

Leale commented afterwards:

"I remember one grower to whom I had given this advice looking at me, and his eyes said plainly what his mind was thinking: 'You're not much of a Briton' . . .

"Truth to tell, I was not feeling particularly heroic at the moment. . . . But in the long run I have no doubt whatever that our right and interests as British people were best safeguarded by sticking to International Law through thick and thin. . . .

"We followed the example of those who take partners for life. We espoused the Hague Convention 'for better for worse'."

It might have been thought that, when dealing with the Nazis, any appeal to the rules would have been a waste of breath. But, Nazis apart, the German delight in all rules and regulations included respect for the rules of war. It even seemed that some of the civilian-life lawyers in the *Feldkommandantur* greatly enjoyed the chance of exercising their wits in argument against such first-rate legal brains as Sherwill, Coutanche and Duret Aubin. Such arguments, however, sometimes got a bit too much for Count von Schmettow, as a plain soldier of the old school.

On one occasion Schmettow wanted part of the St. Aubin's Bay sea wall raised, so as to shield military traffic on the coast road from observation at sea. Coutanche protested that though the States were responsible for maintaining the wall, they could not be asked to raise it to serve a military purpose; and Schmettow gave in. "All right," he said, "for Heaven's sake don't let's have another argument over the Hague Convention just for one sea wall."

On another occasion in Jersey the Germans wanted to requisition the iron railing round churchyards for use as scrap. Duret Aubin appealed to the Hague Convention, and Dr. Casper immediately told him: "I take back the Order."

Sometimes there was a compromise. Once, when a German gun position was flooded by a high tide, it was agreed that the Jersey Fire Brigade would pump out enough water to safeguard anyone from drowning, but not enough to save the ammunition. After this triumph of diplomacy, the joke went round the *Feldkommandantur* that Jersey would obviously be an ideal place to hold international conferences after the war.

One of the indisputable obligations on the islands, under the Hague Convention, was to pay for the cost of the Occupation. It was an obligation which was interpreted differently at different times: in practice it might mean the States paying the wages of everyone working for the Germans, paying rent to the owners of requisitioned property, providing the cost of Army transport, even paying the Germans' laundry bills. And the Hague Convention was held to cover the following curt instructions issued in Guernsey soon after the Occupation began:

"The following goods are to be sent to the Commandant each week for consumption at Government House:

500		Cigarettes
50		Cigars
10	Bottles	Champagne
10	„	Whisky
10	„	White Wine
10	„	Red Wine

"Orders have been given to Messrs. Le Riche's Stores to provide these goods, and the account will be sent to the States Office for payment each week."

A brief word may be said here about Occupation finance —which John Leale continued to deal with in Guernsey, and for which Edgar Dorey was the responsible member on the Jersey "Superior Council".

The first German Orders fixed the rate of exchange at 5 marks to the £*—a gross over-valuation of the mark. The German soldiers used their "Occupation Marks" to

* Changed to 8 marks on July 9, 1940; to 9.60 in September 1940; to 9.36 in September 1942 and thereafter. In August 1939 the mark had been quoted at 11.10 to the £.

buy goods, the shopkeepers paid the marks into the banks, being credited in sterling, and the States in turn bought the marks from the banks. The States paid some of their marks back to the Germans for the cost of the Occupation. But the surplus marks accumulated could only be used for purchases in France—paying for the goods bought by the Joint Purchasing Mission in Granville. The French were parting with actual commodities and only getting paper money in return.

This system lasted, however, till 1942, when an arrangement was made through Barclays Bank, and the French Bureau de Change, for trade between France and the islands to be financed by credit balances, to be adjusted after the war. Curiously enough, this arrangement ended with the balance on the side of the islands. This was earned in the first place by the export of Guernsey tomatoes to France, while imports from France were mostly paid for in ways which evaded the new arrangement.

Paying for the Occupation meant that all States budgets acquired deficits. Income tax was sorrowfully raised in Jersey from 9d. to 4s., and in Guernsey from 1s. 6d. to 5s. For the rest, the States met their financial problems by bank loans or overdrafts—used in part to buy the Occupation marks from the banks. The effect of this was purely inflationary; but it could not be avoided so long as the Germans went on bringing in Occupation marks, and the States continued to buy them—thus, in effect, guaranteeing the German currency. John Leale considered whether he could stop taking the marks: but without the promise of the States to buy them they would have been worthless, and he thought the confusion caused by a worthless currency would be the greater evil. "Wasn't it Lenin," he recalled, "who said that the first ingredient for a revolution is to destroy the value of money?"

For a time, German Occupation marks and British currency circulated side by side. Then Gresham's Law began to operate, and the British notes and silver disappeared, being hoarded or taken to France to be sold on the Black Market.

Both Guernsey and Jersey printed notes for 5s., 2s. 6d., and even lower—those in Jersey being designed by the famous local artist Edmund Blampied. As this cheap paper money suffered the wear and tear of Occupation, the new notes became known as "Dirty Berties"—named after the popular States' Treasurer Herbert Ereaut.

Eventually, but not till the end of 1943, the Germans decided to seize all British notes held by the banks, giving Occupation marks in return. This had rather been expected from the beginning: in fact a proposal had been made, just before the Occupation, to withdraw all British currency. Guernsey had always issued its own notes, which circulated together with British notes, and the idea was to make them sole legal tender for all the islands. There turned out, however, to be insuperable difficulties in getting Jersey to accept Guernsey money.

When the Germans finally seized British currency notes, the banks were not altogether unprepared. In Jersey, some £38,000 worth of notes were hidden by Edgar Dorey and Ereaut in a cupboard in the basement of the States Treasury, where they escaped detection for the rest of the Occupation. In Guernsey, John Leale had all £10 and £5 notes burned—having first, characteristically, carefully made a list of all their numbers, so that he could claim for them after the war.

CHAPTER XVIII

AN EDUCATION FROM THE DAME

Sark is Sark, always remaining something rather apart. Though there was throughout a certain wary watchfulness on the part of the Germans, and a sharp pitting of wits on the side of the Sarkees, the Occupation there was the most benevolent in all the islands, and Sark sometimes had its own way of dealing with the problems which arose.

For instance, when the Order came from Headquarters to confiscate all wireless sets over the Symes-Nicolle affair, the Germans went across to Brecqhou, separated from Sark by a narrow sea channel, to collect the sets belonging to Mr. Lyons, the Bailiff on the farm there, and his farm workers. They took William Carré the Sénéschal with them, and Carré declared flatly that Mr. Lyons's set was far too big to carry down the steep path to the boat. Eventually they compromised by sealing the wireless up. Then Mr. Lyons brought out a bottle of wine, and they had a party. It ended up with the Germans begging them to sing *God Save the King* and *There'll Always be an England*, and they obliged with great pleasure.

Later on, in return for this hospitality, the Germans invited Mr. Lyons and his farm workers to come over to Sark for a party on Boxing Day.

Just before Christmas, William Carré the Sénéschal went to see the German Commandant, and asked for an extension of the curfew till midnight for two nights. He put his case with some eloquence, and at the end the Commandant said: "Let's work this out: till midnight for two nights running . . . You know, I think it would be much better to extend the curfew till 3 a.m., for four nights running. . . . Would the people approve of that?"

On a small island, it was easy enough for the formalities of wartime enmity to be forgotten sometimes, and for spontaneous friendships to spring up. Philip Guille, forty years a fisherman and one of the finest men in all the islands, had photographs of the King and Earl Haig in his sitting-room. He expected the Germans to tell him to take them down. Instead, they liked to come in and see them and have a chat, asking him about the days when Guille served under Haig in the Royal Guernsey Light Infantry, and what the First World War was like.

There was never any doubt about Mrs. Hathaway being in command of the situation on Sark from start to finish, and she provides an excellent example of the danger of judging behaviour under an Occupation by any hard and fast rules. Unlike Coutanche, Carey, and Leale, she never hesitated to extend pleasant hospitality to the Germans, and her Visitors' Book had the signatures of most of the leading figures on visits of inspection from time to time. (The German garrisons, like any other soldiers, put on a wonderful show of spit and polish on these occasions, and then relaxed in their shirt sleeves again the moment the brass-hat sailed off.) Mrs. Hathaway's Visitors' Book grew full of such expressions of German gratitude as "Many thanks for lovely afternoon", and "Always delighted with nice reception." The Germans were ready to do favours in return. Once, when Bob Hathaway had mentioned his despondency at the fact that his wine cellar would never last out the Occupation, an officer coming back from leave brought him a precious bottle all the way through France. On another occasion Mrs. Hathaway had broken her glasses, and Prince von Oettigen arranged specially for them to be mended in Paris.

But Mrs. Hathaway, unlike the authorities in the other islands, was able throughout to refuse to sign any orders at German dictation. Once someone asked her whether, after the war was over, she would not be ashamed of the German compliments in her Visitors' Book. She retorted: "I've done nothing to be ashamed of—there's nothing to be gained by opposing the Germans openly and being rude to them. No, I think the book will have rather a curiosity value!"

As the drinks were passed round in the Seigneurie, and they all chatted together, Mrs. Hathaway's knowledge of German would often allow her to pick up advance information on plans they were making, and she could send warnings to Guernsey.

A regular visitor was Raymond Falla, in his capacity as Agricultural Officer for the Bailiwick, and he would go back to Guernsey remarking: "It's an education to see the Dame dealing with the Germans". She would remain seated while German officers would walk up her drawing-room, bow, kiss her hand, and then walk back with another bow. She would rebuke them fearlessly and peremptorily with such phrases as "But you can't do that—I won't allow it!": or (more frequently) "Oh, dear no, that's *not* the way the *British* do things.... In Britain we *never* shout..."

Mrs. Hathaway made a point of leaving banned anti-Fascist books, like *Sawdust Cæsar* and *The House that Hitler Built*, prominently on her shelves where her guests were certain to see them. She was never asked to remove them.

But her policy of entertaining the Germans intensified the island feuds, and led to the opposing faction complaining bitterly that she was too friendly to the Germans.

To the true-born Sarkee, who looks on anyone outside Sark as a foreigner, there was not so very much inherent difference—loyalty apart—between receiving peace-time tourists from England and war-time visitors from Germany. The English-born residents were not so ready to invite Germans into their homes; though some of them found the Germans pleasant enough to deal with. There was, for instance, the gentle and grey-haired Miss Margaret Toplis, daughter of the well-known artist William Toplis. The Germans would often come to look at her father's work, and when some of them stood to attention and saluted the paintings she could not laugh, because their appreciation was so genuine. She had a pet magpie, Dukey, of whom the Germans grew very fond, feeding it with titbits and macaroni. One day a high-ranking German officer, visiting Sark, was furious to see Dukey perched on the rifle barrel of one of the guards.

Miss Toplis was once relieving a mood of war-time depression by chopping firewood and repeating with each swing of her axe: "I hate Hitler! I hate Hitler!" Suddenly she looked up to see a German officer watching her. She waited aghast to see what would happen. But all he said was: "You are right, Madam. War is not good." Then he shook his head and walked quietly away.

There were some who had to act as hosts to the Germans involuntarily. Among them were two English ladies,

132

Miss Duckett and Miss Page—sometimes known as Bucket and Spade. Just before the war they had put all their savings into buying the Dixcart Hotel. Miss Duckett, a strong personality who coached the Sark girls in hockey, ran the bar; while Miss Page, gentle but equally firm, looked after the rest of the hotel. They were horrified when they learnt they would have German officers billeted on them, and agreeably surprised to find them—apart from the Nazis—well-behaved and courteous. Miss Duckett, serving them drinks behind the bar, would tell them roundly that "England will win the war even if it takes ten years." Miss Page, on one occasion when the Germans wanted to commandeer her favourite writing-desk, was moved to protest sharply: "You're nothing but a plague of locusts." The Germans meekly left the desk alone.

As in all the islands, the population was subject to a number of bureaucratic rules, regulations, and instructions on what crops should be sown, how they should be grown, within what hours fishing was permitted, and so on: all with a certain disdain for local conditions. Bob Hathaway was to describe the Seigneurie as like the Information Bureau at the Grand Central Station in New York, with the Germans giving all the information.

One of the biggest jokes was when the Germans, in spite of all warnings, insisted on putting up a hut near the narrow neck of land known as La Coupée, which funnels the wind in any gale. The Sarkees said the hut would blow into the sea, and one night it did. (But the Germans did not go into the sea with it: an embroidered version of the story told later.)

There was another mishap when the Germans, ignorant of the ways of primitive paraffin stoves, set fire to the thatched roof of their headquarters, the Bel Air Hotel, and burnt it down.

The Sarkees derived some amusement from watching the Germans gradually discovering that the laws of island farming differed somewhat from their own continental variety, and that the fishing depended more on the tides than any man-made hours. Gradually the rigid timetable

133

for fishing hours was relaxed. But a rule about taking a German guard in each boat, to prevent escapes, was still enforced. The guards came from what was supposed to be the German equivalent of the Marines; but in fact most of them were pre-war office workers, bank clerks and so on, who suffered dreadfully from sea-sickness. It is to be confessed that the Sark fishermen sometimes stayed out much longer than necessary, owing to some alleged reason of current or tide, for the pleasure of watching the guards getting sicker and sicker. . . . But, all the same, fellow feeling could often, in the confines of a small boat, prove stronger than international hostility: some guards were generous in sharing cigarettes with the fishermen, and some friendships sprang up between them.

While the Sarkees initiated the Germans into some of the mysteries of seamanship, the Germans reciprocated with lessons on Continental cooking. The Sarkees, for instance, learnt how to smoke eels the German way, and developed quite a liking for them. Lobsters, in peace-time a rich source of revenue for Sark through sales in luxury hotels in London, almost became a staff of life: Mrs. Hathaway, in fact, was to complain that she became sick of the taste of them.

Mrs. Hathaway not only had to cope with the Germans, but with all the shortages caused by the Occupation. She turned one room of the Seigneurie into a workshop for making clothes—out of blankets, tablecloths, or anything else available. The men of Sark went to work in colourful coats and jerkins made from old curtains. Slippers were made for children by cutting up the under felts of carpets. But when children outgrew their shoes, often there was nothing to be done except to cut a hole to let their toes poke out in front.

Mrs. Hathaway's duties even included examining the school children's heads when they got lice, owing to the acute shortage of soap. She used two knitting needles to part their hair.

A serious problem was caused by the departure of Sark's only practising doctor before the Germans arrived. A nursing sister came to the island, but a complication was that she was expecting a baby. When the time came, it turned out to be not one baby, but twins: as there was no one else on the island to do so, they were delivered, with characteristic efficiency, by Mrs. Hathaway herself. The problem of medical attention was then met by bringing over an elderly doctor from Jersey; but later it was mostly undertaken by the German army doctors, who did it with a conscientiousness and care still remembered gratefully by the population to this day. Nothing seemed too much trouble for them; in case of serious illness they would call out a boat any time of the day or night to take a patient to hospital in Guernsey.

A bright and intelligent girl named Phyllis Baker, daughter of a Sark farmer, learnt German so quickly that when the islanders were sick they would ask her to go with them to the German doctors and interpret for them. Soon she went regularly with the doctors on their rounds. A day came when she herself fell ill, and a young German medical orderly, Werner Rang, was sent round to her home with a clinical thermometer and some pills for her. He arrived at the door, but could not speak a word of English, and Phyllis Baker's mother knew no German. So Phyllis called down for Rang to come upstairs and tell her what he wanted: and that was the beginning of a romance which was to continue.

We must not forget to mention the children on the island, to whom the Occupation brought new joys. Cars were introduced—the first they had ever seen in Sark—and the soldiers loved to give the children rides on them. The Germans were so particular about driving carefully that the unaccustomed cars did not cause a single accident during their whole stay.

Only one crisis broke the tranquillity of the early years in Sark. That was when a German Army doctor was found murdered in his bed. The Germans immediately feared this was the beginning of a desperate resistance movement, sworn to kill the occupying force one by one. Mrs. Hathaway assured them firmly and authoritatively that the idea was ridiculous because Sark people did not commit murders—there had not been a murder there for hundreds of years. But for a time the Germans were in a state of jittery tension, and a number of restrictions were clamped down.

Everyone had to report at Headquarters twice a day. Fishing was forbidden completely. A five o'clock curfew deprived many residents of their usual round of evening visits to play bridge. Then, after about a week, the body of the murdered officer's batman, together with a hammer, was found down a well—which had been in use all the time, but without any ill effect. For some reason it was assumed that the batman must have murdered the officer and then committed suicide, and the tension and restrictions ended. Later, stories came back that another German soldier had confessed to murdering the officer and the batman too. But the true details were never satisfactorily established: so our account of this episode can only remain as unsatisfactory as a detective novel with the last pages missing.

CHAPTER XIX

MEN WHO WANTED TO FIGHT

After the Battle of Britain, the war began to pass the Channel Islands by. Even the airfields fell into neglect, the Luftwaffe moving on to other fronts, and the only reminder of the battles being fought overseas was an occasional raid by Allied bombers. There was little to distract the islanders from concentrating their thoughts on their own pressing problems, with food usually foremost in their minds.

But the tragedy of war was to touch them from time to time, in simple human terms. Such, for instance, was the story of François Scornet, the leader of a band of French boys who sailed from Brittany, in January 1941, in an attempt to join the Free French Forces in England. The eldest of them was twenty-one: François Scornet himself was twenty.

They had little idea of navigation and, coming on the coast of Guernsey, mistook it for the Isle of Wight. They landed in triumph, lustily singing the Marseillaise, and were immediately seized by the Germans. It appeared that the story of their adventure had come to a farcical ending; but from now it turned into purest tragedy.

The boys were taken to the public gaol in Jersey, where their courage and cheerful spirits were undaunted: they would scandalise the German guards—and the Jersey prison governor—by singing patriotic songs, and drawing caricatures of Hitler and Mussolini on the walls of their cells.

They were tried by the Germans in the Old Committee Room of the Royal Court. François Scornet insisted on taking full responsibility as leader. He was sentenced to death for "favouring the actions of the enemy by wilfully supporting England in the war against the German Empire". The Germans claimed, in justification of the severity of this sentence, that Scornet was a liberated prisoner of war.

On the morning of March 17, 1941, Scornet was handcuffed, taken from his cell in St. Helier Prison, and put on a lorry with his own coffin. With him also was a Catholic priest, Father T. P. Maré. They drove to St. Ouen's Manor, where the priest administered the last rites of the Church. At twenty minutes past eight, facing a firing squad before an oak tree in the grounds of the manor, and calling *"Vive la France!"*, François Scornet was shot.

Some time afterwards his father and mother received his last letter.

"My dear parents, my very dear parents, the end of my life is at hand. I am going to die for France, facing the enemy bravely.

137

"I forgive everyone. *Vive la France. Vive Dieu.* For the last time I embrace you."

Scornet's companions were imprisoned and treated so brutally that, of the fifteen, four died. Another, Jacques Poisson, escaped and was afterwards killed fighting with the Maquis.

It was natural enough that some young men who had stayed in the Channel Islands should now want to follow the example of the young Frenchmen who had tried to reach England and fight: but their position was more difficult. Escaping was discouraged as likely to bring reprisals on those left behind. But there could be nothing but admiration for the exploit of Denis Vibert, the only man during the Occupation to reach England direct from Jersey.

Denis Vibert had been trained for the sea, and was an expert navigator. His first attempt was in November 1940. Getting away in his boat at night, he reached the Roches Douvres, some rocks about twenty miles west of Corbière, and rested there during the day, hoping to make for England when darkness came on again. The Luftwaffe was then so active around the island that he felt he would be spotted by daylight.

As he waited, however, an unfriendly wind sprang up. It raged on throughout the night, and the next day. Vibert stuck it out for four days, hoping each morning would bring calm weather. But in the end his food gave out, he fell ill with influenza, and he decided that his only chance was to return to Jersey. On the way back his boat struck a rock off St. Brelade's Bay and sank. He swam ashore, and was lucky enough not only to land undetected, but to find that his absence had not been discovered by the Germans.

Undaunted, he started planning a fresh escape early in 1941. He found a boat, took it to his father's house in Bel Royal, painted it sea-green inside to camouflage it from the air, and got two out-board motors.

This took some months. Then there was the problem of getting the boat to a hiding place from which it could be launched. The Bel Royal district was thickly populated with Germans. Every shed and private garage was known to them, and some had even been requisitioned.

Vibert hired a small garage between the main road and the beach. To put the Germans off the scent he acquired a farm tractor which, with as much noise and fuss as possible, was driven to the garage and installed there. Then the tractor was quietly removed, and the boat was taken to the garage after dark on a lorry well disguised with potato barrels. Here, out of sight of passers-by or inquisitive Germans, Vibert and two friends got the boat ready to launch. Rowing on muffled row-locks, Vibert pulled out to sea.

He rowed for four miles before starting his motor. Some hours later he was startled by an enemy E-boat which nearly swamped him with its wash, half-filling his boat and ruining his store of food, but failing to notice him. In mid-channel next day, he ran into rough weather, and the boat was pitching badly. His out-board motor got flooded, and phuttered to a standstill: trying to fit his spare motor, Vibert lost it overboard. There was nothing left but the oars. For three days and three nights, with no food nor water, and only occasional rests, Vibert rowed on towards England. During the third night of this feat of endurance, he was picked up by a British destroyer two miles from Portland.

Vibert promptly volunteered for the R.A.F,. and served with Coastal Command.

Those who could not hope to emulate Vibert's example had been looking for something they could do, however small, towards helping the Allies and hindering the Germans.

In March 1941, Colonel Schumacher, the *Feldkommandant*, announced that on account of "an act of sabotage" the curfew was to start at 9 p.m. A special meeting of the States in Guernsey was addressed by Victor Carey, the Bailiff, and by John Leale, President of the Controlling Committee. The "sabotage" in question turned out to be the cutting of a German field telephone wire. According to a newspaper report, Carey said:

"A few days ago an ill-disposed person or persons deliberately and maliciously cut a telephone cable in two places ... and thus performed an act of grave sabotage. Such an act was not only stupid but criminal, as it involved those participating in it with the penalty of death, and it also brought the population of the whole island under the grave displeasure of the German authorities.

"It is the duty of any individual who has information with regard to the perpetration of this act of sabotage to inform the police immediately, as unless the culprit is brought to justice we do not know what further penalties the population may incur. I can assure you that I will take all possible steps to bring the perpetrators of such acts to speedy justice, so that the safety of the population as a whole may be safeguarded."

Without going so far, John Leale called on the States "to condemn such acts, as on the one hand utterly foolish, for they do no sort of good to anyone, and on the other hand as wicked, because they bring in their train inconvenience and maybe suffering imposed on everyone."

Sixty Guernseymen were made to spend their nights for the next fortnight patrolling a stretch of telephone wire near the scene of the crime. Carrying out this senseless punishment was apparently as much of a nuisance to the Germans as everyone else. A little while after, another telephone wire was discovered cut in a field. It was inspected by a German military policeman and a Guernsey policeman. The German looked hard at his opposite number: "I think," he said, "the wire has been broken by a cow." The Guernseyman solemnly agreed that a cow had trodden on it, and no more was said.

The business of cutting telephone wires was plainly futile. Similar incidents in Jersey produced similar results: the lines were mended again in a moment, and a number of citizens in the neighbourhood were kept out of their beds to patrol the spot. Obviously nothing was to be gained by attacking the Germans with pinpricks, and being punished by general inconvenience.

Loyalists in the islands were still looking for other means of showing their spirit when someone in London thought of the "V" campaign: an invitation to those in occupied countries to defy the Germans by chalking up "V for Victory" signs. This plan was eagerly adopted by some Channel Islanders. But it was bitterly condemned by the authorities there as something which, without doing any real damage to the Germans, would irritate them inordinately and bring reprisals on the civilian population. Victor Carey, as Bailiff of Guernsey, was to declare afterwards that the "V" campaign gave him his worst moments of the whole Occupation.

So angry were the Germans, and so anxious were the authorities, that the appearance of "V" signs in Jersey brought forth an official notice:

Any person who can give information likely to result in the discovery of the person or persons responsible is requested to communicate IMMEDIATELY with the Constable of St. Helier or the Chef de Police of St. Saviour.

This notice was signed by Duret Aubin, the Attorney-General, as well as by the Constable and Chef de Police in question, and it aroused considerable criticism.

Three days later the following notice was published in Guernsey, signed by Victor Carey, as Bailiff:

I have been informed that the letter "V" has appeared written up in public places in the island....

Should the culprit not be discovered, the population may be penalised in the same way as in the case of acts of sabotage.

The culprit or culprits must be discovered within 72 hours of the publication of this warning. May I warn my fellow islanders against committing these foolish acts, which accomplish nothing but merely bring grave consequences in their train?

The seventy-two hours elapsed without any response. There was another stormy interview between the elderly Victor Carey and the German authorities, at which the unfortunate Carey was shouted at furiously. Soon afterwards the following notice appeared in the press:

REWARD OF £25

A reward of £25 will be given to the person who first gives the Inspector of Police information leading to the conviction of anyone (not already discovered) for the offence of marking on any gate, wall or other place whatsoever visible to the public the letter "V" or any other sign or any word or words calculated to offend the German Authorities or soldiers.

This 8th day of July, 1941.

(Signed) VICTOR G. CAREY,
Bailiff.

The Bailiff is said to have explained later that the Germans had threatened to deport a number of leading residents to Germany unless the culprits were discovered, and that "it seemed to him in the best interests of the population that the notice should be published".* The present authors can only add one comment as a result of their own inquiries. It seems that Victor Carey may have been guided by advice from G. J. P. Ridgway, who had succeeded Sherwill as Attorney-General. Ridgway, who was already a sick man at the time, died soon afterwards, so we have no way of knowing what explanation he would have offered. He may have felt that the offer of a reward was a dramatic way of pacifying the Germans while harming no one—no information was laid, and the £25 was never claimed.**

* Cortvriend: *Isolated Island*, p. 205.
** One of Ridgway's friends has written to us: "I knew him as an extremely astute lawyer . . . here was a bit of cunning that worked well to quieten the Germans. It is exactly the sort of thing he would have done and chuckled over."

But the offer aroused bitter feelings in Guernsey. Neither Leale nor any member of the Controlling Committee carried dissent to the point of resigning, but one member commented that the appropriate reward would not be £25, but thirty pieces of silver. A cruel cartoon was passed from hand to hand, representing Victor Carey in the role of Judas Iscariot hanging from a tree.

Even greater indignation was caused next month when reference was made—obviously unthinkingly—to British forces as "the enemy". On August 11, 1941, the following notice appeared over Carey's name in the *Guernsey Evening Post*:

Attention is called to the fact that, under the Order relative to protection against Acts of Sabotage, dated October 10, 1940, any person who hides or shelters escaped prisoners of war shall be punished with death. The same applies for the hiding or sheltering of members of enemy forces (for instance, crews of landing aircraft, parachutists, etc.). Anyone lending assistance to such persons in their escape is also liable to the death sentence.

Some of the curious uses of English in this notice made it obvious that the Bailiff's name had simply been put on something drafted by the Germans.

So far as the "V" campaign was concerned, neither warnings nor offers of rewards served to stop the incidents or to catch culprits. On the contrary, evidence of German anger gave a new impetus to the campaign. Chalked "V's" appeared on walls everywhere, and policemen were sent round with buckets and sponges to try to remove them. Cardboard "V's" would be dropped through letter-boxes or put down on shop counters; or two matches would be left in the form of a "V" wherever a German might see them.

It was ironic that the only people convicted and punished for making "V" signs had done so rather as jokes. In Guernsey a man named de Guillebon conceived the idea of chalking a "V" sign on the saddle of a German soldier's bicycle, so that the "V" would be transferred to the seat of his trousers. He was detected—some say given away by an informer—and sentenced to a year's imprisonment in France. In Jersey, two young sisters, Kathleen le Norman and Mrs. Lilian Kinnaird, were seen playfully making "V" signs with their fingers. Both of them were under twenty, and Mrs. Kinnaird had a young baby. Nevertheless they were sentenced to nine months in the notorious gaol at Caen.

Meanwhile a characteristic move towards calming the situation had been made by John Leale. He asked the Germans: "If you really don't want people putting up 'V' signs, why don't you put some up yourself? That would soon stop them." It is not known whether Leale's suggestion had anything to do with it, but in fact the Germans decided to reply to the "V" campaign in exactly this way, not only in the Channel Islands, but throughout Europe. German "V" signs appeared everywhere, and the *Guernsey Evening Post* explained the matter as follows:

VIKTORIA—Victory, shouted the soldiers of Frederick the Great after they had won the battle. . . . Proud of the victories gained by their comrades on the Western Front, the German soldiers have now begun to display the "V" sign . . .

THE LETTER "V" CAN ONLY BE ATTRIBUTED TO THOSE WHOSE COLOURS HAVE NEVER BORNE RETREAT, BUT ONLY VICTORIES, CLAIM THE GERMAN PEOPLE.

It was promptly pointed out that the usual German word for victory was not "*Viktoria*" but "*Sieg*", which begins with "S". The German "V", said humorists, must stand for "*Verloren*" (Lost), or perhaps for "Verminous". But, on the whole, the German counter-propaganda was successful, though "V" signs were to appear occasionally for the rest of the war.

One instance was a Christmas card secretly printed by

Stanley Green, a cinema-projectionist and general handy-man in St. Helier, who was also a printer and lithographer in his spare time. The card had two black lines which came together to make a "V" when it was folded, and had these verses in between:

> If we have whispered truth,
>   Whisper no longer;
> Speak as the tempest does,
>   Sterner and stronger:
> Still be the tones of truth
>   Louder and firmer,
> Startling the haughty one
>   With the deep murmur;
> God and our charter's right,
>   Freedom forever!

CHAPTER XX

MRS. GREEN AND MRS. FERRIS

In the Channel Islands, in 1941, such verses were little more than a dream for the future. But there were always some people ready to suffer for their outspokenness, even though they might use such homely prosaic words as those of Mrs. Winifred Green—no relation to Stanley Green—in Guernsey.

Mrs. Green, a dark-haired and spirited young woman, was married to a plumber in St. Peter Port. Her two children had been evacuated to Scotland, and to fill the void she got a job as a waitress in the Royal Hotel, where one of the foreign employees was a fervent admirer of Hitler. This servant, like everyone else, knew of Mrs. Green's hero-worship of Winston Churchill, and would nettle her by greeting her daily with "Good morning, Mrs. Green—*Heil Hitler!*" To which Mrs. Green would retort: "Good morning—*Heil Churchill!*" Staff lunches became a battling ground with the rest of the staff looking at one and then the other. "Heard the news, Mrs. Green?" her tormentor would enquire, "Germany has taken Jugoslavia"—or Greece, or Crete, or whatever the latest conquest might be. Sometimes Mrs. Green would choke down furious tears. Sometimes she had her answer ready. One lunch time she was asked: "Heard the news, Mrs. Green? We've got the *Hood*." A few days later, Mrs. Green had her revenge: "Heard the news? We've got the *Bismarck*."

So it went on, with bitterness increasing until the final act came in this little daily drama. "Would you like some rice pudding, Mrs. Green?" asked her adversary one lunch time from the top of the table.

"Yes, please."

"Only," came the reply, "if you say '*Heil Hitler*'." The rest of the staff sat still, expecting an explosion. It came. Said Mrs. Green: "To hell with Hitler for a rice pudding —and one made of skim milk at that!"

Soon after, on the morning of October 13, 1941, German Military Police called at the Royal Hotel and told Mrs. Green to come with them—she was being court-martialled at eleven, in twenty minutes' time. She only had time to take off her apron, put on her coat, and go straight to the court. All the proceedings were in German, translated to her through an interpreter, and no one appeared to be defending her. Evidence was taken from the hotel employee, and from herself. Did she admit she had said what she did about Hitler and the rice pudding? She most certainly did admit it. Whereupon she was sentenced to six months' imprisonment at Caen.

Mrs. Green, though bewildered by the speed of the court-martial, was thankful for the absence of bullying. Throughout she had been worrying about her husband, who up till now knew nothing of what was happening. She asked, and received, permission to call under escort at her home. Then she quailed at the thought of the neighbours gathering round, and instead went straight to the gaol. Later the soldiers escorting her, whom she described afterwards as two "very decent young Germans", went to her home and broke the news to Mr. Green.

She had two weeks in the St. Peter Port prison before being marched down to the boat which was to take her away. She walked erect through the streets, looking straight ahead; not ashamed, but somehow embarrassed by the townsfolk's sympathetic looks.

She was the only woman on the boat, which was full of German soldiers. They crowded round her, asking what she had done. When she explained, one of them said: "Politics —they always cause trouble"; and another echoed that ageless sentiment of soldiers in every army: "Why don't the politicians get in the front line, and shoot each other?"

Mrs. Green had five days at Granville prison in a cell with French prostitutes. They greeted her with much kindness, sharing their biscuits with her, and showing her the knack of making a straw palliasse comfortable. Arriving at Caen, Mrs. Green was put in a cell with two fellow Channel Islanders, the young and pretty le Norman sisters —Kathleen le Norman and Mrs. Kinnaird—who had been sent from Jersey for making "V" signs.

Though food was scanty, consisting of cabbage soup and baked potatoes, their greatest hardship was the complete lack of any work to do. Mrs. Green resolved that if she was ever likely to go to prison again it would be for a criminal rather than a political offence: then she would at least have hard labour. As it was, Mrs. Green and the le Norman girls were always trying to devise ways of passing the time. Playing cards were not allowed, but they made them from scraps of cardboard, and played Snap, Sevens and other nursery games. Mrs. Green managed to borrow a needle and thread from another prisoner, tore a piece of her sheet, and embroidered on it, in an effectively painstaking pattern: "*Heil Churchill*; R.A.F.; Caen Prison 1941", ending with a triumphant "V" sign. She knew that if this was found she risked having her sentence prolonged, but even more she hated idleness and being beaten by her surroundings.

The most important possession in prison, Mrs. Green found, was the calendar each prisoner made for herself from a scrounged bit of paper. Every morning, as soon as she woke, each inmate would cross that day off although she still had to live through it. Mrs. Green also noticed that short-term prisoners sharing cells with long-term prisoners would delicately hide away their calendars, so as to avoid rubbing in the contrast in their lot.

The worst thing in her cell was the sanitary bucket. This was chained to the wall—a relic of the days when women prisoners would empty it over the wardress—and as it was never scoured it smelt abominably, especially when empty. There were, of course, no screens in the cell, or any other opportunities for privacy, but the three women, with a good temper which can only be described as heroic, helped and cheered each other up and in four months did not have a single quarrel. When they got lice in their heads they combed each other's hair. They had cosmetics, and carefully made up their faces every day, to keep up morale. But the lack of baths and the shortage of water—they each had one and a half pints a day for all purposes—tried them sorely, and sometimes they would even strain the bits of cabbage out of their "soup" and use the water to wash their feet.

Eventually a letter reached the prison authorities from Mrs. Green's husband, pointing out that his wife had had no defence at her court-martial. It was a technical point, but some official was sympathetic; and Mrs. Green was told that the remaining few weeks of her sentence were cancelled. She sewed her embroidered piece of sheet—now the size of a tea tray—in between the lining and cloth of her coat, planning to have it framed when she returned home. She also smuggled out as a memento her prison mug, winding knitting wool round it and sticking through a couple of knitting needles. She said goodbye to the le Normans, feeling no elation at her own freedom, for they had still several more months to serve; and went back to work at the Royal Hotel, where she was known ever after as "Mrs. Churchill".

There was another case in Jersey, which had a less happy ending.

Mrs. Ferris, the invalid wife of a retired Indian judge, lived quietly with her husband in the Ommaroo Hotel. She greatly prized a jewelled R.A.F. badge given to her by her airman son, and always wore it on her dress. One day a Jersey woman, who was friendly with Germans who lunched in the hotel, pointed out this brooch to one of them. He sent a waiter across to ask Mrs. Ferris to remove it.

The next day, when the same German came in again, he noticed that the brooch was still in its place. He summoned both the hotel proprietor and Mr. Ferris. Both refused to ask Mrs. Ferris to remove the brooch; and Ferris himself, who could speak fluent German, became exceedingly angry. He was collected the next day by the German military police, and taken up to the *Feldkommandantur* in College House. Here, with perhaps impudent forthrightness, he still refused to stop his wife wearing the brooch. He was imprisoned in the local gaol, and later sent to France.

After some months he returned to find that his wife's health had been made worse by her anxiety, and that she was now bedridden. Subsequently, he was again deported as a British-born "undesirable". Mrs. Green failed to survive this second parting, and died in a nursing home while he was away.

CHAPTER XXI

HITLER'S GLASS CASE

The German attack on Russia, in June 1941, revealed a reversal of strategy. Previously, the coast of Europe had been regarded as a jumping-off place for the invasion of Britain; now the Atlantic Wall was planned to make Germany secure against any attack from the West, while Hitler settled accounts with Russia in the East. The Channel Islands had special importance in this defence system: only the Pas de Calais area was fortified as strongly. And their fortification preceded the rest of the Atlantic Wall by about a year.

It appears that Hitler had always taken a personal interest in the islands. In the early days he had boasted to the Soviet Ambassador in Berlin that he was eating British tomatoes from Guernsey: and he thought the islands would make ideal centres for Dr. Ley's Strength Through Joy Holiday Camps—architects actually arrived, in the very early days indeed, to make preliminary plans for them. By February 1941, Hitler had started complaining that the Channel Islands were not defended strongly enough; and he ordered that a heavy coastal battery was to be sent to Guernsey, and medium batteries to Jersey and Alderney. His directive had one interesting addendum: the reinforcement had to be done in such a way as to "keep out the 'Sea Lion' threat"—i.e. to appear as part of preparations for a forthcoming invasion of England.

The German C.-in-C. of the islands, Colonel von Schmettow, still remained far from satisfied with what was being done, and asked for more.

On June 15, 1941, Hitler issued further orders that the Channel Islands had to be reinforced immediately, as a British attack on them was to be expected soon. Guernsey and Jersey, said Hitler, must have at least one reinforced

Infantry Regiment each, sixteen tanks between them, and artillery. Preparations should also be made for permanent defence constructions. Hitler followed this by calling a conference on June 25 to discuss Channel Islands defences, and more and more soldiers came in.

The subject came up again at a conference held by Hitler with his naval chiefs on August 26, 1941, and the Minutes recorded the following interchange:

What are *The Führer's* intentions with regard to the future status of the Channel Islands?

Are they to belong to the Greater German Reich even if the French coast near them is not in our possession?

The Führer wishes to retain the Channel Islands; he would like to fortify them as strategic bases.

Count von Schmettow still complained that his troops lacked sufficient weapons and equipment. His chance came on October 5, 1941, when he was visited in Jersey by Hitler's Adjutant, General Schmundt. Schmettow said that his troops were so lightly armed that a strong raiding force could land at any time, knock on the doors of the German barracks, and take the men away as prisoners. His troops, explained Schmettow, could best be called "Canada Commandos", since they were plainly destined for prisoner-of-war camps in Canada.

This typical appeal by Schmettow, always ready to back up a serious argument with a dry joke, had an immediate effect.

On October 18, 1941, Hitler called yet another conference in Berlin on the defence of the Islands. According to notes made by Captain Voss, the Naval representative, Hitler said that Britain badly needed a prestige victory, owing to the situation in Russia and the state of morale in England. The most likely objectives would be the Channel Islands, the airfields of which could be used for attacking Brest and the other Atlantic U-boat bases. The British, said Hitler, had landing craft capable of putting ashore heavy vehicles and tanks as well as troops. An attack might be made on all three islands,* probably under a smoke screen after an air and sea bombardment. If the British once re-established themselves in the islands, neither the German Navy nor Air Force would ever be able to get them out again. As proof of this, Hitler cited "the conduct of the British in Malta, where they have held on in spite of the fact that tens of thousands of bombs have been dropped on them."

Hitler repeated that he had no intention of handing back the Channel Islands after the war. They were to be fortified as permanent German strongpoints like Heligoland. As part of the post-war plan. St. Peter Port could be made into a U-boat base.

Hitler went into more detailed plans for fortifying the islands in a secret directive he signed two days later, on October 20, 1941. This declared that though an attempt to invade Europe was unlikely, they must expect small-scale English operations "for reasons of politics and propaganda", and particularly an attempt to regain the Channel Islands.

Therefore, said Hitler, work must be continued at full speed to convert the Islands into *"eine unangreifbare Festung"*—an impregnable fortress. Progress reports had to be sent to him personally at the beginning of each month. Foreign labourers of the O.T., or Organisation Todt, could be brought in to do the work. Eventually English people in the islands—i.e. those not island-born—would have to be deported to the Continent.

According to the minutes of another conference later that month, *"The Führer* has no qualms about evacuating the purely British population." Hitler complained that the guns proposed did not have sufficient range; they must be capable of outranging any naval guns.

From then onwards Hitler sent more and more artillery and fighting equipment into the islands. Count von Schmettow reciprocated by sending Hitler, as a Christmas present, a special copy, bound in red leather, of the book on the

* Jersey, Guernsey, Alderney. The Germans seldom seemed to bother much about Sark.

islands written by Hans Auerbach. (Schmundt read parts of it aloud to Hitler on Christmas Eve.)

The policy Hitler laid down was carried out with fantastic thoroughness, far beyond anything Schmettow had asked. By 1944 the islands could boast as great a strength in artillery and fortifications as were to be found strung out along the whole 1,000 kilometres of coastline from Dieppe to St. Nazaire. And this concentration was hardly the happiest of Hitler's intuitions, diverting substantial fighting strength from the main fronts. If the islanders had indulged in the most vigorous resistance and sabotage movements possible, they could never have done more to tie down enemy forces than was done by Hitler's private obsession.

His policy was strongly opposed by Field Marshal von Witzleben, the German Commander-in-Chief in the West, and by General Hilpert, Witzleben's Chief of Staff. They pointed out that the islands were not operationally important either for Britain or Germany: if they had been, Britain would have fortified them long ago. They did not even provide any worthwhile harbours for use as naval bases. But no arguments would prevail against what Hilpert once described as Hitler's *"Inselwahn"*—"Island madness". German Army Commanders on the Continent soon learnt that it was useless to ask for any men or equipment earmarked for the islands. It became a common saying that "Hitler has put the islands under a glass case."

In the Channel Islands, in 1941, the people did not have the benefit of Hitler's directive to explain what was happening and why. To them the new policy was revealed only in steps and stages—it was nearly a year later, for instance, before the English-born residents were deported. All that was seen by degrees was the arrival of more and more troops; the unloading of apparently unlimited quantities of cement at the ports; the sight of strongpoints and gun positions rising all over the islands; and the arrival of thousands of foreign workers to build them.

Hitler's demand, in June 1941, for more troops on the

islands had been met by bringing in a complete Division, the 319th Infantry Division. With further reinforcements, including heavy Naval and Army batteries, tanks, and an extra reconnaissance section, the German strength on the islands once rose as high as 36,000 men.

Since the Commander of the 319th Infantry Division, Major-General Müller, was senior in rank to Colonel von Schmettow, he became Commander-in-Chief, with von Schmettow reverting for a time to the position of Commandant in Jersey.

General Müller, who established his headquarters in Guernsey, was in some ways the counterpart of the choleric Colonels in the British Army, beloved of caricaturists, who ask candidates for commissions "Do you hunt?" It is not true, as once reported, that he issued a specific order that all officers who wore spurs had to be able to ride. But any young officer, particularly if the General noticed he had spurs on, might be told to report for a ride with General Müller, and woe betide him if he did not come up to the standard expected.

Apart from a fondness for horses Müller had, by some standards, few endearing qualities. A short, red-faced bachelor with high blood-pressure, he looked as if he might explode at any moment. He had a habit of watching groups of soldiers at work or on parade from a distance; and if displeased by anything he saw, he would suddenly gallop into their midst to deliver furious castigations or lay down punishments, while the offender flung himself on the ground in the traditional Prussian Army fashion. It was a typical enough incident, for instance, when Müller stopped a column on the march and demanded that they all took their boots off, so that he could catch those with holes in their socks.

Another new appointment (in October, 1941) was the replacement of Colonel Schumacher as *Feldkommandant* in Jersey by Colonel Knackfuss, whose name for a time was to become a music-hall joke in England. Knackfuss was stocky, aggressive, and very short. (Once he was furious, entering a soldiers' mess at dinner time, because they did not stand up for him; and it turned out that nobody had noticed his head bobbing along just above the level of the ranks of seated soldiery.) The Prussian effect of Knackfuss's appearance was accentuated by an eye which glared through a monocle.

The Jersey authorities had at least the advantage of discussing civilian administration direct with Knackfuss, whereas there was less chance of getting concessions from the frightened subordinates in the branch of the *Feldkommandantur* in Guernsey. In fact, Guernsey had the worst of it both ways, since on the military side it had the immediate presence of General Müller and his headquarters.

And in yet another way, Guernsey was at a disadvantage as the new influx of troops poured in. Jersey, with its bigger tourist industry, had almost unlimited hotels and boarding houses to accommodate them; but in Guernsey many private homes were requisitioned. Householders never knew when they might be turned out; either to make way for German soldiers, or else because they happened to live near the coast in a "Defence Area", destined to be covered with mines.

The new defence systems, marked by eruptions of concrete all over the islands, was probably one of the most remarkable pieces of military engineering ever accomplished, greatly admired by Allied experts when at last they had a chance to inspect it, and incorporating every latest idea. (Within four years, the explosion of the first atom bomb made it old-fashioned.) Observation and fire control posts, with concrete many feet thick, directed the fire of heavy guns, ranging in size up to the famous "Mirus" battery. This consisted of four 30.5 c.m. guns which had started life on the Russian battleship *Czar Peter V*, a ship brought into Sebastopol by White Russians after the Revolution, and later bought by the Danish Navy. Captured when Denmark was invaded, the guns were mounted and installed in Guernsey, concealed by dummy cottages which traversed with them. They had a range of thirty-seven miles.

Perhaps the most heavily fortified island was Alderney,

with a fire control system like a huge unsinkable battleship. It had six batteries of heavy guns, each with independent electrical power, so that any one of the six could go on firing even if all the others were knocked out.

Vast tunnels were bored for storing ammunition; even hospitals were put underground. The underground hospital at Jersey, consisting of seven long tunnels with smaller intersecting ones, could take about 800 beds; that in Guernsey, 600 beds. But they were only used for one short period—after the invasion of Normandy in 1944, when it was expected that the islands might be attacked or bombed. In spite of all the labour that went into them, and the excellent equipment and elaborate arrangement for ventilation, they were always damp inside from condensation and water seepage. It was noticed that patients would go in comparatively fit, and come out looking pale and ill.

There were smaller underground hospitals in Alderney as well.

Some of the strongpoints, made of reinforced concrete up to six feet thick, were ingeniously camouflaged to look like cottages. They were faced with granite blocks, and provided with dummy doors and dummy windows—in one case a window pane even had a painted flower in a painted flowerpot.

As a final defence against invasion, massive anti-tank walls were built wherever there was a beach suitable for landing craft.

To carry cement and materials, the Germans built light railways in the islands—previous railways had been closed down through the competition of buses. The opening of the two-mile St. Helier-Millbrook railway was attended with great ceremony. Count von Schmettow cut a tape and blew the whistle of the engine, which set out bearing flags and a laurel wreath encircling the legend *"Heil dem Führer"*. The occasion was further celebrated by a commemorative dinner at the Pomme D'or hotel.

Some constructions had a more permanent value, like the Beaumont powerhouse in Jersey, and a main water system for St. Anne's in Alderney.

In all this Edgar Dorey, responsible for financial affairs in Jersey, shrewdly saw a chance to score a point for the islands. He argued that it was now unfair for them to bear the whole Occupation costs, since their fortifications were not just for the islands themselves, but were key-points in the whole Atlantic Wall defence system. Therefore, he said, the islanders were being called upon to bear a disproportionate burden. This argument was accepted, a proportion of the Occupation costs being returned as a credit in Paris which could be used for buying goods from France.

One German soldier, watching the concrete mixers at work on the fortifications, remarked to an islander: "You never thought in 1939, when you sang *We'll hang Out the Washing on the Siegfried Line*, that the Siegfried Line would come right over here." But there were some Germans who were distrustful enough of Hitler's intuitions to doubt the value of all these vast erections. One day in Jersey, Edgar Dorey was talking about them with Dr. Casper of the *Feldkommandantur*, and ventured to point out how useless they were. Casper shrugged his shoulders. "I suppose it's the same in every country," he said. "War contractors must live." Another German soldier, when the same point was put to him, remarked philosophically, "It's better than being on the Russian Front."

CHAPTER XXII

WORKERS AND SLAVES

The labour force to build the island fortifications was provided by slaves from the Organisation Todt. According to one estimate, 18,000 of these foreign workers had arrived by the beginning of 1942. The first to come were

French unemployed, mainly from docks areas. Then came men of a very different stamp: Spanish Republicans who had taken refuge in France after the Civil War and had been seized when France surrendered. There followed Poles, Czechs, Belgians, Dutchmen: then a large number of Russians—civilians as well as soldiers—captured on the Eastern Front. Next came Algerians and Moroccans.

Some of these foreign workers were ordinary criminals, straight from prisons or prison camps. Some were skilled workmen who had joined the Todt Organisation voluntarily, tempted by attractive rates of pay. Some, doing clerical work, had every appearance of being well-paid and well dressed. Some were French youths, from all social classes, seized arbitrarily and indiscriminately while waiting in cinema queues.

But if the workers were of varied types, there seems little doubt about the almost uniform callousness of their guards and overseers.

In winter the Todt labourers were taken from their billets before daylight, and not seen again until the population was confined indoors by the curfew. The islanders only had occasional glimpses of them, dressed in tattered clothes, shuffling along with nothing but rags or bits of old motor tyres bound round their feet. In the middle of the day their soup lorry would come round, and each would produce some improvised receptacle to receive his ration —perhaps nothing better than an old jam tin. One worker was seen drinking his soup out of a bowler hat: another, by contrast, carried a saucepan which he also wore as a hat on his head.

Most of the men were so hungry that they would rush the soup lorries as soon as they arrived, eager to be first. But it was noticed that the older hands would wait till the end, because the soup was thicker at the bottom.

Once John Leale saw the body of a foreign worker thrown on top of a heap of stones on a cart; he had obviously died at work, and was being removed on the first conveyance that came handy. On another occasion one of them could be seen by passers-by in the plantation at the

Half-way. He was lying on the ground, he was covered with lice, and he seemed to be dying. He lay there all day.

But the sight which told most vividly of some of the men's plight used to come on Sundays, at the place near St. Peter Port where the sewer discharges into the sea. There were always a number of fishes waiting there for any food scraps; and foreign workers armed with baskets or nets could be seen paddling in the sea amid the refuse, trying to catch the fish to eke out their food supplies.

The Todt workers were usually billeted in empty houses without furniture, where they slept on the floors and lived like animals.

Those who knew the German reputation for cleanliness and scientific efficiency were amazed at the neglect of the most elementary sanitary precautions. Even with their own soldiers, they would sometimes billet thirty in a house which had a septic tank and soakaway designed for six people, so that the ground would be permanently flooded with sewage. The most primitive arrangements were made in the Todt workers' camps. In one case a privy was placed over a stream which, a little lower down, supplied a German gun battery with its water.

Towards the end of 1941 a serious typhus epidemic gave the German Army doctors a chance to protest against the danger of infection spreading from the Todt workers to the troops; and thereafter the living conditions and food of the workers improved. But brutal treatment continued of those who tried to escape, or committed other misdemeanours. The islanders only had occasional glimpses of a world of horror hidden away in their midst.

It was a half-open door which gave Edmund Blampied, the Jersey artist, an accidental glimpse of a Russian prisoner hung upside down by the ankles, a favourite form of punishment. In Guernsey a house in the Vale, ironically named "Paradise", was used as a prison for Todt workers, and those who lived in the neighbourhood could hear the screams which came from it. In charge of "Paradise" was a brutal sadist, a huge man who delighted in trussing up his victims with a length of rope, beating them about the

159

head and body, and then leaving them dangling in the hall from the banisters of the staircase.

The Guernsey police co-operated with the Germans in catching escaped foreign workers—on the ground that they could only live by stealing from local people. One policeman, after taking an escaped French boy back to "Paradise" and seeing how he was treated, vowed that he would never take anyone back there again. Men who had been in "Paradise" had an unmistakable mark for months afterwards: they would shy away and cringe at the slightest gesture which they could mistake for a hand raised against them.

(The German police, however, were just as brutal in their treatment of German offenders whom they caught. It seemed routine procedure to beat up the prisoner after any arrest. Once a German and a Guernsey policeman had co-operated in catching a cat burglar. He was taken to the prison, where two or three Germans took turns in beating him. They then politely handed over the cosh to the Guernsey policeman and invited him to have a turn too; he seemed to go down in their estimation when he refused.)

Several people in the islands took great risks helping escaped foreign workers. Many Russians in Jersey were sheltered by two ladies, Mrs. Metcalfe and her sister. But pride of place must go to Dr. R. N. McKinstry, the Jersey Medical Officer of Health, who undertook the essential job of providing faked ration books and identity cards for those who escaped. McKinstry was a witty Irishman whose fighting spirit gave him a natural sympathy for anyone in trouble; and he even made a point of always carrying sets of faked cards on him, ready for distribution.

In Guernsey the French Consular Agent, M. Lambert, became known throughout the island as a strong friend of any fellow countryman in trouble. Lambert, a short, round, white-haired Frenchman with shining bright eyes, was a familiar sight pedalling furiously on his bicycle, always bent on some mission or another—among his particular charges were about ninety French prisoners of war who had been sent to Guernsey. Once he found in the roadway, sobbing with terror, a young French boy who had escaped from his Todt overseers. For over a year the boy lived and hid from the Germans in a tool shed at the end of M. Lambert's garden.

One escaped French Todt worker actually built up a prosperous store with Black Market goods. But he was informed on by a rival shopkeeper, rounded up by the Guernsey police, and handed back to the Germans.

CHAPTER XXIII

"ALDERNEY, ISLAND OF NIGHTMARE"

Only scanty news reached the other islands from Alderney, where the Germans were almost on their own to do as they liked: the rumours spread of cruelties worse than anywhere else. Occasional reports came back from reliable witnesses. One of them had seen Russian prisoners unloading cement at the harbour. They were all covered with the cement, only their bloodshot eyes showing through the masks of cement dust on their faces. Many were barefoot; and when anyone climbed the ladders to get on board the ship, his hands might be smeared by blood from their feet.

One of the workers at the harbour, knocked from a twenty-foot wall, broke his legs. He was left lying without help till that evening.

After the end of the war, accusations of mass shooting and other atrocities on Alderney were made by some of the men from Jersey and Guernsey who had gone up there to work for the Germans; and also by the before-mentioned Mr. George Pope, who declared that he had kept a record showing 1,000 deaths.

It is true that a number of foreign workers were buried

on Alderney, in a cemetery on Longy Common; the burials were seen by a man named Tom Creron, a Scot from Guernsey, who looked after a flock of sheep for the Germans, and was thus more free to move about the island than most people. He saw the bodies being buried in sacks from time to time, but his recollections of how many were buried were naturally hazy. The present writers also interviewed all others who had reported atrocities on Alderney, and were still to be found, but we were unable to satisfy ourselves that they were satisfactory witnesses.

Mr. Pope failed, on request, to produce to official investigators his record of 1,000 deaths. Disinterments in many different places also failed to give proof of atrocities on the scale reported. There were rumours that some of the bodies were flung into the foundations of defence works, and concrete poured over them. This is hard to disprove. But it is suspicious that the identical story is attributed to many different concrete defence works in different places in all the islands; and we have been unable to find any eye-witness story which stood up to examination.

This irresponsible atrocity-mongering had its usual effect in tending to bring all such stories into discredit. But there seems little doubt about evil things happening on Alderney during the Occupation. The treatment of the Todt workers there may have been little worse, or even better, than on the other islands. But there were also on Alderney "political prisoners"—the euphemistic name used for Hitler's victims from the concentration camps in Germany, some of whom were sent to work on Alderney. They occupied what can be described as the only German concentration camps ever established on British soil.

Whether these camps were better or worse than their counterparts in Europe we have no way of knowing. Some of the political prisoners were assigned to the Todt Organisation, and supervised by Todt overseers; but other camps were run, as in Europe, by the S.S. The prisoners had the usual concentration camp blue-and-white striped "pyjama" uniforms, with the usual different coloured squares or triangles or stripes to distinguish different classes—Jews, criminals, homosexuals, "*Schutzhäftlinge*," and so on.

One camp was near the airfield, and men grazing cattle on the airfield could just see the rows of kennels for Alsatian dogs guarding the entrance. The prisoners were marched out to work each day, and made to sing as they marched.

One can hope that their sufferings were less than in Europe, because otherwise the handful of British people on Alderney would have come to know more. Beyond that there is only guesswork. It is certain that there were none of the mass shootings reported afterwards, for the shootings would have been heard. It may be that, on a small island, a common humanity could even mitigate some of the cruelties of a concentration camp; but otherwise it is likely that no one will ever know what silent horrors may have taken place behind the tall barbed wire fences which, at the time of writing, still have their rusting remains on Alderney.

"*Aurigny; ile du silence, du cauchemar et de l'épouvante*"—"Alderney; island of silence, of nightmare and of terror." Thus wrote a French woman conscripted to act as a cook for one of the O.T. camps: and the story of Alderney can only be guessed at now from such phrases in a few letters which chance has preserved.

CHAPTER XXIV

SPIES INSIDE THE FORTRESS

With the islands now holding important concentrations of German troops and armaments, it naturally occurred to a good many people that there was scope for spare-time spying on behalf of Allied Intelligence. For the most part, however, these efforts were necessarily somewhat amateurish. The most important organisation was in Jersey, and was led by Major W. Crawford-Morrison, the A.R.P. Controller, together with the two Major Manleys (both brothers) and Major L'Amy. Working under cover of the A.R.P. organisation, they made their plans in the Picquet House on the Royal Square (now the manager's office in the National Provincial Bank); and they met there regularly on Saturday afternoons, with a German military band playing a few yards away in the Square.

Crawford-Morrison, who had fought with the Black Watch in the First World War, had the use of a car as A.R.P. Controller. He would call on the officer in charge of every new gun battery, politely asking to be notified the first time it fired its guns, so that he could warn people in houses nearby to open their windows in case of blast. In this way he was able to get together some precise details about the German artillery.

At another time he noticed that Ober-Leutnant Zepernik, von Schmettow's A.D.C., had a map of the German defence system on the wall of his office. So he would drop in to see Zepernik as often as possible, to chat about some A.R.P. business, and each time would ask Zepernik as a favour to get him some cigarettes from the canteen. During the minute or so that the obliging Zepernik was out of the room, Morrison would memorise the map square by square.

Major L'Amy, who won an M.C. in the First World War, acted as States Surveyor; and therefore had every excuse for taking the road, armed with a theodolite, to spy out German positions. To get further information, men were told to enrol as lorry drivers for the Germans. Another agent was Frederick Cook, who acted as gardener for Colonel Knackfuss at his home, Linden Court. One of Major Morrison's men called at Linden Court regularly to pick up any information Cook had gleaned, meeting him in the glasshouse in the garden. Cook, a downright fellow from Devonshire, was one of the colourful characters of the Occupation years. Once Morrison's agent arrived to hear Colonel Knackfuss splashing in his bath upstairs, while

Cook was listening in to the B.B.C. on his wireless downstairs; on another occasion, Cook managed to steal all the medals off Knackfuss's tunic for devilment, without Knackfuss suspecting the culprit. On yet another occasion, Touzel Bree had brought Knackfuss a present of some prize melons, which Knackfuss said he would send on to friends in Germany. Cook proposed to pump the melons full of arsenic weed killer with a garden syringe, and was only dissuaded with the utmost difficulty.

Eventually, drawing on these various sources of information, Morrison and L'Amy made a complete schedule of military locations, each with a map reference, so that the German defences could be charted by anyone in England with an ordinary Ordnance map of Jersey. This schedule was photographed down to a size little bigger than a postage stamp by Stanley Green, the operator at West's Cinema. Green was one of those handymen whose technical knowledge extended to photography and printing as well as film projection. He had already run risks cutting German telephone wires, and we have mentioned his "V" sign Christmas cards. He will be coming into our story again.

Unfortunately it was one thing to collect information, another to find means of getting it to Allied Intelligence. Major Morrison's most ingenious idea came from reading a book called *Gold Fever*, which described a method of simulating tuberculosis. He went to Dr. McKinstry, the Jersey Medical Officer of Health, and asked for an X-ray of the chest, having first applied to his skin a little Iodex— a form of ointment which produced a most convincing shadow on the lung in the X-ray photograph. Dr. McKinstry forwarded the photograph to the German authorities, asking that Major Morrison should be sent for treatment to a sanatorium on the French Alps—from where Morrison was certain that he could get his photographs back to England via Switzerland. Unfortunately, however, the Germans refused to let him go.

Nevertheless, Major Morrison found ways of getting copies of the photographs out on the boats to France: and another copy, as we shall relate later, he took out himself.

Another attempt at intelligence work led to tragedy. In May 1942 three Jersey boys—one eighteen, and the other two only fifteen—tried to escape to England, taking with them a suitcase containing photographs of German defences.

They were some way out to sea before they realised that their boat had a leak, and that they could not keep pace baling out. They began to throw their things overboard, but the water still gained, and the boat sank. One of the boys could not swim; the other two, after desperate efforts to save him when he was struggling in the water, had to leave him to drown. Eventually they got ashore, and the next morning were found naked on the floor of a deserted bungalow, huddled together for warmth, with their wet clothes in a heap on the floor beside them.

Unhappily some of their military photographs were washed ashore and discovered by the Germans, who reacted violently. The two boys were sentenced to prison on the Continent where one died of tuberculosis and the other suffered all the horrors of the Nazi prison system, but just survived.

During 1942 the Germans proceeded with their work in consolidating and strengthening their island fortresses, not forgetting systematic measures for keeping up the morale of their troops. The soldiers in Jersey already had their own paper, the *Deutsche Inselzeitung*; a similar service was now provided for those in Guernsey by the institution of the *Deutsche Guernsey Zeitung*. It regaled the troops with Goebbels' propaganda and reading matter about *"Englische Nervosität"*, *"Timoschenkos Katastrophe"*, etc.; while students of British politics were able to learn in November 1942 that *"Cripps ist ausgebootet"*. The most popular feature of the *Deutsche Guernsey Zeitung*, however, was the column of jokes called *Lach mit, Kamerad!* wherein the conquering soldiers of the *Herrenvolk* were able to amuse themselves with assorted humour: —

What is the difference between a paraffin lamp and a woman?

When a paraffin lamp is cleaned, it burns with a clean flame and doesn't go out. When a woman is well cleaned, she always goes out.

Is he honest?

Yes, he spent eight years in charge of a public bathing establishment, and he never even took a bath!

From which it can be seen that the standard of humour of the German Army is very much on the same level as that of the B.B.C. Variety Department.

Sparing nothing to ensure the morale and well-being of their troops, the Germans also proceeded with typical thoroughness to provide brothels in Jersey and Guernsey, whole establishments complete with French prostitutes being brought in for the purpose. Landing in St. Helier, the girls were marched by their Madame up to a house near the Headquarters of Colonel Knackfuss, who happened to be away at the time; when he returned they were peremptorily removed to the Maison Victor Hugo. In St. Peter Port, the brothels were set up in houses in Sausmarez Street and George Road, and on the road to Forrest. They were plainly marked, in the evenings and on Sunday afternoons, by the German soldiers waiting outside to get in.

Such institutions had been unknown for very many years. They aroused some indignation and caused some curious problems.

Despite protests, civilian doctors were ordered to carry out a medical examination of the inmates twice weekly. In Guernsey the task was arbitrarily assigned to the head of the States V.D. clinic; in Jersey the doctors chose one of their number by drawing lots from a hat.

Another problem was food rationing: there was a protest when the Germans laid down that the girls were to be given rations on the scale provided for "Heavy Workers". When this order reached St. Lo, some official there with a

Gallic sense of humour sent a long detailed official questionnaire as to the exact justification for claiming "Heavy Worker" allowance: asking whether the work in question was skilled or unskilled, continuous or intermittent, and so on. This questionnaire was duly forwarded to the *Feldkommandantur*. It came back with a pen stroke through all the questions, and the reason for the extra rations was written boldly in the one word *Kriegsnotwendigkeit*— "necessity of war."

The girls were often generous with their food supplies. They had, of course, a good deal more sympathy for their fellow countrymen in the Todt Organisation than for the Germans whom they served, and one of the neighbours in George Street once saw a curious sight. A girl was leaning out of the window, holding a mug of soup on the end of a long string. A little farther along, a French Todt worker was leaning from the window of his billet. The girl gradually swung the mug in longer and longer arcs until the Todt worker was able to seize it.

The brothels also raised a financial problem, since the girls wanted to send their earnings—some of them were making £100 a month or more—back to France. This task fell by chance on that highly respectable and respected institution, Barclay's Bank. The girls paid in money in "Occupation Marks", in return for credits in France. This process caused a vigorous but unavailing protest from Guernsey, because the marks were of course valueless paper, and the payments in France were at the expense of the States' holding of francs there. "Thus," wrote an indignant States official when the arrangement was first proposed, in words which might have been put differently, "the transfer would cost the States the full amount transferred, and we would get nothing from the brothels!"

Nor was this the end of the trouble. The Manager of Barclay's Bank in St. Helier persuaded the proprietor of the brothel to collect the money for him. But in St. Peter Port the bank would be crowded by thirty to forty prostitutes, who all came in at the same time once a week. To obviate this embarrassment, the Manager even tried for a short time calling on one of the brothels himself for the purpose of collecting the money from the girls. Sometimes he would have talks with them: more than one told him that they were working in the brothel because they were saving up money to get married.

CHAPTER XXV

CONFISCATIONS AND EXILE

Early in 1942 there arrived at the *Feldkommandantur* in Jersey the Baron von und zu Aufsess, who was later promoted Chief of Administration. He was thus one of the most important figures on the German side so far as the civil population were concerned, as well as one of the most interesting ones.

Baron von Aufsess was a Bavarian nobleman, who lived in a fairy-tale castle at Oberaufsess with a high-born wife as delightful as any princess in a story book. He was a man of the most varied talents: a true countryman, broadly built and broad-shouldered, an expert on the timber and crops on a big estate; and at the same time he was a successful lawyer. But he was also an artist, with a rare talent for camera work and stylish gifts as a writer; and he produced a book of photographs of the Channel Islands which was one of the few good things to come out of the Occupattion.

Baron von Aufsess was soon called upon to exercise all of his ability and finesse in his dealings with the island authorities, for during 1942 a succession of repressive measures were ordered.

In June, Berlin suddenly decreed the confiscation of all wireless sets—which had not been done even in Occupied France. The order went direct to General Müller's Headquarters, and the *Feldkommandantur* ascribed the reason to "military necessity". This seems genuine. Hitler still had an obsession that the Channel Islands would come first in any invasion of Europe; and the B.B.C. was promising to broadcast instructions to people in Occupied countries as to how they could help when the time came. The banning of wireless sets in the Channel Islands was a fairly natural reply.

All the same, the local authorities protested vigorously: though not vigorously enough to please everyone. In Jersey there appeared, pushed through letterboxes, a half sheet of paper with a typed and roneoed message headed *Bulletin of British Patriots No.* 1. It said that the Hague Convention gave the German authorities no right to confiscate wirelesses—or cycles, or any other personal property—and it emphasised how scrupulously the islanders had observed the Convention!

> "The Occupying authorities cannot point to one single hostile act of the population towards the forces of Occupation. We have, in fact, carried pacification to the point of seriously compromising our honour . . .
>
> "For our part, we refuse to comply with the confiscation order. It is for you to decide . . . what your own attitude is to be. But whatever your decision, be careful to give the German authorities no cause for offence in your dealings with them . . . Thus you will give them no justification to take reprisals . . ."

Inevitably, copies of this leaflet reached the Germans, who were not impressed by its moderation. They demanded that the perpetrator should come forward. When nothing happened, they seized ten respected Jerseymen as hostages and put them in gaol. The hostages were, in some cases, very fearful of what was to happen to them and, in others, critical of the leaflet that had landed them in trouble. So it was with relief that they learnt that, two brothers having made a full confession, they themselves were to be released.

The men responsible were Herbert Gallichan, who worked in the local food office, and his brother George, who had helped in distributing the leaflets. Herbert's main concern now was to save his brother, a married man with two small children to look after. He took all the blame he could on himself, being sentenced to five years' imprisonment, and his brother to one. George came back to the island after serving his sentence at Dijon, but Herbert spent the rest of the war at Wolfenbuttel concentration camp.

More troubles for the islanders came after the Dieppe raid in August 1942. One gun position at Dieppe had been attacked from the cover of surrounding houses. The result was a general German order, in the Channel Islands and elsewhere, for the destruction of all houses overlooking gun batteries. In Jersey, Count von Schmettow did his best to ignore the Order, thinking it unnecessarily harsh, except in cases where the military reasons seemed overwhelming. A place known as "Egypt", in the north of Jersey, was levelled ruthlessly. Thereafter, whenever visiting Generals complained that the Order had not been strictly enforced, Count von Schmettow would make a point of taking them out to see Egypt.

In September 1942 there followed the harshest shock of the Occupation—the deportation to Germany of people born in England. It seems that Hitler feared that English-born residents would be those most likely to help any Commando raids, or the attempt at re-capturing the islands which he always feared.

At the time, the Order puzzled the Germans in the islands as much as the islanders themselves; and the reason for its exact timing remains as much a mystery as any other of Hitler's intuitions. Another puzzle is the insistence on definite numbers being deported—1,200 from Jersey, 800 from Guernsey. This suggests that Hitler may have wanted a certain number of Englishmen as pawns in some possible bargain: perhaps to exchange for interned Germans.

The deportations were, of course, a complete breach of the original German promise, in the last paragraph of General Richthofen's ultimatum, that: "In the event of peaceful surrender the lives, property, and liberty of peaceful inhabitants are guaranteed." An immediate protest against the deportations was in fact made by Colonel Knackfuss—both to the German Commander-in-Chief in France, and to General Schmundt, Hitler's Adjutant. Knackfuss telephoned Schmundt, a personal friend. When he put the receiver down, Knackfuss turned to Baron von Aufsess, who was in the room at College House with him, and said, "It's hopeless." Schmundt had made it quite clear that the order had come from Hitler himself.

The news of the deportation came to the islanders without any warning. At half-past eight on the morning of Tuesday, September 15, Louis Guillemette had just reached his office in St. Peter Port when the telephone rang. It was Dr. Brosch at Grange Lodge.

Brosch said he had an urgent and important letter. Startled by the tone of his voice, Guillemette asked: "Is it good news or bad?"

"Bad."

A meeting was called with the Bailiff.

To protests from Victor Carey, Dr. Brosch replied he was certain that nothing could be done to rescind the Order; and he added (truthfully) that he did not know the reason for it.

In Jersey, Coutanche and his colleagues protested and even discussed resigning in protest. But, after much talk, it was decided that the lot of the islanders would be much worse if the entire civil administration was given over into German hands.

On the Tuesday afternoon, the following abrupt statement appeared in the local newspapers:

NOTICE
Jersey, den 15. September, 1942.

By order of higher authorities the following British subjects will be evacuated and transferred to Germany:

(a) Persons who have their permanent residence not on the Channel Islands, for instance, those who have been caught here by the outbreak of war.

(b) All those men not born on the Channel Islands and

16 to 70 years of age who belong to the English
people, together with their families.

Detailed instructions will be given by the *Feldkommandantur* 515.

Der Feldkommandant,
(*gez.*) KNACKFUSS, *Oberst.*

Within twenty-four hours, the first shipload of deportees
had been taken from the islands. Others followed in quick
succession.

This cruel and apparently senseless uprooting of people
from their homes, to be sent into exile in an enemy land,
caused something approaching panic. One man killed himself after making a suicide pact with his wife, who took
poison but vomited it up and was nursed back to recovery.
Some young girls of English parentage escaped deportation
by quickly marrying Jerseymen.

Men and women employed by the Germans were automatically exempted. Some exemptions were also allowed
on the grounds of bad health or essential work. At the end,
Baron von Aufsess had to reject other appeals by saying:
"I am sorry, but I have to provide the numbers."

In all the islands, young people volunteered to go in the
places of the elderly or the ailing, usually unsuccessfully.
But three young men in Jersey, who had arrived with the
party of Conscientious Objectors in 1940, were allowed to
go instead of a clergyman and his family.

In these days of sad partings there was still room for
humour. One deportee, on leaving the bank, was heard to
shout back to the clerk: "Don't forget to transfer my over-
draft to Berlin!"

Those who could stay did their best to help those who
had to go, with gifts of ill-spared clothing. Women stayed
up all night, mending and making children's frocks, pants
and coats out of blankets and curtains and any other
materials they were given. Officials and local tradesmen
combined to give the deportees a good send-off with hot
meals, hot soup, and rich and rare presents of tobacco and
cigarettes. At St. Peter Port there was a little incident which

told of worse hardships than the islanders had yet been asked to endure. A can of soup was accidentally knocked over, so that it lay in puddles on the rough quayside. In a flash, some Todt workers standing nearby were down on their knees and scooping it up in their hands to drink it.

The final partings were taken with dignity and high spirits. In St. Helier, the deportees marched down to the harbour with heads erect, carrying their luggage, between lines of steel-helmeted German guards. Some even wore small Union Jacks in their hatbands. Their fellow-islanders lined the streets watching, mostly in unhappy silence, but every now and then there would be a sudden defiant cheer.

So high did feelings run that the Germans feared demonstrations—and in Jersey they got them. The crowds overlooking the harbour shouted: "One—two—three—four! Who the hell are we for?" And the deportees, and the onlookers themselves, yelled in answer: "Churchill!" "England!" "Jersey!" A party of youths defied the German guards, shouted at them, and played football with one of their helmets, while one boy, more daring than the rest, punched a German officer. Fourteen were arrested, and later sentenced to one month's imprisonment.

The islanders waited anxiously for news of how their exiles fared. After a while letters started coming back from internment camps in Southern Germany. The single men had been sent to Laufen; those with families, and single women, to Biberach and Wurzach. Although living conditions varied, the poor food was supplemented by Red Cross food parcels. The children were well cared for, and the German Red Cross sister at Biberach was beloved by every child there.

Monotony and lack of exercise were the worst privations, but those who volunteered to go out working in the beautiful surrounding countryside found Bavarian farmers so friendly that they could even listen to B.B.C. broadcasts.

Among those sent to Biberach were a Mr. and Mrs. Dunkley of Ramsgate, who had innocently gone to Guernsey for a holiday in the spring of 1940. Their holiday was to last for five years.

174

There also arrived in Biberach Mr. and Mrs. Roche, the Jersey Airport Controller and his wife; and Mr. and Mrs. Topley, a retired British Army sergeant who had settled with his wife in St. Peter Port. With the philosophy of an old soldier, Mr. Topley told his wife, "We're lucky—we're getting a Cook's Continental tour for nothing"; and Mrs. Topley replied: "If the Germans have got such a lovely country as this to live in, why do they want to come bothering other people?"

CHAPTER XXVI

"APPLE," AND THE HAND OF STEEL

About this time there cut across the Channel Islands story a group of men rather different in type from any before or after. Among their leaders was Geoffrey Appleyard, and they were Commandos; that is, they were one of those little bands of immortals, like the few of the Battle of Britain, who won the war and freed the world (the Channel Islands included). No army can carry on without its rank and file of faithful fighters, but it also needs its élite. Appleyard was one of the élite.

"It's not enough just to do our duty," he once said to a friend. "We must do *more* than our duty—everything we can, to the absolute limit." Or, as he wrote to his father: "I think we set out on these excursions very much in the spirit of Cromwell's injunction—'Put your trust in God, and keep your powder dry.' We'll do everything humanly possible to make them successful, and after that, we'll put our trust in God, and in our belief in the righteousness of what we are striving for and in our cause."

Brave men sometimes sound naïve when trying to put

their fighting faith into words; there was really nothing of pious phrase or conventional platitude about Appleyard's character. It is true he was deeply religious; before setting out on a raid he and some of his comrades would kneel and pray, privately and quietly, for courage and success. They were the modern counterparts of the mediaeval Crusaders. But when they went into battle it was with the same zest with which they had lived their lives. Geoffrey Appleyard, son of a Yorkshire motor engineer, had been a champion ski-er and oarsman before the war, as well as taking a First in engineering at Cambridge.

It was in 1940, when he was 23, that he joined a newly-formed Commando Group. After adventures in West Africa, they turned to the Channel Islands and the west coast of Europe. These raids were very different affairs, by now, from the farcical pioneering attempts in Guernsey in 1940. Their success was to be recorded in a typically Churchillian turn of phrase: "There comes out from the sea from time to time a hand of steel which plucks the German sentries from their posts with growing efficiency."

Appleyard—later known officially as Major Geoffrey Appleyard, D.S.O., M.C. and Bar, but usually known unofficially as "Apple"—took part in three Channel Islands raids. The first was on the Casquets, the famous lighthouse on a barren rock west of Alderney, which was being used as a German naval signal station. The raid was led by Major March-Phillips, D.S.O. (known as "Gus"); others of the party were Anders Lassen, the legendary Dane who won the V.C. and M.C. with two bars, and Captain Graham Hayes, M.C.

Appleyard, who had got to know the Channel Islands during schoolboy holidays, navigated their boat. "It was pretty nerve-racking," he admitted afterwards, "as it's a notoriously evil place and you get a tremendous tide race around the rocks." But they landed safely in the darkness, and Appleyard climbed eighty feet of spiral staircase to find the Germans completely unprepared—"I have never seen men so amazed and terrified at the same time." Seven Germans were taken prisoner without a shot being fired on either side, although the lighthouse men had a box of stick grenades open and ready for use.

The German in charge of the lighthouse, taken by surprise in the office below, actually fainted. Others were caught in bed—it was now one o'clock in the morning—and taken to England in their pyjamas. One of the sleepers was wearing a hair net, and was at first mistaken for a woman.

Getting off with the swag of prisoners and captured code books, Appleyard fractured his leg sliding down the rock to the boat. This accident saved his life afterwards. Unable to walk, he went as navigator on the next two raids, but had to stay in the boat off shore.

Five nights after the Casquets success, the Commandos landed on the small island of Burhou, near Alderney, and found it deserted. Then, on September 12, 1942, a party of eleven landed near Cherbourg. They ran into a German patrol which called up reinforcements, and none got back to Appleyard, waiting in the boat. March-Phillips was killed. Graham Hayes escaped through France to neutral Spain, but was handed over by Franco's officials to the Germans, and shot.

Within a month, although his leg was still not right, Appleyard was out raiding again—this time on Sark. Anders Lassen still survived to come with him, and they took three other officers—Captain Dudgeon, Pinkney, Ogden Smith—and five men.

Appleyard had spent a holiday on Sark with his family some years before the war. They were somewhat mystified when, at home on leave, he ran through an amateur cinema film they had taken there: he was refreshing his memory of the place where they had stayed. He decided he would go ashore on the promontory known as the Hog's Back, on the south side of the island, and then cross the Dixcart Valley—avoiding Dixcart Bay itself, because he thought the beach was certain to be mined.

It was nearly midnight, on Saturday, October 3, when they landed on rocks which Appleyard had often used for sunbathing. Climbing the steep cliff, dangerous with shale and loose rock, they cut through a barrier of barbed wire and then advanced cautiously inland. From time to time they lay down quietly to listen for any sound: but they heard nothing, except for one scare when a seagull suddenly flew over.

They had a tense moment when Appleyard saw on the right a wireless mast, an Army hut and some figures standing in front of it. He crawled towards them, and his men were ready to fire, when it suddenly occurred to him that none of the figures ahead had moved since he first saw them. Then he realised that the hut was the butts of a rifle range: the figures were dummies for target practice: and the wireless mast was a flag pole.

They pressed forward, cautiously and silently with their rubber-soled shoes, up to a path leading inland. Hearing a German patrol approaching, they dodged down in the undergrowth and were not spotted. As the men of the patrol went sleepily past, thesy heard one of the soldiers swearing, and the others laughing at him.

They went across the Dixcart Valley, through thick gorse and bracken, and came on a little house, known as La Jaspellerie, standing by itself in the middle of a lawn. They broke a pane in a French window on the ground floor, under the catch, and rushed inside with their guns at the ready. They pushed open door after door on the ground floor, but found no one; then they went upstair and along a corridor. Suddenly a door opened.

A woman came out dressed in a nightgown.

She asked: "Is the house on fire?"

It turned out that her name was Mrs. Pittard, and that she was now living alone, her husband having died a few months earlier. She dressed and joined them downstairs. They asked her about the German defences; she could tell them the whereabouts of some of the guns, but knew little about what sort they were. They asked for a map of Sark, and she went upstairs to get one.

She gave them a copy of the *Guernsey Evening Press*,

with the Deportation Order signed by Colonel Knackfuss, providing the first news of it to reach England.

One of the Commandos noticed a loaf of bread on the table, ready for Sunday morning breakfast, and said they would like to take it back to England to be analysed. Mrs. Pittard said quickly that it was all she had for a week, so they just cut off one corner.

"We want German soldiers to take prisoner," said Appleyard. "Are there any near here?"

"In the building up the valley," she said. "It's the Annexe to the Dixcart Hotel."

The Commandos all shook hands with her in turn, and then they disappeared into the night.

Appleyard was now on very familiar ground. They passed a large yew tree, under which his younger brother had found a half-crown piece on the peaceful holiday that now seemed so long ago.

There was a German sentry ahead. Anders Lassen crept forward to where the sentry was pacing very slowly to and fro on his beat. He was obviously very tired and sleepy. Anders drew his knife from its sheath—it was the first time he had used it, and he did not like it. He waited until, from the sound of the German's steps, he knew he had reached the end of his beat and was turning round.

The others, listening behind, heard nothing but a sudden gasp. Anders dragged the German behind a bush.

Time was now getting short. The door of the Dixcart Hotel Annexe had jammed, and they made some noise pushing it open. They were dazzled to find themselves in a brightly lit room, which fortunately had nobody in it. Five rifles were stacked in a corner.

They went through and found themselves in a passage with several doors. At a sign from Appleyard, these were thrown open simultaneously. In the inner rooms were five Germans, sound asleep and half-dressed in bed. They were hastily seized, secured and bundled outside.

The trouble began when they were out in the open, and the Germans realised how small the British party was. One prisoner broke away, ran screaming towards the hotel, but was recaptured. The others started shouting and making as much noise as possible to summon assistance. Soon all of them were kicking and struggling madly. Appleyard knew that once the alarm was given his position would be desperate: he ordered that any who tried to escape should be shot. But the scuffling went on; others broke away and were fired at; soon they were left with only one, who was scared enough to do what he was told.

They made their way down to the Hogs Back, with the sound of roused Germans shouting behind them. Their prisoner, an unsoldierly specimen with thick glasses, was by now frightened only too thoroughly; he suddenly collapsed, and Lassen had to carry him along. Nevertheless, helped by bright moonlight as they climbed down the cliff, they managed to get back to their M.T.B. with their one prisoner, and the valuable information given by Mrs. Pittard. It turned out that the prisoner, and the other four men in the Annexe, were Engineers who had been working on the harbour boom defences.

The success of this raid threw the Germans into a fury and a fluster. Miss Duckett and Miss Page, in the Dixcart Hotel itself, had heard nothing of the commotion in the Annexe: but at four o'clock that morning they were awakened by a thunderous knocking on the door. A German officer pushed his way in, shouted "You have the British here!", and proceeded with his men to ransack every room in the hotel. The two ladies stayed up in a state of suspense the rest of the night, drinking mint tea. At day-break the secret Military Police arrived too. The mystified Miss Page and Miss Duckett had no inkling as to what could have happened until, through the windows, they saw Germans carrying two coffins up to Mrs. Hathaway's horse-drawn van, which had been commandeered as a hearse. "Then," Miss Page explained afterwards, "we were thrilled to bits to think our own boys had been here." But for weeks the two women were questioned by the Germans, who would not believe that they knew nothing of the raid at their doorstep.

The German Commandant in Sark was court-martialled

and relieved of his post for leaving men sleeping on their own, and all German troops were thereafter billeted inside a central perimeter. There had been no sentries where Appleyard landed, because the currents were so treacherous and the cliff so steep that the Germans did not think a landing possible there. They guessed that the landing must have been made by someone who had lived on Sark, and decided that he must have been told of the German defence arrangements, and of the fact that men were sleeping in the Annexe, by Sark people using carrier pigeons.

Strangely enough, Mrs. Pittard was not questioned until about a month afterwards, a month during which—she was still living alone—she had slept little at nights, on edge lest the British might come raiding again, or the Germans might come to arrest her. She was given away by the window pane which the Commandos had broken to get into her house, and soon she was forced to tell the whole story of how she had helped them. She was put into the meat van used as a Black Maria, taken to the quay, shipped to Guernsey, and imprisoned there. She spent the first week in a solitary cell, weeping and wondering what would come next. She was the only woman in her section of the prison, but was treated with courtesy; she was given privacy, and even allowed to dry her hair in front of the Governor's sitting-room fire. After eleven weeks, without any reason being given, she was suddenly released and allowed to return home.

But the raid had repercussions far beyond Sark. As soon as he heard the news, General Müller ordered the redoubling of guards throughout the Channel Islands, and the carrying of weapons. The curfew hour was altered from 10 p.m. to 9 p.m. And Berlin Radio was soon broadcasting angry accusations:

"Sixteen British fell upon a German working party consisting of one N.C.O. and four men, whom they tied up in their shirts with a thin but strong cord. The men were not allowed to put on more clothes, but were led off to the beach, and when they resisted this improper treatment the N.C.O. and one man were killed by bullets and bayonets,* and another soldier was wounded."

As a reprisal, the Germans ordered the chaining of 1,376 prisoners taken at Dieppe, and the chaining of 1,376 German prisoners in Canada was promptly ordered in reply. The theme of indignation—"German soldiers had their hands bound in deplorable and outrageous fashion" —was continued at length for some days. This was not such unmitigated hypocrisy as the British public assumed at the time. In the fight for life which had developed on Sark, the Commandos had no chance to think of niceties. But on their way back in the M.T.B., comparing notes on what had happened, they realised that the binding of prisoners might be represented as technically against the rules of war. Anders Lassen was so upset at the possibilities for German propaganda that he volunteered to go back alone, find the bodies, and remove any ties round their wrists. But Appleyard had to rule that the chances of doing this successfully were too small, and the risks involved too great: moreover they now had on board a valuable prisoner and valuable information, and their first duty was to get these back to England.

When they arrived, Appleyard was summoned to see Churchill in his room in the House of Commons. Churchill began by growling "What have you been up to, my boy?" and then put an arm round his shoulder and congratulated him on the information he had got.

The handling of the matter by British propagandists can hardly be called happy. The first official statement on the raid merely said that "Five prisoners were taken of whom four escaped after repeated struggles, and were shot while doing so." *The Times* Diplomatic Correspondent said that the German allegations were "based on the flimsiest foundation," and were merely a pretext for "German terrorist methods". It was not till the following Saturday

* The mention of bayonets seems to have been a mistaken reference to the sentry knifed by Anders Lassen. We have found no mention of the killing of the sentry in either British or German official sources, so it remains subject to an element of doubt; but we have taken our account from a source which should be reliable.

that Whitehall officially admitted that the hands of prisoners on Sark *had* been secured. According to the new official statement, "The hands of the Germans were tied so that arms might be linked with the captors." (Another version again was to be given later in *The Green Beret*, the official history of the Commandos, which implied that only one prisoner had been bound.) The truth seems to be that each man secured his own prisoner in his own way; and that in the confusion, with men shooting and shouting in the dark, nobody could know exactly what happened. Appleyard's official report, for instance, shows he believed four of the Germans had been shot.

Whitehall was on much stronger ground in saying that the circumstances on Sark amounted to a battle, and that "there is a wide difference between what is appropriate to a prisoner in safe custody, and to prisoners in the course of a battle." But German propagandists were not likely to lose any chance of magnifying the matter. The Guernsey *Star* quoted Lord Haw-Haw*: —

"The British Government takes refuge in flimsy excuses, and the argument that humanity varies according to circumstances. The German Supreme Command have never deemed it necessary to resort to such a distinction. They have observed a standard of chivalry in which the British Government evidently does not believe . . ."

It must be admitted that the Germans were not the only people who resented the Sark raid. People in Sark had previously been able to wander freely almost anywhere over the island: now paths to the shores were mined and forbidden. Many years later a Sark lady still had an aggrieved tone in her voice as she remarked to the present authors: "We were all getting on all right during the Occupation, until the Commandos spoilt everything by coming and murdering two German soldiers . . ."

Others rejoiced that Britain had not forgotten them: and

* Whom, curiously enough, it referred to openly as Lord Haw-Haw; it was only later that he was known as William Joyce.

from the point of view of the war as a whole—admittedly difficult to see in perspective from a small island—there is no doubt about what was accomplished by Appleyard and his men. The thousands of mines round Sark and the other islands could have been used against Allied soldiers when the landing came in Normandy. Every gun on the island was a gun wasted for Hitler; every soldier meant one man less for other fronts.

What Hitler thought of the effectiveness of the raids was shown plainly enough by his order of October 18, 1942, that captured Commandos were not to be treated as prisoners of war, but "slaughtered to the last man".

Towards the end of 1943 there was another Commando raid on Sark, led by Lieutenant McGonigal. At the first attempt they landed on Derrible Point, but could not get across the narrow neck of land dividing it from the rest of the island. The second time, trying another way, they reached the top of the Hog's Back, and followed Appleyard's route. The Germans, however, had prepared for just such a return visit. McGonigal and his men, feeling their way forward cautiously with blackened faces, had to keep to the path because of the noise they made when they tried going through the gorse on either side. Suddenly there were violent explosions, as the two men coming last were badly wounded by mines. The others tried to drag them clear with toggle ropes tied round their legs; but it then appeared that they had come right through a minefield, because more mines went off as they retraced their steps. The fresh explosions killed the two men. The rest of the party managed to get back to their boat, though all but one were wounded.

The Germans heard the mines exploding and sent out patrols to investigate. They found nothing till daylight, when they came on the two men lying with their grotesquely blackened faces, and a flecked trail of blood, left by the wounded, leading back to the sea.

That was the Commandos' last visit to Sark. Meanwhile Appleyard, Lassen and the others had passed on to other exploits in other theatres of war; but the memory of their attack remained in the minds of the Germans, and kept them ever fearful of their return. As General Warlimont, of the German Supreme Command, wrote immediately after their raid: *"Es gibt daher keinen Abschnitt, der sicher ist. Der Feind kann zu jedem Zeitpunkt und an jeder Stelle landen."*—"Nowhere can be considered safe. The enemy may strike at any time and any place."

ELIMINATING THE UNRELIABLE

When the German High Command discovered the help given by Mrs. Pittard to Appleyard, fresh deportations were ordered from the islands. The fact that the Commandos had been able to get valuable information from a British resident proved that "unreliable elements" still remained. An Order had been issued previously for the registration of all former officers of the British Army; and towards the end of January, 1943, they were summoned for medical examinations. At St. Peter Port this took place in the Regal Cinema,* which by now was in a gloomy and dilapidated condition, with holes in the carpets, patches of damp on the walls, and padding missing from the seats and arm rests. There was a macabre incident when an old soldier was brought in who had spent many years in a mental asylum. The idea of being examined by German doctors tipped the balance of his mind once more, and his screaming echoed round the empty theatre, while four men tried to hold him as he struggled.

Deportations to Germany, of those found medically fit, followed in February.

In Jersey, Duret Aubin secured one of the greatest triumphs for his policy of patiently trying, whatever the

* Later known as the Odeon Cinema.

rebuffs, to work with the Germans, and thus have an opportunity to argue every possible point. When the Order came for the registration of former Army officers, this was understood in Guernsey as meaning what it said—all who had held the King's Commission at one time or another. They were a very numerous class in the islands: including, for instance, men like John Leale, who had been for a little while in the Royal Guernsey Militia in the First World War.

Duret Aubin decided he would try and argue the scope of the Order in Jersey down to former *Regular Army* officers. As soon as he heard of it late one afternoon, he dashed off to College House, caught Dr. Casper just as he was leaving the *Feldkommandantur*, and they walked up and down under the trees of Bagatelle Road discussing it.

"*We* don't look on a person as a soldier just because he's held some temporary war-time commission," said Duret Aubin. ("I'm afraid," he said afterwards, "I had to be a little rude to temporary officers and gentlemen.") "Are you going to call a man a retired British Army officer if he's just some clerk who happened to go into the Army for a few years? You Germans are supposed to be a military race: you'll make yourselves the laughing stock of Europe."

Strangely enough, this argument was solemnly accepted, and Duret Aubin may thereby have saved many men in Jersey from being deported.

Among those who could not escape deportation was Major Crawford-Morrison—the A.R.P. Controller who had organised a secret service, producing the list of fortifications which was photographed down by Stanley Green of West's Cinema. Morrison took one set of photographs to Germany with him, in the hope of finding some way of getting it through to England. Unfortunately he was now regarded with some justifiable suspicion by the Germans—who soon afterwards closed down the A.R.P. organisation completely —and he was interrogated and searched on his way to Biberach. They probed the lining of his coat and all his clothes, and even searched between the leather of his shoes;

but fortunately they did not look at his old cap, which he had thrown aside carelessly just before the search began. The photographs were tucked away in the lining.

It was not, however, till 1944, when one of the internees was repatriated to England for health reasons, that Morrison was able to send back this particular set of photographs with him.

In Guernsey, John Leale and others in official positions were excused deportation. But there was no exemption for Major Sherwill, although he had been re-appointed Attorney-General on the death of G. J. P. Ridgway some months previously. Sherwill was not surprised, for he knew the Germans had not forgotten his part in the Symes-Nicolle affair. What hurt him, however, was that the names of his wife and two young sons were also listed for deportation.

He remarked to Baron von Aufsess, who had come over from Jersey for relief duty: "I can understand your getting rid of me, but how on earth can it help you Germans to deport women and children?" Sherwill went home, and forgot what he had said; but a little later he learnt that his wife and sons could stay. He was puzzled, but never asked why the change had been made, being thankful enough to know his family were remaining in their own home. (May Sherwill and the boys moved down to a flat in the basement of Havelet House, where they soon had seventy Germans—who behaved with perfect consideration—billeted above them.)

It was not till after the war that they were told, by von Aufsess himself, what had happened. Troubled by the taunt about the military value of deporting women and children, he had appealed to General Müller. But Müller's reply was typically short: *"The women and children must go!"*

Baron von Aufsess thereupon told May Sherwill that she and her sons were to stay; but he left their names on the list of deportees, so in due course they were officially recorded as having gone. Thereafter, Aufsess was in constant anxiety lest General Müller should find what he had done, for Mrs. Sherwill was still prominent in amateur dramatics. But fortunately for all concerned, General Müller was not interested in the theatre, and never associated the actress May Sherwill with the Attorney-General's wife.

Sherwill was made leader of the batch of 150 deportees who left Guernsey. They sailed from St. Peter Port on a wet February day, with dismal rain and a keen wind blowing: but they were able to keep up their spirits well enough to ensure a brave show. As the boat cast off, Sherwill and a party of men, standing in the bows, gave three cheers for the King: and then, as they headed towards the grey seas outside the harbour, there came the sound of strong voices singing *There'll always be an England*.

With this group of deportees, and another small party which followed it, were included more people from Sark. Among them was Mrs. Pittard, who had barely recovered from the strain of her husband's death, the Commando raid and her subsequent imprisonment: and throughout a long night she had walked up and down her house trying to decide which belongings to take, and how to hide her valuables. In their Dixcart Hotel up the valley, Miss Ducket and Miss Page were facing the same problems, fearing that this might be the end of the venture into which they had sunk all their savings; and wondering, like all of their fellow deportees, whether they would ever come back.

All three women eventually joined the Channel Islanders at Biberach, but Miss Ducket and Miss Page had some unpleasant experiences on the way, being first sent to a prison camp at Compiègne. Here they were herded into a filthy room, and had nothing for food except swede water and a little bread, with sugar and margarine every second day. Also in the camp were Todt workers. Miss Page said afterwards that "They looked barely half alive, squatting in blankets and trying to coax a few sticks into a fire. The Germans, as they walked through their rooms, would kick these pathetic bundles with their boots and send them flying."

Later they were transferred to Biberach, changing trains in Paris, where they crossed on foot from one station to another in a dejected looking crocodile, with saucepans and any other possessions strapped on their backs.

After eighteen months Miss Ducket and Miss Page, as "unattached" women, were moved on again, and quartered on the second floor of a lunatic asylum at Liebenau. They had lunatics, with their sad crazy noises at all hours, above and below them.

Another deportee from Sark was Robert Hathaway, the Seigneur. He made no appeal against his Deportation Order, explaining afterwards that "I wasn't going to ask those damned Germans for anything." And so he ended up in Laufen, where for over two years he and Major Sherwill shared a double-tiered bunk, with Sherwill sleeping on the top and Hathaway down below.

Two years of such close proximity would test the nearest and dearest friendship; and it is not surprising that some antagonism was to develop, on one side at least, between the two men. Each reacted to the confinement in characteristic fashion. While Sherwill was soon helping to run things as British "Camp Senior", Hathaway stuck in his room with dogged American determination and announced his refusal to set foot on German soil, except in so far as he was actually forced. He could not avoid the daily parade: but he sometimes had a pipe in his mouth, and when the parade was called to attention he would promptly put his legs apart. According to his account later, the German sergeant came up to him one day and said: "I want to ask a favour of you: would you mind not smoking on parade?" Hathaway replied: "Now you've asked me that way, I will never smoke again."

At the end, he was excused parades entirely, on the ground of ill health.

For the rest, Hathaway occupied himself breaking every rule and regulation in the camp. He said afterwards: "When I found that no one was allowed to have more than 1,000 cigarettes, I made a collection of 10,000. When there was a limit of two tins of tobacco, I collected twenty-two. When I found no one was allowed to have more than 500 marks, I got together 15,000."

They were so well supplied with Red Cross parcels at Laufen that some of them even posted cigarettes back to Guernsey and Jersey. The only things Hathaway asked his wife to send from Sark were onions, useful in giving some sort of flavour to the interminable soup. Mrs. Hathaway, with her usual resourcefulness, also managed to send something even more welcome. All she had left now in the way of drinks at the Seigneurie were a bottle of whisky and a bottle of brandy kept for emergencies. First she sent a little of the whisky in a bottle hidden in a case of onions: she used a Boots medicine bottle with a label "EYEWASH". It got through safely, so she followed it with a little brandy in a bottle labelled "SLEEPING DRAUGHT".

CHAPTER XXVII

THE HIDDEN WIRELESS

Two small boys were jostling one another for places in a queue outside a St. Helier shop.

Said one: "If you don't stop pushing, I'll tell the Germans your father has a radio."

Returned the other: "If you do, I'll tell the Germans your father hadn't the guts to keep his own, but comes and listens to ours instead."

With the confiscation and prohibition of radio sets, the most common Occupation offence against the Germans was keeping hidden wireless and listening to the B.B.C. And with this came the ugliest feature of the Occupation: the informers who were ready to betray neighbours with sets. Sometimes the threat might be made as a joke; but it was actually carried out by petty little anonymous letters each betraying some festering spite to an extent which amazed the Germans themselves. Sometimes it would be a way of paying off a grudge against a neighbour; sometimes even members of the same family would denounce each other after some family quarrel.

Fortunately the Post Office sorters in Jersey made a point of watching letters addressed to the *Feldkommandantur* and German secret police, and in this way over four hundred letters from informers were detected and "lost".

Penalties varied. For a time, sentences were sometimes imposed of fifteen months imprisonment—one of the dreaded longer-term sentences which meant going to a prison on the Continent, and perhaps never returning. But there were few people who did not, at some time, disobey the order; and the result was largely a matter of luck. Sometimes the whole thing was rather a joke; for a period so many people had short sentences that they were told to go home and wait their turn to go to prison. Sometimes an illicit set could bring utter tragedy.

Among the lucky ones we may mention, for instance, Mr. W. J. Corfield, the highly respected Manager of Barclays Bank in St Peter Port. Corfield, having much regretted giving in his own radio when demanded, learnt of an elderly widow who was now regretting having kept hers, since she feared it might cause her to be deported. The only problem was to move the set; it was a biggish one, hard to conceal if removed by day, and impossible to move by night because of the curfew. (By now, of course, motor transport was a forgotten luxury.) Corfield, however, managed to borrow a butcher boy's bicycle with a delivery basket. As he was wobbling his way along, with the hastily wrapped wireless set perched on front, he turned a corner and found approaching him a column of German troops, goose stepping and singing in unison with their eyes fixed resolutely ahead. In grave danger of toppling off and spilling the wireless at their feet, Corfield paddled madly forward between the marching column and a hedge by the side of the road. Fortunately the sight of a highly dignified Bank Manager riding a butcher boy's bicycle, however unusual in most times and places, was unlikely to excite any comment in Guernsey in 1943. Corfield got through safely and was able to deposit the set in the strong-room of his bank, to which thereafter he disappeared mysteriously at a regular time every day.

Once, to his consternation, the Germans ordered a search of all safe deposit boxes in bank strong-rooms. But the search was carried out with a typical mixture of thoroughness and stupidity; it took place upstairs, with Corfield down in the strong-room sending up the boxes to be searched batch by batch and then returned to him. He was thus able to transfer the wireless set from box to box down below, and it passed undetected.

There was less good fortune for Canon Cohu of St. Saviour's Church, Jersey.

Cohu was a retired Indian Army Chaplain, and a familiar figure; greyhaired, half bald, and full of courage and cheerfulness in the darkest days. He thought he should do all he could to keep up the spirits of his parishioners: and did so in a spirit of defiance verging on foolhardiness, which earned him the disapproval of the island authorities. At the end of one Sunday evening service, for instance, Canon Cohu invited his congregation to conclude proceedings by singing *God Save the King*, which they did with such heart and voice that half of St. Saviour's must have heard it. Strangely enough, the Germans made no protest: but Ralph Mollet, the Bailiff's Secretary, one of the congregation, spoke to the Attorney-General about it, who spoke to the Dean of Jersey, who unsuccessfully urged on Canon Cohu a policy of greater caution.

It went without saying that Canon Cohu kept his wireless set. He found a convenient hiding place in the organ loft of St. Saviour's Church, and invited his parishioners to listen to it. The Canon made little secret about this possession: he would gaily shout the latest B.B.C. news to passers-by in the streets. On his hospital visits, he would cheer up the patients by telling it to all and sundry as soon as he got inside the wards, including the maternity wards. This was even more dangerous; for a proportion of the mothers were obviously enough on friendly terms with

Germans, because they were having babies by German soldiers.

It was inevitable that the German secret police would hear of Cohu's wireless set. The Church was searched, the wireless seized, and Cohu and a number of his leading parishioners imprisoned. Cohu was sentenced to four years, two others named Tierney and Nicolle to three years, and others had shorter sentences. The case caused something of a stir, and one of the more cautious members of the congregation did not go to Church for six months afterwards for fear of being implicated.

Life in prison has a way of bringing out the best as well as the worst in people, and Canon Cohu proved himself a brave man and a Christian. He kept his companions fit and cheerful by leading them in gymnastic exercises every morning, and then leading them in prayer and hymn singing. And when he was moved on to France, he made a point of taking off his clerical collar, so that he would not receive any preferential treatment.

On the Continent, like so many others, they were transported from prison to prison, under conditions of increasing harshness and degradation. In June 1944 Canon Cohu's wife had her last letter from him. After the war it was learnt that Cohu, Tierney and Nicolle had all died in prison or concentration camps.

Stories of hidden wireless sets usually followed a set pattern. First, an informer's letter, or a tip picked up through careless talk. Then came an arrest, a search, and an interrogation under blinding light and sometimes brutal treatment.

In these years, many had cause to be grateful to Mrs. Perkins, the buxom and commanding Assistant Matron of St. Helier Prison. She would try to visit new prisoners when they came in, sometimes praying with them—she was a devout Catholic—and sending out messages to their families, who might not have heard about their arrest. Sometimes these messages were just in time for the secret wireless to be removed before the *Geheime Feldpolizei* search party arrived. To get a chance of seeing the prisoners, Mrs. Perkins tried to keep on friendly terms with the German guards, and would use some such excuse as that the new arrival was a cousin, or a former sweetheart. Once one of the guards remarked to her: "Madam, for so good and Christian a lady you have had a great number of sweethearts."

Since any misdemeanour during the Occupation would lead to a routine search of a man's house, and since the search was as likely as not to reveal a wireless set, the most freakish mischances could lead to the savagest penalties.

A dentist named Edward Ross, and his wife Nan, had been shocked by the plight of the Russian prisoners of war in Jersey. One Saturday afternoon, in September 1942, they set off on their bicycles to find some of them. They took bread and cheese to give away, and also a rough sketch map showing the latest position on the Russian Front, which they thought would cheer the prisoners up.

After a while they came across a working party of Russians, barefooted, ragged and thin. The Ross's got off their bicycles and sat in some long grass by the roadside, as if to picnic. To their surprise the German guards approached and questioned them, saying they were in a prohibited Defence Area.

Mrs. Ross, afraid that they might be searched, tried to push the map of the Russian Front down into the grass. The guard saw her; in a panic she jumped up and ran away, trying to swallow bits of the map as she ran. She was caught and roughly hauled back. Meanwhile her husband was seized and kicked.

Both were taken to the prison in St. Helier. The *Geheimefeldpolizei* searched their house—and found their wireless set. Then the Germans tried to force the Ross's into false confessions. They said: "You have been holding B.B.C. news parties." Mrs. Ross denied this, for in fact only she and her husband had used the set. "If you do not tell the truth," she was then told, "you will be shot!" Whereupon Mrs. Ross, with a touch of the heroic which later made her smile, retorted: "Then I shall die happy, knowing I have told the truth."

They were sentenced to six months' imprisonment at Coutances, in France. Just when the six months were up, instead of being freed they were sent on to other prisons and separated. Only after many entreaties was Mrs. Ross allowed to see her husband and say goodbye to him, both wondering whether they would ever see each other again. For by now they knew enough of Nazi justice to realise that the fact that they had served their sentences did not mean freedom. They were caught in the system and might be sent on, from prison to prison, to end in some concentration camp. There was no knowing what would be the eventual outcome of their innocent and well-meaning Saturday afternoon bicycle ride.

Mrs. Ross found herself in the infamous "hostage prison" at Romainville. In her room were crowded fifty-six women, a mixture of prostitutes and French patriots. One, "Aunt Yvonne", had been caught helping prisoners of war to escape back to England, and was sent to Ravensbrück and a gas chamber. Among the others were the mother and five sisters of the Maquis hero Gilbert Renault, who had been arrested as hostages. Sometimes women with young children and even babies were brought in; there were heartbreaking partings when the mothers were sent on elsewhere. Mrs. Ross never discovered what happened to the children.

Meanwhile her husband, sent to Compiègne Prison, had providentially been able to smuggle a letter out to the Swiss Red Cross in Paris. As a result, the Ross's were reunited in an internment camp at Vittel, where life was relatively pleasant. Their one tragic memory concerned some Jews who had been living in Vittel with forged American passports, and who were caught by the S.S. and put into a commandeered hotel opposite the camp. The Ross's watched helplessly while several tried to kill themselves jumping from top floor windows.

The stories of hidden wireless sets have one hero. Jack Soyer, a Jersey wood merchant, was sentenced because of his set to twelve monnths' imprisonment in France. He made a daring escape and, though over forty, joined the Maquis. He was later killed, and many French men and women joined his funeral procession to mourn the islander who had fought for the common freedom of France and the islands.

Two others arrested in Jersey for a wireless set were Mr. Peter Painter, and his high-spirited son and namesake. It was generally believed that they had been given away by an informer. When their home was searched, the Germans also came across an old Mauser pistol. The fact that it was merely a souvenir of the First World War was counted as no excuse for not handing it in.

They were thrown into St. Helier gaol until, on a cold winter night, without any warning or any chance of getting warm clothing, they were put on a boat for France. Thereafter no word was heard of them. Every attempt to get information from the Germans had no results. It was not till after the war that their story was learnt when a fellow prisoner, a Frenchman, wrote to Mrs. Painter.

It then appeared that father and son had been sent to the Cherche Midi prison, then to a camp in Alsace, then a Krupps factory in Silesia, then to work on a canal. Ill-clad in the bitter cold, their health broke down. Peter got bronchial pneumonia. He and his father were in one bed in their camp. Peter died in his father's arms.

The French friend and fellow prisoner wrote to Mrs. Painter: "Before breathing his last, your son thought of you, Madame, so his father told me; he also thought of his sisters and of his brother who, he hoped, was in the Air Force and who would avenge all those who have suffered in concentration camps."

Painter himself survived. But when the big Russian advance came from the East, all the prisoners were sent back into Germany. Painter, with many others, was put in an open truck for a journey which took five days, in rain and snow and bitter cold, and without food. On the third day he died.

Yet, such was the complexity of the German character, that while men like Cohu and the Painters were suffering brutalities or death for the crime of listening to broadcasts from London, some islanders were able to do so freely through the chivalry of other Germans—who themselves risked death if they were discovered by their own secret police. When Dr. Lorenz, the chief medical officer, was visiting Sark for the day, he would go first to the Seigneurie, and leave his portable wireless there while he went round the island (not knowing that the Dame had her own wireless set hidden in a rabbit hutch). On Alderney, Clifford Bichard the mason once had a room in the same billets as a German with a set, who would pointedly go out for a walk at five to nine every night so that Bichard could slip into his room and listen. Then he would come back and ask cheerfully, *"Neues gut?"*

Towards the end of the war Baron von Aufsess of the *Feldkommandantur* in Jersey would drop in every day on Ralph Mollet, the Bailiff's secretary, to ask him the B.B.C. news.

Even inside St. Helier Prison the German guards—unlike their masters, the secret police—were sometimes kindly and good-natured men. Mrs. Perkins, the Assistant Matron, actually grew to trust two of them to the extent of letting them listen to the B.B.C. news on the wireless hidden in her private sitting-room in the prison.

Count von Schmettow had got to know an old lady acting as caretaker at a house which he visited as German Commandant in Jersey. One afternoon, driving there on his own in his car, he carried inside a mysterious parcel wrapped in sacking. It turned out to be a wireless set. He told the old lady, "I know you would like to listen to your own country." Thereafter, each time he came he brought the wireless set in the car with him, so that the caretaker could use it while he was there.

CHAPTER XXIX

PIPES, TRIPES AND ERSATZ TOBACCO

To most islanders, as the slow years of Occupation were counted by—1940, 1941, 1942, 1943 . . .—they were marked not so much by the occasional highlights of excitement and fear, as by the monotony, the wearisomeness of routine restrictions, the scarce and dreary food. By now few people, except for farmers and those who could afford Black Market prices, were not suffering from under-feeding in one form or another; and food was the one endless topic of conversation.

The staple diet came down to turnips, parsnips, carrots, coffee made from acorns, and tea made from blackberry leaves.

Sugar beat syrup became another feature of the Occupation. Housewives would struggle, and sometimes in exasperation, weep over their first attempts to make it. The process involved stewing the sugar beet and rendering down the liquid for hours, and the art lay in stopping it boiling over or burning. The expert practitioner found she could eventually get 2 lb. of black treacly syrup from 10 lb. of beet, and it could be used as a sweetener for puddings, a substitute for jam, and even—when the sugar ration completely ran out—to put into blackberry leaf tea. There were some who always hated the taste of the syrup; but children often grew genuinely fond of it.

As was to be expected, the children got preferential treatment throughout the Occupation, with priority full-cream milk, and extra sugar and fish-liver oil when possible.

People who were fortunate enough to live near a slaughterhouse had a special advantage. They would go down and beg for the blood and intestines of animals. The blood they baked into "black pudding", with the addition of breadcrumbs and suet. The intestines, after being thoroughly washed out, were boiled down to yield a yellow fat which could then be used to fry slices of the black pudding. "Pipes and tripes" became a much sought-after delicacy.

There were some cases of oedema of the legs, due to malnutrition, among the elderly and less robust during the winters. But usually the cumulative effects of under-feeding showed themselves not so much in illness as in lethargy and a slowing down of the physical and mental processes. When Dick Johns, the Guernsey Labour Officer, had cases of men fainting at work, the hours were cut from 8 a.m.—5.30 p.m. to 10 a.m.—4 p.m. People's memories seemed to function more slowly; they would find themselves fumbling for words in conversation. There were strange instances of absent-mindedness, like the lady who went down the town shopping in her dressing-gown, and the farmer who went to milk an old grey mare, and found himself sitting beside it with a pail. John Leale noticed that writing letters took him longer, and that his legs often had a tendency to go to sleep.

After the shortage of food, the shortage of soap came next in importance. The tiniest cuts would fester, as the skin could never be kept really clean. Skin diseases were hard to clear up. "Occupation ulcers" was the name given by one Jersey doctor to a type of indolent and fairly prevalent ulcer of the leg. In hospitals, operation wounds were slower in healing; the stitches would be taken out on the fourteenth day instead of the eighth or ninth.

Medical supplies were often a problem. We have mentioned how, through the initiative of Butterworth, the Boots Manager in St. Peter Port, drugs were imported from Germany. This traffic was abruptly forbidden by the Germans in 1942, presumably because of their own shortages. Other supplies came from France, largely owing to a stroke of good fortune. One day Raymond Falla, over in Rennes for the Purchasing Commission, got violent toothache. He went to a chemist for oil of cloves, and noticed that the shelves were well stocked. Being Falla, he contrived to linger and talk. Eventually he walked out with a letter of introduction to the chemist's wholesale dealer, a man named Langlois, who not only agreed to supply the Channel Islands, but became a personal friend of Falla.

The work of distributing imported drugs among the different chemists was undertaken, with great success and without payment, by Boots—a firm which already had a special connection with Jersey. (Its founder, Jesse Boot, married a Jersey girl whose business acumen had a great deal to do with the firm's expansion.) The bond was made even stronger by the Occupation, the Manager of Boots in St. Helier, Reginald Gould, winning official thanks for his "really unselfish service" to the people of Jersey.

Great ingenuity was shown in finding substitutes for scarce goods. Tinctures were made with brandy. Cuttlefish were ground down for toothpowder. Gould produced a substitute for Parrish's Food—phosphate of iron—by the simple method of putting wrought iron nails in phosphoric acid. The greatest all-purpose medicinal substitute was carrageen moss (sometimes known as Irish Moss). Its collection from the seashore was vigorously organised by Mrs. Butterworth, wife of the Boots Manager in St. Peter Port; and it was used for cough medicine, hair cream, and even (bleached and sold in packets) to make a kind of milk blancmange.

Cosmetics came in occasionally from France. The demand for lip-sticks was so great that one of the chemists made them out of white wax, olive oil, and carmine—but this was frowned on by the others, as wax and olive oil were very scarce, and needed for urgent medical purposes.

One of the greatest deprivations, of course, was tobacco. It might have been expected that many would even have welcomed the heaven-sent encouragement and opportunity to learn to give up smoking. But, strangely enough, smokers found that the craving for tobacco did not leave them even months after there was no tobacco to be had—probably because it would dull the pangs of hunger. The most remarkable substitutes were tried out: even dock leaves and rose petals were rolled for cigarettes.

Like many other islanders, the Coutanches in Jersey grew tobacco in their garden, and found by hard experience the best way of curing it, after several times nearly knocking themselves out by smoking it when it was too green. The Bailiff also tried smoking dried cherry leaves in his pipe.

The shortage of fuel produced a crop of other problems. On her rare visits to her hairdresser, who still contrived to give perms and sets with home-made sachets and hairpins made of wreath wire, Mrs. Coutanche would set out with a bundle of twigs, to swell the fire used for drying the customers' heads. In fact, a large part of her energies went into gathering wood and twigs, to keep a kitchen fire going for the servants, and another in her drawing-room. Once, when the artist Edmund Blampied and his wife were ill, they were heartened to see Mrs. Coutanche calling upon them, dragging down the road behind her a precious gift of a great branch of dried wood.

Transport became more and more primitive. When Louis Guillemette, secretary to John Leale in Guernsey, lost the use of his car, he used a motor bicycle for travelling the three miles between his office in St. Peter Port and his home in St. Sampson's. When his motor bicycle broke down he bought a bicycle. Then his bicycle, like most bicycles in Guernsey sooner or later, was requisitioned by the Germans. He finished the Occupation walking.

The fortunate might be seen getting about the islands in farm carts and strangely ancient carriages. It may be remembered that, in 1940, Messrs. Domaille and Sons had offered bicycles from £4 19s. 6d. each. Within a few years, bicycles were a rare luxurious means of transport, selling at £50—and at this price they might have tyres consisting of a hosepipe with a rope through it. Even bits and pieces of bicycles were counted precious.

A feature of the Occupation were the "Exchange and Mart" advertisements in the newspapers, wherein one scarce commodity would be traded for another. Sidney Bisson, in his pleasant book, *Jersey, Our Island*, noted such bargains as 1,000 saccharine tables for five sacks of coal, a bicycle tyre for a circular saw, an electric razor for a baby's layette, a pair of budgerigars for a pair of trousers, and a guitar for a text book on economics. Or we can take a typical enough sample of offers from a single issue of the *Guernsey Evening Press*:

Rear wheel cycle, as new, 26 in. x 1½ in. for what permissible.

Men's leather gaiters, for sweet corn, or what permissible.

New dark green cardigan, woollen, for sugar beet syrup.

Wheelbarrow wheel, iron rim, for what permissible.

Ewbank wringer, as new, rubber rollers, for lady's pyjamas.

400-day all-brass clock, for sweet corn.

Cigarette papers, inner tube 28 in. x 1½ in., for sweet corn or what permissible.

The phrase, "or what permissible", was because the bartering of rationed foodstuffs was forbidden. It could be used as an euphemism for "what *not* permissible". In less law-abiding Jersey the same purpose was served even more flagrantly by the magic words "or what?" or "for what?" Thus, for instance:

An undervest, a belly band, and a pair of bedsocks—for what?

Discerning readers of small advertisements noticed another blind—a farmer promising a reward for the return of a pig or other lost animal. What had usually happened was that the pig had been slaughtered illegally and sold in the Black Market, the farmer telling inquiring officials that it had strayed or been stolen; and the advertisement would be part of the game.

Some indication of some food prices can be got from one auction sale in Guernsey in January, 1943. For a half-pound packet of Orange Pekoe tea, sold pre-war at 1s. 5d., the bidding started at £5. The tea was finally knocked down for £7 7s. 6d. to a man who explained that he and his wife had not tasted real tea for over two years. Other closing bids were a tin of Bisto (pre-war 9½d.) sold for 23s.; a half-pound of tapioca, 16s.; packets of strawberry jelly crystals, 10s. each.

At another auction, single eggs sold for 8s. each.

Life in the Occupation was not all greyness, even for those who had no Black Market friends. There were amateur dramatic shows, and concerts, and French and German films; some islanders still say nowadays they wish they could have such good films again, instead of the usual Hollywood variety.

On the whole the Germans did not interfere much with entertainments, though music by Mendelssohn and other Jewish composers was forbidden, and the song *Kiss Me Good-night, Sergeant-Major*, was banned from one concert programme on the ground that it lacked a proper respect for military sanctities.

Once exception was taken to a notice in the *Jersey Evening Post* of a performance of *The Merchant of Venice*. The dramatic critic, under the pen name of "First Nighter", praised the way Shylock had been played, saying that the strength of the performance lay in not portraying the Jew as a wholly evil character, but in showing how he made himself unhappy by his own actions. By some slip, this notice went straight into the paper without being seen by the German censor. Next day a storm broke.

The Germans demanded that Arthur Harrison, the Editor, should tell them who "First Nighter" was; not uncourageously, he refused. So the Germans contented themselves by summoning to College House the actor who had played Shylock, and severely reprimanding him for not being completely villainous.

Though the curfew made conventional entertainment difficult, at least it introduced the innovation of all-night parties. Young people, with their own food and drink, would trek to the host's house and dance and sing and play games until exhausted; then they would curl up in rugs on the floor for some sleep before curfew ended, and they could walk home for breakfast.

At afternoon tea parties ladies would take their own provisions with them, and the new conventions were most properly observed. For example, Mrs. Coutanche's guests in Jersey would hand their wisps of paper containing blackberry leaf tea to the maid on arrival, with perhaps a nicely baked potato to warm up; in time these would be served in the drawing-room on the old family silver and china, each lady selecting her own portion. On leaving, the ladies would be given back their folded wisps of paper, or whatever other receptacles they had brought.

The sale of spirits remained forbidden. But Dr. McKinstry, the Jersey Medical Officer of Health, pointed out to the Germans that this was somewhat harsh for ex-Indian Army colonels, and others who for decades had been used to their daily tot. One of the Germans remarked, "But are there not complaints for which spirits can be prescribed?" Dr. McKinstry took the hint, and every week would authorise sufficient prescriptions to use up the supply of spirits available. Some strange reasons were given for needing them, and more than one teetotal old lady found she urgently required brandy, afterwards selling it on the Black Market.

Perhaps the greatest source of comfort in these years was the Red Cross message service, which would bring twenty-five words of news, however occasional and erratically delivered, from children and others evacuated to England. Once when Charles d' Authreau, the Jersey Assistant Postmaster, complained of the delays in getting messages through, a German *Sonderführer* remarked philosophically that "the fault lies with our common enemy, the Generals."

Messages were supposed to be entirely personal, but different devices were tried for getting through news about the war and the Occupation. "Uncle Joe" and "Uncle Jerry" were frequently mentioned, and so was "Mr. Cassius" (of the lean and hungry look) when food became short.

CHAPTER XXX

BATTLES OF WORDS AND BATTLES OF WITS

Even the Occupation did not end all traditional rivalry between Jersey and Guernsey. At Granville, where the Joint Purchasing Commission functioned, it was said to be not unknown for a Guernseyman to see goods in a packing case with a chalked address "JERSEY", rub it out, and substitute "GUERNSEY"; or vice versa in the case of a Jerseyman. (It all depends on who is telling you the particular story.) Since most ships from France called at Jersey first, there might have been a tendency for Jersey to get the best of it: but a most valiant fight was put up by Alfred Sarre, a Guernseyman living in Jersey who acted as representative of the States of Guernsey there.

One day a consignment of pit props, meant for German ammunition tunnels, arrived at St. Helier. Nobody knew what to do with them—by some clerk's error, the manifest had not been filled in properly. Sarre thought quickly.

"It's all right," he said. "I know all about it; they're for Guernsey."

Unfortunately the officials in Guernsey were not very quick at the uptake on this occasion: to Sarre's embarrassment, he got a puzzled message asking what the pit props were for. Urgently he replied that they were to be chopped up for firewood quickly and lively, and no questions asked about where they came from . . .

It is pleasant to record, however, some acts of kindly mutual help between the islands. Once, for instance, Guernsey sent Jersey 1,000 candles, a rare gift indeed; and

Guernsey could offer a loan of foreign currency derived from its sales of tomatoes. Jersey, with its greater food resources, sent potatoes—and later flour—in return, though some Guernseymen thought Jersey might have done more. When Alfred Sarre first raised the point with a senior Jersey official, he was told that "There'd be a riot here if we sent wheat to Guernsey." And on another occasion an offer of firewood from the Jersey Fuel Officer was vetoed by higher authorities.

One occasion when the two islands ended at cross purposes came after the Germans had ordered severe ration cuts in April, 1943. Colonel von Unger, Chief of Staff to General Müller, was returning from a visit to France when he saw an attack by Allied planes on ships plying between Granville and the islands. Several were sunk. Now these were ships on which German sailors were carrying food to the islands at the risk of their lives. Colonel von Unger was furious at what he saw; and orders were given to *Feldkommandantur* 515, through "Section A" at St. Germain, to cut rations on the islands.

On April 30, 1943, a notice appeared in the island papers:

The British Military Command . . . disregarding the fact that the population of the Channel Islands are their OWN COUNTRYMEN, are attempting in every way to jeopardise the continuous supply to the Islands by increased NUISANCE RAIDS. If in consequence of these raids the RATIONS of the ISLAND POPULATION have now to be decreased, the population can thank for this their countrymen ON THE OTHER SIDE OF THE CHANNEL. Churchill and his supporters will not achieve any military success from such nuisance raids. But it characterises their notorious lack of scruples that they do not refrain from exposing their own fellow countrymen to sufferings that could be avoided. THE POPULATION OF THE ISLANDS, HOWEVER, MAY AT LEAST KNOW THE CULPRITS.

It was plain that the ration cuts were not really due to any shortage caused by shipping losses; they were a punishment—a reprisal. As such, they might be contrary to Article 50 of the Hague Convention, which forbade collective punishments on a population on account of acts for which they were not responsible.

There followed one of those legal arguments which would have been dry and dreary but for the conviction that the result might literally be a matter of life or death. Men could not go on working without proper food. And if the principle were admitted that the islanders could be punished for legitimate acts of war by the Allies, where would such reprisals stop?

The Bailiffs of Guernsey and Jersey were allowed to confer together by telephone. (With the Germans listening in.) Victor Carey asked, "Have you put the new rationing order into operation yet?" and Coutanche replied "No, and we don't intend to." They then agreed that each would appeal to the "Protecting Power" by sending a letter to the Swiss Ambassador in Berlin. Victor Carey of Guernsey also suggested that a Swiss Government representative should be asked to visit the islands.

The immediate result of this telephone conversation was a new rationing order, with something of a retreat on the side of the Germans; the only important remaining cut being in the bread ration. The Guernsey authorities pursued the argument, on the ground that even this reduction—allowing less than 3 lb. of bread a week—was bound to have a bad effect on health. They were then flabbergasted to be told by a triumphant Dr. Kratzer, at the Guernsey *Feldkommandantur*, that the new ration scale had been accepted without protest by Coutanche in Jersey.

It was said bitterly, in Guernsey, that there was plenty of food in Jersey, so it would make little difference to them in the end. But if Jersey did not protest, the Guernsey authorities felt helpless.

The Germans refused to allow another telephone conversation with Coutanche.

In the following August, however, the previous bread

ration was fully restored, so Coutanche could say that his tactics had been justified. It seems that there were divisions on the German side as well as between the islands; Count von Schmettow, as Military Commandant in Jersey, was not immediately concerned with food rations; but he had opposed the cuts, saying the proper course was a Diplomatic Protest on the sinking of ships. During the arguments, Coutanche was asked to go to Schmettow's Headquarters (and to park his car where it would not be seen outside). Whether their talk had anything to do with it or not, the final upshot was another victory over outside interference from St. Germain; and one *Feldkommandantur* official remarked: "The Bailiff of Jersey is a remarkable man."

In spite of a variety of divisions and side issues, the battle of words and paper beween the German occupiers and the island authorities usually took place along fixed lines. The islanders said the civilian rations were dangerously low for health, and should be increased: the Germans retorted that the food supplies were a good deal better than pretended, and that the islands could really do more towards feeding the Occupation army.

Some German accusations were well founded.

In Jersey, for instance, the parishes took it in turn to supply the Germans with eggs; and it was amazing how the hens would stop laying in each parish when its week came round. There were few occasions when Touzel Bree, the Jersey Agricultural Officer, had not some trick up his sleeve. Once he appealed publicly for those with spare potatoes to donate them to the States. A few personal friends, at his urgent personal request, did so: though they were much mystified about it, as the response to the appeal was bound to be negligible. The explanation came later. It turned out that, if some statistics Bree had given the Germans earlier had been correct, he would have had no potatoes left. When the Germans queried why he had nevertheless issued the usual quantities, he could say, "Ah, yes, but these are the potatoes which patriotic people gave me to save the ration . . ."

Once, in Guernsey, the Germans bluntly questioned some statistics on cattle, produced by Ernest de Garis. They told Raymond Falla, the Agricultural Officer, that "you have more cows than you admit." Falla's dark eyes became reproachful. "If you don't believe us, then you must count them for yourselves," he said.

The Germans knew that any attempt to do so would end in ridicule, with calves and heifers disappearing as if by magic. Nothing more was said.

At one time the Germans put their men into every mill in Jersey to try (with laughable absence of success) to check how much flour was being ground, and where it was going. A proposal to put a German soldier on every farm was rejected by Baron von Aufsess, on the realistic ground that it would create more Black Marketeers.

Another line of attack in the endless battle between occupiers and islanders was for the Germans to argue that, if the islanders would only work harder and organise production with Teutonic thoroughness, there need be no food problem at all. Dick Johns, the Guernsey Labour Officer, was told "You should run your glasshouses like motor car factories"; and he would protest that Nature did not work that way. We need add nothing to this extract from Louis Guillemette's Minutes of one meeting at Grange Lodge:

"Colonel Knackfuss (*Feldkommandant*) . . . suggested that as Guernsey's principal industry before the war was catering for holiday makers, the inhabitants had become unused to hard work. This suggestion was strongly denied by all the Guernsey representatives."

Another frequent subject for discussion was the mounting number of paper marks which Guernsey was getting from the Germans in payment for real goods and services. It was protested that nobody knew what the marks would be worth after the war. We quote, again, from Guillemette's Minutes of one frank discussion:

"Colonel Knackfuss (*Feldkommandant*) said that this was a political question which could be solved by the nation which won the war. Jurat Leale remarked that Guernsey might well be the loser whichever side won. Dr. Casper replied that if Germany won, Occupation Marks would keep their value; if England won, then that country would attend to the matter."*

All these discussions took place through interpreters, since few of the island officials bothered to learn German, and they usually pretended to know even less German than they did. The Germans on their side were much more venturesome in talking English, though not without occasional slips. "I know," one of them remarked once to an islander, "you are all longing to see our backsides." And on one occasion, at a meeting between Dr. Brosch of the *Feldkommandantur* and the Guernsey Controlling Committee, he once protested in the heat of an argument: "I will *not* allow the Committee to play with my person."

CHAPTER XXXI

SOME OF THEM WERE FRIENDS

During the negotiations over the bread ration "reprisals" after the attack on shipping, Louis Guillemette, as secretary to John Leale, met Major Kratzer at Grange Lodge. In his position, Guillemette got to know the Germans as well as anyone: and after this discussion with Kratzer he wrote in his diary:

* In the final upshot after the Liberation, people holding marks were allowed to convert them into sterling at the prevailing rate of 9.36 to the £.

"A bread ration of under 3 lb. a week . . . and there was I talking to a German—and laughing with him too —who I knew to be hating the very thought of the task he was called upon to do.

"As a background to this grim Alice-in-Wonderland conversation, I looked out into an expanse of sunlit greenery with the wind playing magically in it. And in one corner of that cheerful looking room the radio was playing a delightful cello concert."

Guillemette's appreciation of music—in private life he was much in demand as a church organist—gave him one special bond of contact with some of the Germans. It was, in fact, impossible to see the same man day after day, getting to know something of himself and his background and his family, without friendships springing up between some islanders and their German opposite numbers.

Guillemette had nothing but praise for the way Kratzer, one night during a quarrel over bread rationing, had a boat rushed to Sark to take off an urgent appendicitis case; and Guillemette also grew friendly with Kraft, the German interpreter. Seventy-year-old Dr. Symons, who had come back from retirement to look after Guernsey's medical services, found a good friend in Dr. Lorenz, the Chief German Medical Officer and an anti-Nazi. Lorenz would drop in to see Symons and, in the trusted privacy of his home, the two men would sit and curse Hitler together. Down on the waterfront, the international camaraderie of all sailors still prevailed in St. Peter Port. The German harbour boss was now *Kapitänleutnant* Obermeyer, a typical sea-dog with no particular dislike for anybody, and a liking for anything that came out of a bottle. He was not only of the same age as Captain Franklin, the Guernsey Harbour Master, but they had both served in the old days in square-rigged sailing ships, and they found that their two ships had once laid beside each other in Hamburg harbour.

On occasions at night the two men might be heard singing sea shanties together. Guernsey fishermen learned the knack of dropping in to see Obermeyer at a slack time when he was alone, ostensibly to talk over some matter like a fishing permit; it would not be long before the hospitable Obermeyer would bring out a bottle and they would be drinking amicably together. The toast was usually the same—the end of the war.

By now the balance of the war was shifting slowly to the side of the Allies, with the mounting air offensive by the R.A.F. against Germany, and the German reverses on the Russian Front.

The Forces in the Channel Islands, at any rate, seemed to regard 1943 as the turning point in the war: and the decisive event was the German defeat in North Africa. After this the more intelligent Germans obviously realised that, sooner or later, Hitler was finished. As for the islanders themselves, they got some pleasure from repeating the story of the Guernseyman who was told by a Todt officer that the war in Africa was over. "Oh, really," said the Guernseyman politely. "Of course, I haven't got a wireless now, so I hadn't heard. *Who won?*"

But win or lose, as the war went on taking its toll of both sides, it was hard to exult. There was little gloating over the bombing of Germany among those who had day-to-day dealings with Germans whose wives and children lived in the bombed cities, and who would wait for news of them after every raid. And there were few who did not sympathise with Count von Schmettow when it was learnt that his only son had been killed fighting on the Russian Front. Among those who conveyed their condolences to him were Coutanche, Duret Aubin and Mrs. Hathaway. Previously, when Mrs. Hathaway's son had been killed in an air raid on Britain, Count von Schmettow had visited Sark specially to offer his sympathy.

Louis Guillemette wrote in his diary:

"With all the bombing in Germany, the Germans show very little bitterness, though some of them have lost their homes, and all know their families are in danger. I have a feeling now that most people look upon the war as something permanent and outside human control, and that it is this almost subconscious outlook which kills bitterness."

One event which made for happier relations on the islands was the departure of General Müller, in September, 1943. He was sent to a Command on the Eastern Front, where he was reported to have been taken prisoner by the Russians. His place as Commander of the 319 Infantry Division was taken by Count von Schmettow, who had been promoted to Major-General the year before, and now once more became Commander-in-Chief of all the islands. Schmettow moved to Guernsey to take up his Command, and was succeeded as military Commandant in Jersey by Colonel Heine.

One of Schmettow's first acts was to make changes in the German Command on Alderney. From then onwards the treatment of the Todt workers there is believed to have improved.

So far as the civilian population were concerned, Schmettow stuck to the policy of avoiding repressive measures; though the actual administration—Schmettow was always more of a soldier than an administrator—was mainly in the hands of Colonel von Helldorf, his Chief of Staff, a six-foot Prussian with a monocle. Schmettow was so punctilious in avoiding unnecessary destruction to civilian property that Coutanche once paid him the compliment of saying that he would never question any Order signed by Schmettow personally, because he knew it would not have been made unless it was unavoidable. There were times when military necessity was considered to be overriding: the de Saumarez Memorial was so prominent a landmark in Guernsey—and it had a heavy battery near it—that von Schmettow ordered its destruction, ignoring a protest that this was against the Hague Convention. The Memorial was duly toppled to destruction by an explosion of dynamite which blew two windows out of John Leale's house.

On the other hand, when a gun position was being mounted on Gorey Castle in Jersey, Schmettow specially consulted Major Rybot of the Société Jersiaise, for advice on the best way to place the gun without destroying anything of historical value on the castle.

(If Count von Schmettow cost Guernsey the de Saumarez Memorial, he also saved it the Grandes Rocques Hotel. Once—much later on, when the war was nearly over—an over-enthusiastic German *Stützpunkt* commander found this hotel was blocking the arc of fire from his guns, and demanded its demolition. Count von Schmettow went up personally and showed how, by siting the guns differently, they could cover the same ground without disturbing the hotel at all. "The war may not last for ever," said Schmettow dryly. "If we knock the hotel down we may only have to pay for it later in war damages.")

The deterioration in the calibre of the occupying troops, after the crack soldiers of the early days, continued steadily. By now they were mostly elderly men in spectacles or very young boys. Once the outspoken Dr. Symons was complaining at the *Feldkommandantur* of a shortage of teats for feeding bottles, and asking urgently for more to be imported from France. "You'd better be quick about it," he said. "You may soon be needing them for your own troops."

Even by 1943 there was a growing feeling that the Germans, almost as much as the British, were welcoming anything which brought the end of the war nearer. The day after the news of the Italian Armistice, some German soldiers were playing leapfrog in the streets and singing the old (pre-Hitler) Austrian National anthem.

Sometimes, Allied bombing raids brought home some reminder of the price of war, and the price still to be paid for victory. At times there were frequent visitations from the R.A.F., the most successful being a low level attack by three Beauforts, in January, 1942, which smashed up two ships in St. Peter Port. Civilian dock workers were sometimes killed in these raids, making it difficult to get men to work at the docks, and many Germans were killed too.

Louis Guillemette recorded, in his diary, how one night a dance in the Grange was interrupted by a burst of anti-aircraft fire. British planes, attacking ships in St. Peter Port, were twisting and turning over the Russel and everyone was smiling excitedly for the rest of the dance.

"But afterwards," wrote Gueillemette, "walking down the Grange, German ambulances began to roar past us on their way to and from the harbour. Sitting next to the driver of one ambulance, on its way to hospital, was a young sailor with a wounded shoulder and a look of stunned amazement which we could not forget. We went soberly home after that."

Once the German anti-aircraft guns shot down one of their own planes by mistake. The wreckage of the plane was scattered over Jethou and Herm; and a boat was sent out, with old whisky crates, to collect what could be found of the pilot's body.

Towards the end of 1943 the turn came for the Germans to sympathise with British bereavement. A British cruiser, the *Charybdis*, was sunk by two German torpedo boats in the Channel. Some time later, by some random choice of the winds and the tides, the bodies began to be washed ashore on Guernsey, Sark and Jersey. Nineteen young men who had served in the *Charybdis*, mainly engine-room ratings, became items in an official report on the recovery of the corpses, from the island police in Guernsey to the President of the Controlling Committee:

Sir,

I beg to report that between 13th and 15th Novmber, 1943, the following bodies have been recovered from the sea, 18 on the coasts of Guernsey and one on Sark.

1. Found on beach near Douet du Moulin, St. Peters, 8.5 a.m. 13.11.43, ——— ———, Royal Marines, dress, blue battle dress, body very decomposed, 5′ 11″ in length. Identity established by Pay Book, effects, wallet containing photographs and English addresses on paper. . . .

6. Found on beach at Perelle Bay, St. Saviour's 8.45 a.m. 14.11.43, ——— ———, dress, sailor's blue trousers, khaki pullover, black socks, brown sandals, body very decomposed, length 5′ 10″. Identity established by life-

belt with name thereon, effects 2s. 5½d. cash, one French coin, two keys. . . .

The list went on, with the phrase "body very decomposed" appearing in every item. They had been three weeks in the sea.

As soon as they heard of the bodies being washed ashore, the Germans arranged a mass funeral with full military honours. It was taken as an opportunity for the islanders to show their loyalty and give their thanks to the men fighting for their freedom, and the response was moving and overwhelming. There were over seven hundred wreaths, and no censorship on the inscriptions. "They died that we may be free."

The year 1943 saw the last two Commando raids on the islands—both made without meeting any Germans. On the night of February 27, Captain Porteous, V.C., had taken his men to Herm. He was asked to establish that artillery could be landed on Shell Beach to provide supporting fire for any assault on Guernsey. The Commandos satisfied themselves that Shell Beach was not mined, by the simple but nerve-straining process of walking up and down it. They then went on in earch of Germans to take prisoner, but failed to find any because (although they did not know it at the time) there were no Germans there. Apart from a brief period when light A.A. guns were set up to protect shipping in the Russel, Herm was never occupied.

Jersey had its only Commando raid of the war on the night of Christmas Day, 1943. Led by Captain Ayton and a French Lieutenant, a party of four men, including three other Frenchmen, landed on the North Coast about an hour before midnight. They wanted to take a prisoner, and they knocked up a farmhouse to ask where a German could be found.

After hammering on the door they heard talking inside, but it was many minutes before a frightened and unfriendly woman appeared at a first-floor window. She refused to give them any help, but pointed out another farmhouse.

Here they tried again, and a farmer appeared who was so overcome by fear at the sight of them that he could hardly speak. Then his brother came down, almost equally afraid; but gradually Ayton got them talking, and got information on German defence arrangements. The brothers reported that there was no resistance movement on the island, and that the population as a whole was not hostile to the Germans. They said there was no shortage of food in the countryside, though conditions were bad in St. Helier. Finally the two farmers became enough at their ease to offer the Commandos a glass of milk each, and to say they hoped they would come again soon.

The Commandos found a German strongpoint, but there was no way in, and no sentry outside they could capture. They went back reluctantly to their landing point; and here, while waiting for the boat to take them off, Captain Ayton touched a mine which exploded and wounded him critically. They managed to get him back to England—mindful of Hitler's order that any Commandos taken prisoner would be shot—but he died in hospital.

Nobody came to investigate after the mine exploded, though another half an hour elapsed before they left. The Germans had grown used to hearing mines being sprung by rabbits from time to time. The visit remained unknown both to the Germans and almost everybody in Jersey, with the exception of one frightened woman and two friendly farmers.

CHAPTER XXXII

JOURNEYS TO HORROR

While life in the islands went on with courtesy and sometimes mutual respect between the rulers and the ruled,
there were a growing number of islanders whose experiences on the Continent, if they had been known, might
have served as a reminder of why the war was being fought.

There was Stanley George Green, for instance, the Chief
Operator at West's Cinema in St. Helier. It may be remembered that he had photographed down the plans of German
fortifications for Major Crawford-Morrison and Major
L'Amy, and had also cut telephone wires, without being
caught. So it was one of the ironies of war that he should
eventually have been arrested because of something for
which he was not responsible. The Germans found that his
assistant operators had wireless equipment hidden some-
where in the roof of the cinema. They were taken away and
later, on January 16, 1944, the *Geheime Feldpolizei* called
at Green's house with three cars and picked him up. His
wife and two sons watched him go with foreboding.

Green, without trial, was shipped to France. Eventually,
imprisoned in France, he had a fellow prisoner in Yeo-
Thomas, the British agent, whose story was subsequently
told in *The White Rabbit*. Green noticed that Thomas
looked in a bad way, having already been brutally treated:
but he heard him shout, in reply to German questioning,
"Go to Hell! God save the King! "

Green was put in solitary confinement and found it hard
to sleep, because of the crying of women prisoners in the
same block. He saw a German guard shoot a young lad
who had his hands tied behind him, and he saw Yeo-

Thomas beaten with the butt end of a rifle for shouting out the news that the Allies had landed in Normandy—for by now it was June, 1944.

Green, like other Channel Islanders, was caught up in the general panic evacuation of prisoners back into German concentration camps.

From Fresnes he and others were herded into a cattle truck for a journey of five and a half days. By now he had severe dysentery, and was suffering from kicks in the stomach. But he noticed that many of his fellow prisoners were in a far worse state.

There were five French women—two of them very young —who had been caught helping the Maquis. Green could not talk French, but there was a French doctor among the prisoners; and from him, in a whisper in a corner of the truck, Green heard of the obscene tortures to which the two girls had been subjected. Another of the five was an old lady who had the nails torn off one hand with pincers. She died while they were travelling, and Green helped to cover her body with his coat.

Arriving at Buchenwald, Green and his fellow prisoners were stripped, doused in disinfectant, shaved completely all over their heads and bodies, and given an old pair of trousers and a thin smock.

The women—all had been stripped together—were then marched off elsewhere, some to the camp brothel which served the S.S. The men slept in the open for six weeks on heaps of stones; bare-footed, bare-headed and without any covering. At nights it was bitterly cold and often it rained. Then they managed to find room in one of the block houses —the long, wooden buildings of which the concentration camp was made up. The number of deaths from murder or semi-starvation or disease were always making vacancies.

Every day the death cart piled with bodies would drive through the camp to the crematorium, which had, in brass letters over its doorway, the words *"Fire Cleaneth All Evil."*

In Buchenwald, Green met Bill Symes—the cousin of

Jim Symes from Guernsey, who had been arrested after smuggling out messages to a British agent in Spain. Symes had arrived in Buchenwald, like Green, in a cattle truck. After one attempt at escape, the train was stopped, and Symes and the hundred other prisoners in the truck were made to undress and heap all their clothes on one side. They travelled naked in this way for four days, with no means of sanitation.

British prisoners in Buchenwald were rare; and as peculiarity of any sort attracted the special attentions of the S.S., Stanley Green got into the habit of strolling about with his arm casually crooked, hand on lapel, over the "E" on his breast which stood for *Engländer*.

Green owed the recovery of his liberty, and probably his life, to Major Sherwill. By now his elder son, Leslie Green, had been deported to Laufen, where Sherwill was the British "Camp Senior". Green managed to smuggle out of Buchenwald a letter to Leslie telling him of his whereabouts, and Leslie took it to Sherwill. Thereupon Sherwill went to his German Camp Commandant, secured his help, and in less than a week Green had been transferred to Laufen.

For Bill Symes, release also came from Buchenwald, by a million to one chance. He broke orders by writing a postcard to his wife, who was now in Taunton, and smuggled it out among the postcards which French prisoners were allowed, at rare intervals, to send to their families. By some freak it was actually delivered in England. The result was an official demand from the British to the German Government, for Symes to be moved to conditions more fitting for a British subject: and he was also transferred to Laufen.

There was no such freakish good fortune for other concentration camp victims: for Mrs. Louisa Gould, for instance, who used to run a small grocer's shop in Jersey; or for her brother, Harold le Druillenec, a hearty young schoolteacher. Mrs. Gould's kindness was to bring about her own death, and horror upon her brother. But, on the morning when a ragged and starved young Russian came to her door in Jersey, begging help, she could not foresee what was to follow for herself—and perhaps, even if she had, she might still have urged him inside her home. For Louisa Gould was warm-hearted, and a mother with two sons of her own. She had just learnt that one of them had been killed in the Navy. She looked at the Russian, an escaped prisoner-of-war. He was about the same age as her dead son. She said: "Come in."

The young Russian received much kindness from Mrs. Gould and her family, and the few trusted friends who knew who he was. They called him Bill. (His real name was Fyodr Polycarpovitch Bourriy.) Dr. McKinstry, the indefatigable Medical Officer of Health, provided him with a faked ration book and other papers, and in time Bill's English became so good that he mingled freely with the townsfolk, got a job, and even joined Boots Library in St. Helier.

Mrs. Gould's family were convinced that it was a petty informer with a spite against them who brought disaster on them all. One night, in a pub, a well-known member of the German secret police was overheard boasting that he was on the track of the escaped Russian. A warning was telephoned to Mrs Gould in "Jersey French," the local *patois*.

"Bill" himself got away in time. Mrs. Gould hurriedly tidied up her home to remove any trace of her recent guest, but a Russian dictionary was overlooked. It was found by the secret police when they came to search. They then also ransacked the homes of her sister, Mrs. Ivy Foster, and her brother, Harold le Druillenec. In each of their houses they found the inevitable hidden wireless set.

And so on June 22, 1944, came a court martial. Mrs. Gould was sentenced to two years. Mrs. Foster and le Druillenec were each sentenced to five months' "simple" imprisonment for having radios. This should have meant nothing worse than a few months in the local gaol—and this was all it did mean for Mrs. Foster. But the German Reich was now entering the first stages of panic and dis-organisation which led towards its end, and le Druillenec found himself, with Louisa Gould, helplessly borne away into their enemy's chaos.

They were put on a boat for France. Its holds were crammed with political prisoners being evacuated from Alderney. Le Druillenec noticed that, beyond their ragged-ness and their animal-hunger, they all had the same look in their eyes—peculiarly wide-open, staring and piercing. Later, le Druillenec was to understand that this was the mark of men living in constant fear and watchfulness, never relaxing, never knowing what lay ahead. At the time their inhuman look merely puzzled and chilled him. He talked in French to one of the prisoners, who told him they had been sent to Alderney from Buchenwald, and were now going to Neuengamme. This was only a name to le Druillenec, but he gathered enough to realise that these prisoners were part of the dreaded Nazi concentration camp system—and so, now, was he.

In France, le Druillenec was parted from his sister. Long afterwards he was to find out that Louisa Gould, by what stages of desolation and misery we shall never know, eventually reached Ravensbruck, and died in one of the gas chambers.

Le Druillenec, with other prisoners, started his journey into Germany. After three days in a closed cattle-truck, crowded in without sanitation, they reached the great central concentration camp of Neuengamme. To shouts of *Raus! Raus!* from their guards they somehow got out of their truck, caked with their own dirt, and nearly starving.

And so le Druillenec, still tenaciously clinging to his great natural cheerfulness, entered a world of its own split off utterly from the one he had left—a world where the abnormal became the normal, where sadism and torture and hunger so transformed men that, within weeks, some were incapable of remembering that there was any other world.

The Kapo, or Prisoner Chief, looked over le Druillenec and the others and said: "You are in here for good. You will never get out. Forget your family, your job, and every-thing you used to do. If you think about all that you will

go mad. Here then is only one think you must think about
—*work. Work for the Reich!*" He suddenly screamed the
words at them in a way which le Druillenec still remem-
bers.

Next morning, le Druillenec and the others were moved
on again to a similar concentration camp at Wilhelmshaven. Here le Druillenec was told that one Prisoner Chief
had beaten more than a hundred men to death, sometimes
for such slight offences as stealing a potato. So acclimatised
was he now becoming to this abnormal world that he
accepted the information without comment; and when he
later saw, and watched, this particular Chief, he found it
credible. Indeed, he found little exaggeration in this world;
what actually happened went beyond anything that could
be imagined or invented.

Le Druillenec's mind gradually grew numbed. If anyone
had told him that he had a wife and small daughter in
Jersey, he would never have believed it. He slowly learnt
the rules of survival, the first being automatic and instant
obedience to the S.S. and the Prisoner Chiefs. He learnt to
shuffle instead of walk, and thus conserve the spare energy
derived from food that was little more than watery soup.
And when the prisoners were marched with tommy-guns
to and from the factory where they worked all day, he
learnt to keep in line without looking to left or right, and
thus not attract the guard's attention. He shrewdly volunteered to train as a welder, because it was a job done
sitting down, and had a higher survival rate because it
conserved energy.

He saw many men die of starvation or exhaustion. He
saw a boy prisoner who had stolen food from the kitchen
beaten to death. He saw another boy first driven stark mad
by torture and then killed. The bodies were exhibited by
way of warning.

The tortures thought up by the S.S. and Prisoner Chiefs
did not possess the merit of causing speedy death. Apart
from routine beatings, a favourite one was hanging by the
wrists tied behind the back until the shoulder blades broke,

or hanging head downwards by the feet. Another was "crucifixion", the hands and feet of the victim being tied to a cross, where he was left to hang till he died. On occasions the men were cut down before they died, so that something else could be tried out on the victim as fellow prisoners were paraded round and made to watch. There were other tortures which cannot be described here.

Le Druillenec said afterwards: "I learnt how hard it is to destroy the human body. I saw men in indescribable agony, whose only wish was to die quickly. But they would go on, hour after hour, showing by their eyes, or by some twitch of their limbs, that there was still life left."

One particular incident at Wilhelmshaven stuck in his mind afterwards. He had made friends with a gifted young Frenchman, a poet who had been in the Maquis. He and le Druillenec were sitting side by side killing the lice on their bodies when the Frenchman, instead of crushing a particularly large louse, cradled it on the back of his wrist and said: "No, let it live. These are the only creatures in this camp who are living their natural life."

The most bizarre occasion was on Christmas Day, 1944. The prisoners were herded into the main hut to find it beautifully decorated, with a Christmas tree on the stage, and lighted candles. Then eight of the Prisoner Chiefs, each of them a sadist and a murderer, sang in unison, tenderly and sentimentally, *Stille Nacht*.

Le Druillenec himself grew in cunning and stealth, always watchful, always obedient; and so, in spite of suffering beatings and kickings, partial starvation and near exhaustion, he managed to survive; though even greater ordeals awaited him in future.

CHAPTER XXXIII

THE UNDERGROUND NEWS SERVICE

It was from Jersey that most of the victims of the concentration camps came; perhaps because of greater bitterness there between the invaders and the islanders, perhaps simply owing to the workings of the same sort of macabre chance by which the victims themselves were selected from among hundreds who broke the same regulations. And those who suffered from Jersey included not only brave men like Canon Cohu, but ordinary criminals and wartime Black Marketeers.

Though Guernsey had fewer victims, it was in Guernsey that the most sustained organisation of subversive activity was carried out, in defiance of the Germans, by men who knew the risks and paid the penalty. This was the G.U.N.S., or Guernsey Underground News Service.

It was started by Charles Machon, a linotype operator on the Guernsey *Star*. Machon, a tall, good-looking man of nearly fifty, had four brothers in British uniforms, and bitterly regretted that his age and his ill-health—stomach ulcers—prevented him playing a more active part in the war himself. His mother, then in her seventies, refused to leave her home during the evacuation, and so Charles stayed in Guernsey to look after her. After a while he began fretting at his inaction. Suddenly he saw an opportunity.

Some families were too poor to own radios, even before the Germans forbade them. Machon told his mother: "People must have news. The least I can do is to help them get it."

225

She warned him: "If the Germans catch you you'll suffer, and so will many more."

He replied thoughtfully: "Don't you worry. Even if I'm caught they'll get nothing out of me."

And so he set about organising G.U.N.S., which became the biggest of the several secret news-sheets in the islands. Four others helped him—Frank Falla, Assistant Editor of the *Star*, who thought of the title G.U.N.S., Cyril Duquemin, a greenhouse worker and near neighbour; and two carpenters, Legg and Gillingham. Machon himself had no wireless set, so the others took it in turn to listen in, take down the news, and then bring it to him. Machon would make several copies on a typewriter which he kept hidden in a deep chair, and Falla in his turn would type many more.

At one stage they were turning out a hundred copies a day. Old Mrs. Machon herself would distribute twelve to tradespeople and neighbours. One would appear mysteriously on the Bailiff's desk every morning, and disappear mysteriously after he had read it. Another was taken round by a milkman in an empty milk can. Another was placed in a pre-arranged book in the Priaulx Library: those in the know would come in and take this book down, appear to glance casually at some of the pages, and then put it back on the shelves.

Three copies were sent to Sark. This could be perilous, as no one could catch the boat without coming under scrutiny, and perhaps being stripped and searched, at the barrier to the harbour. The G.U.N.S. news-sheets, on thin paper tightly folded would get through in a number of ways: sometimes tucked behind a man's hatband, sometimes in the heel of a shoe. Among those who received them at Sark, and distributed them further, were Wakley the carrier and Hubert Lanyon the baker and general storekeeper. One copy was kept in the back room of Lanyon's shop, and trusted customers would look in regularly to see it there.

Altogether over seventy people in Sark saw G.U.N.S. regularly, including some Germans. (Lanyon remarked darkly, after the war, that "I trusted some of them better than I trusted some civilians".) Once, when Lanyon was ill in bed, these Germans were so anxious to go on getting the news regularly that they visited him at his home: and two of them bought him a wireless set so that he could hear one of Churchill's speeches.

All went well with G.U.N.S. for a time, though all knew the danger. With so many copies in circulation, there was always the chance of somebody being careless. Once Frank Falla was horrified to come on a copy lying casually on the counter of a barter shop. It was inevitable that the Germans should eventually learn about G.U.N.S.—and in March, 1944, they found out who was running it, helped by an informer. First they picked up Duquemin, and then went on to Machon's house down the road. "We want that typewriter hidden downstairs in the chair," they said; and he knew that G.U.N.S. was ended.

He was taken to prison and interrogated by the Secret Police. Their methods included rough physical violence, and more subtle measures like being stood in an overcoat before a white-hot stove, and afterwards turned into an icy cell. He was threatened that his mother would be sent to Germany if he did not talk. It seems that the severity of the Germans was largely due to the title G.U.N.S.; they suspected that the organisation did much more than produce a news-sheet, and served as a cover for gun-running, or an underground resistance movement.

Later Machon's mother became ill with shock, and he was allowed out of gaol to visit her. An English-speaking German officer came with him and sat on the other side of her bedroom while mother and son talked together, as it happened for the last time. Machon was cheerful, although already showing signs of the harsh methods used at the interrogation. "We've only got fifteen minutes, Mother," he said. "Never mind," said the German, "we make it thirty."

When Machon left the room for a moment the German drew near to Mrs. Machon's bed and said: "I think I should tell you that your son is a hero.' Then he added:

"Some of your people are no good to you. If you saw the letters we get from your own people saying who has a wireless, you would not believe it."

Frank Falla was in the reporter's room at his office, when the German Police came for him, saying: "You have a radio set: where is it?" Others were caught in the net too, including Hubert Lanyon on Sark. The Germans found out that he had been getting *two copies* of the news-sheet, and unsuccessfully tried to make him tell who else saw it. He insisted that the second copy was simply a spare one which he burnt. Once he was knocked unconscious by a blow which took two of his teeth out. When he came to again he was still muttering automatically: "I didn't send it to anyone. I burnt it."

The Germans staged a trial in the Police Court; Machon, with his indifferent health and cruel treatment, already looking wretchedly ill. The five ringleaders—Machon, Falla, Duquemin, Legg and Gillingham—were sentenced to eight years' imprisonment between them. Lanyon was sentenced to six months, but this was reduced on appeal to four months, so he was not sent on to the Continent.

Machon, after a period in gaol in Guernsey, was sent to Potsdam Prison. Eventually his mother received a laconic eleven-word note from the German authorities:

Charles Machon died 26th Oct. 1944 in hospital at Hameln-Weser.

(*signed*) WALLI,

27-11-44   *Heeresjuistizinspektor.*

Next, Falla and his three remaining companions were sent through France to the prison at Frankfurt-on-Main. Here they found more Channel Islanders—some of them Black Marketeers for whom they formed no liking, and others such as Percy Miller, an ex-C.I.D. man from Guernsey, who had been sentenced to fifteen months for not giving up his radio set. Miller, who had organised his own

228

intelligence system in the prison, told Falla that the average number of deaths and executions was thirty-five a week; and he himself died a few months later. Falla and the others could hear the screaming of prisoners in the condemned cells, and the rattling of their chains—sounds that were to come back in their nightmares for years.

Gillingham, like Machon, died in prison—a month after he had completed his sentence, because he could not persuade his German gaolers to release him.

Falla, Legg and Duquemin were moved on, with seven other Channel Islanders, to Naumburg prison; and here they were joined by Canon Cohu from Jersey, who was still doing his best to sustain hope and courage as, one after the other, his compatriots died in macabre succession. Cohu, repeatedly but vainly, would plead with the Germans from behind his own bars that he should at least be allowed to give them a Christian burial.

Mostly the men died alone in their cells at night, from sheer starvation. Falla found that when the stomach is empty, one of the best ways to make it feel swelled is to drink something scalding; so, when his bitter acorn coffee arrived each morning, it went down in agonising but filling gulps. When he came across a bone in his soup he kept it to suck like a dummy until nothing was left. There was no medical attention at all; when Falla got pneumonia, he lay alone in his cell sweating and fighting it out until it passed, leaving him with a spot on the lungs.

Once he saw a young French boy grab a bone from one of the Alsatian guard dogs. Four Germans beat him insensible, threw a bucket of cold water over him to revive him, beat him again, and then put him back into his cell. He died from pneumonia.

And there in Naumburg prison, for the time being, our story must leave Falla and his companions; waiting with unconscious hope, like le Druillenec in Wilhelmshaven concentration camp, like Herbert Gallichan in Wolfenbuttel, like countless thousands more throughout Europe, for the Liberation which only force of arms could bring.

CHAPTER XXXIV

INVASION AND A THREAT

We have anticipated, and must now go back to the military events of 1944.

The invasion of Normandy was heralded, so far as the Channel Islands were concerned, by a number of spasmodic air attacks. One particularly heavy raid was made on Alderney. Clifford Bichard, the foreman mason from Guernsey, watched with somewhat mixed feelings while American bombers demolished some buildings which he had recently put up for the Germans.

Often pilots attacking the French coast were told, if they missed their targets for any reason, to go on to the islands and dispose of their bombs or their bullets. One young American pilot, Joseph Krebs of Milwaukee, was wounded and had to bale out of a damaged plane, landing in Jersey. As he lay in hospital, he remarked that the one thing he was sorry about was missing the invasion.

"*Ach*," said his German guard. "All this talk of invasion!"

"It's sure coming, buddy," said the American.

The final overture was provided by two raids by Typhoons on the radar station at Fort Grange in Guernsey —part of a systematic plan to put every radar station covering the approaches to Normandy out of action.*

Hitler's "island madness" was unabated. On March 3, 1944, Jersey, Guernsey and Alderney were officially de-

---

* Second in Command of the R.A.F. Second Tactical Air Force, which carried out these raids, was Air Marshal Sir Thomas Elmhirst, later Lieutenant-Governor of Guernsey.

clared "Fortresses" on a priority level for supplies with Cherbourg, Dunkirk and Le Havre. And the minutes of a high-level German conference held on May 2, to discuss likely objectives for the Allied landing, noted that "there is a certain worry about the weak defences of the Channel Islands"—apparently because Hitler did not think that some of the batteries were well enough protected against air attack.

On the night of June 5, 1944, the sound of a hundred planes was heard from Alderney to Guernsey, and as far away as Jersey.

More and more planes followed in wave after wave, and all over the islands men lay awake listening to them. Before daybreak everyone knew that the planes were the harbingers of invasion.

A fully armed German soldier arrived at Coutanche's house on a motor bicycle, with an urgent proclamation signed by Colonel Heine, the Commandant of Jersey, for immediate publication. It called on the islanders to keep calm and refrain from any "acts of sabotage", and threatened that: "Attacks against the German Forces will be punished by death."

German soldiers appeared everywhere in full battle order, carrying rifles and hand grenades, and with sprigs of green leaves to camouflage their helmets. All telephones went dead, the Army having taken over the telephone exchanges. Berlin Radio announced, incorrectly, that Allied parachutists had landed in the islands.

So far as the islanders were concerned. D-Day began brightly with openly interchanged "V" signs, and the mounting excitement was fed by eager rumour. The Allies were said to have landed at Calais, at Dunkirk, in Holland, in Norway; and when the B.B.C. gave the official fact that the landings were as near as Normandy, some people fondly thought Normandy had been chosen so that the Channel Islands would be among the first places to be liberated. There was even a theory that the German garrison was going to be withdrawn at once, so as not to be cut off when the adjacent coast of France was taken by the

Allies. The wildest stories were told and believed—that Alderney had been captured by American troops, that Count von Schmettow and his senior officers had already been recalled. It was rumoured (in Jersey) that all the Germans were leaving Guernsey, and (in Guernsey) that they were all out of Jersey. Perhaps the best story was the one that went round Guernsey, saying that the States had offered the Germans £25,000 to go.

What actually happened was that Rommel and von Rundstedt repeated previous demands to Berlin, even more urgently, for troops to be transferred from the Channel Islands to defend Europe. But Hitler refused, still having his obsession that the British would attack the islands; and he ordered that the subject should never be raised again. At a conference with Rommel and Rundstedt on June 17, he declared that Cherbourg and the Channel Islands had to be defended *"Bis zum Aussersten"*—"To the last."

Jodl, Chief of the Operations Staff at Supreme Command, was more realistic. He did not expect a direct attack on the islands, and said that it was more likely that the British would try to starve out the garrison by a blockade. Therefore, to stretch out supplies as much as possible, he ordered that as many Todt workers as possible should be moved back to the Continent.

This order was followed by a partial evacuation of Alderney. Most of the men there from Jersey and Guernsey were returned to their own islands. Todt workers and "political" prisoners were sent back to the Continent, via Guernsey or Jersey. (As already recounted, Harold le Druillenec went on the same ship with some of the concentration camp prisoners, and their S.S. guards.) Their evacuation had been ordered personally by Hitler, who said they must on no account fall into British hands.

Some of the "political" prisoners went through a transit camp in Guernsey. Their guards flung them basketfuls of tomatoes over the barbed wire, and they could be seen fighting each other for them like animals.

To Admiral Krancke, Commanding the German Naval Group West, occurred another idea for making rations last out on the islands as long as possible. He proposed that any of the islanders themselves who were not working for the Germans or growing food should also be removed, through Granville, to the Continent. The evacuation ships would not be attacked if British civilians were known to be on board; in fact, said Krancke shrewdly, for perfect safety British civilians should be put on the ships *both* going to and coming from the islands.

Fortunately for the peace of mind of the islanders, they never knew of this prospective threat to have them removed. By the time Berlin had agreed to it, Granville had fallen, and the whole idea of mass evacuation was abandoned for the time being.

After St. Malo fell the sounds of battle were heard no longer on the islands; and the islanders realised that the fighting had passed on and left them behind, still awaiting their freedom. But the racing advance of the Allies through France and Belgium raised light-headed hopes. Glib politicians and military experts wrote off the German Army, and only the voiceless soldiers doing the fighting realised the astonishing courage and tenacity with which the Germans were to carry on the battle for months to come. The facile official optimism of the autumn of 1944 had particularly unfortunate results in the Channel Islands. Their grimmest winter lay ahead, cut off from all supplies from the Continent; but it was some time before much thought was given to ways and means of staving off starvation.

Divisions now began to be openly apparent, for the first time, among the German occupiers themselves. One day Duret Aubin went to see Baron von Aufsess, as Chief of Administration at the *Feldkommandantur*, and found him almost in a state of collapse. Aufsess appeared to have been weeping: and to Duret Aubin's surprise and pleasure, he began a violent attack on the Nazi regime in Germany.

One of the officers involved in the July assassination plot against Hitler was a near neighbour in Bavaria, and an old personal friend. Baron von Aufsess's wife, a staunch anti-Nazi who had always refused to give the Hitler salute, had been talking about the attempted assassination, and remarked: "What a pity it didn't succeed." She had been reported to the Gestapo and arrested. Since then Aufsess had heard nothing of her fate.

For a long time he poured forth to Duret Aubin all his hatred of the Nazis. Then he stopped dead, and said: "If you disclose to anyone that I had talked like this . . . ?" Duret Aubin's reassurance went beyond saying.

From then on, the Germans began to split more and more into different groups, some of whom were ready to trust friends among the islanders more than they would trust their fellow Germans.

In June, 1944, there had arrived in Guernsey, as Naval Commander, a fervent Nazi supporter named Vice-Admiral Hüffmeier, who had formerly commanded the *Scharnhorst*. Tall, burly, with something of the Goering build, his geniality masked a hint of fanaticism. It was not long before he was organising study courses on National Socialism for N.C.O.s, and sending disparaging remarks about Count von Schmettow to Admiral Krancke, Flag Officer Commanding Naval Group West.

In October, 1944, the Channel Islands were put under Admiral Krancke for supply and administration. This was partly because the German Generals had plenty of battles on their hands, whereas the Admirals had big staffs but few ships left. Another reason was that Hitler, after the July plot, had become more and more distrustful of the Army, and was putting his faith in the Navy. It was Admiral Doenitz who was entrusted with inspiring "fanatical resistance" in the western ports still held by Germany; and Hüffmeier, a practised and emotional orator, aspired to this role in the Channel Islands, hoping to supercede Count von Schmettow as Commander-in-Chief.

The ordinary Channel Islander, of course, knew nothing of these rifts till months later. The only immediate effect of the liberation of France was that the civil administration —now known as a *Platzkommandantur* instead of a *Feldkommandantur*—no longer got its orders from St. Germain, but came directly under Count von Schmettow.

CHAPTER XXXV

ONE WAY TO FRANCE

Though the liberation of France immeasurably increased the economic hardships of the islanders, there were compensations. To bring the cheering news of Allied victories there was the powerful new B.B.C. Forces transmitter, easily picked up on home-made crystal sets. The B.B.C. gave instructions on how these sets could be put together, and their manufacture was undertaken industriously. The record was probably held by Father Rey of the Jesuit College in Jersey, who made and gave away sixty-three sets during the course of the Occupation. He was fortunate in being able to draw, for raw material, on a huge piece of crystal, kept in the College Geological Museum, which he had picked up as a missionary in Madagascar.

The utmost ingenuity was shown in getting different kinds of crystals. One jeweller in Guernsey cut up a meteorite which had fallen there in 1915, and which turned out to serve the purpose admirably.

The headphones for crystal sets came from telephone receivers.

For a time, in the autumn of 1944, there was also a regular nightly service by an R.A.F. plane dropping news sheets. These were picked up, with great zeal, by the Guernsey police, who handed a few over to the Germans and kept the rest at the police station—where businessmen and shopkeepers, on their way to work, would call in for copies as though they were getting the morning paper from a new stall.

For some people, the greatest advantage of the liberation of France was the opening up of a short way of escape from Jersey, the nearest islands. In Guernsey, it may be remembered, Sherwill had condemned people who escaped as "running away". But since then the position had changed.

In 1940 all men of military age who wanted to leave the islands had been given every opportunity to go. By now, however, a new generation, schoolboys in 1940, had grown to fighting age, and many were determined not to stay tamely under German rule if they could do some fighting in the war themselves. And so a number of young people of spirit, including some young women, set out to brave the treacherous currents and minefields in flimsy crafts, and often with scant knowledge of seamanship. In all, fifty-nine made the attempt from Jersey. Forty-seven reached France safely. Six were forced back, and shot or captured by the Germans on landing. Six were drowned.

A family who helped to make many of these escapes possible was the Bertrams, led by Wilfred Bertram—generally known as Bill. At this time he was in his early fifties, a white-haired, red-faced man widely liked for his jolly good nature. He had been a corporal in the Canadian Victoria Rifles during World War One, and now he ran a farm with his brother Charles and young nephew John, just opposite Fauvic beach on Grouville Bay.

Near them lived Bill Bertram's cousin, Thomas Bertram, with his wife, son and daughter; and the two women would take hot drinks down to the beach whenever escapees were leaving.

It must have been providence which placed the loyal Bertrams and this particular beach together. For it possessed the rare advantage of being accessible to the sea at all stages in the tide; and it also, by some unexplained chance, faced a known channel through the German minefields. It was, of course, overlooked by bunkers and German machine-gun posts, and patrolled regularly—but too regularly. For the Bertrams, by careful observation, learnt like many fellow islanders that it was the Germans' rigidity of habit which gave a chance of outwitting them. If they patrolled, say at 8 p.m., and again at 10 p.m., it was safe to assume that in between they would be relaxing over supper and a game of cards.

After France was in Allied hands, it gradually became known among right-minded people that the Bertrams' beach was a good one to escape from, and the Bertrams the best men to help.

An escape typical of many was that by three nineteen-year-old youths—Peter Crill, Roy Mourant and John Floyd. Crill had a twelve-foot sailing dinghy with an outboard motor, a perilously small boat for such a trip, with its treacherous coastal currents and winds, and the danger of German mines and patrols. But the dinghy was repaired and smuggled, by furniture van, to Bertram's beach. The local fishermen coached the boys on tides and currents, and they siphoned off enough petrol from unattended German lorries to fill their tank. They got regular weather forecasts —from a friendly German in the Met. Office—and fixed their escape for a Saturday evening when they would have the company of another escape boat. The time: just after the Germans' eight o'clock patrol.

Seen off by Bill Bertram, both boats crept out, the boys rowing silently across an eerily phosphorescent sea. After an hour they started their motors.

It was hard to see the compass without showing too much light. John Floyd sat shading it with his coat and shouting back directions. He became very seasick through watching the gyrating compass in the heaving bows, but carried on with his navigating between spasms. Then the engine of the other boat broke down: Crill tossed over a rope, but only brought trouble on his own boat, for the sea washed over their motor and put it out of action too.

After this, unable to restart their motors, both boats hoisted sails, and the other boat went out of sight.

A couple of hours later a frightening accident befell the three boys. Peter Crill was steering, and the mainsheet slipped from his hand. He called to Floyd to grab it, and Floyd did: but as he leaned over the gunwale the boat tipped. The compass fell into the water which was swilling round the bottom, making it useless.

There were no stars to steer by, and there was a great danger of the current carrying them back to the island to be machine-gunned by the Germans.

The boys tried to drop anchor, but found the new anchor rope a mass of knots, and cursed themselves for not having checked it earlier. So they did the only thing possible—which was to do nothing and remind themselves that a boat, left to herself with no sails up, can ride a rough sea remarkably well. By now they were so wretchedly seasick that they almost lost interest in their fate. Soaked and half-frozen, they covered themselves with canvas, taking it in turns to bale.

As soon as it was daylight, Roy Mourant cleaned the plugs and got the engine going. The boys steered slightly north of the rising sun, believing this would bring them to the French coast. Soon they were cheered by seeing several birds, and towards the afternoon they saw a tower on the horizon. About two miles off-shore their engine stopped again and they began rowing desperately: eventually, to their relief and delight, reaching a deserted coast—France.

Peter Crill then realised that they had felt too ill to touch their small emergency bottle of brandy. The others refused it, so he drank the lot, by way of celebration; but, never having touched it before, fell flat upon the beach.

Another exploit of escape was that by eight Jersey boys, led by Bernard Cavey, who joined together to map German military positions, and then take out their information to the Allies. Each reconnoitred one section of the island and noted gun batteries, strongpoints, ammunition dumps. Then they looked for a boat to make their escape, but without success. So they conceived the daring idea of attempting the sea passage to France in two canoes and a rubber "Folboat". One canoe and the "Folboat" actually reached there, and Cavey saw his information delivered to the War Office.

The other canoe began leaking and had to turn back. The boys were arrested by the Germans when they landed and put into prison. But two of them, Frank Killer and Peter Curwood, managed to escape. Armed with a thick blanket and a stirrup pump, they put the blanket over the broken glass coping of the high wall, hitched the stirrup pump to an iron peg, and threw its long hose over the wall. In this way they surmounted the glass, and then climbed down the hose to the street; though, when Frank Killer's turn came, the blanket slipped and the glass cut his arm badly.

They went into hiding for the rest of the Occupation, sheltered by different friends, who braved heavy punishment. Frank Killer had his hair dyed black and, like so many others, was provided with a faked identity card and ration book by the obliging Dr. McKinstry.

Another group of Jersey boys, instead of taking out information, stole some weapons and ammunition so that they could help any attempt by the Allies to recapture the islands. One of them, James Houillebecq, came under suspicion. His home was searched, and a list of the stolen weapons was found there; though his parents managed to destroy a list of the other boys who had been helping him. Houillebecq died in Neuengamme concentration camp a few weeks before his eighteenth birthday.

Sometimes attempts at escaping to France could also lead to tragedy, as was inevitable when novice seamen tried their luck. Once a newly-married couple and two boys set out from Rozel. Their engine failed and they drifted helplessly till they struck a rock off La Saline Bay. They were only two hundred yards from shore, but though they shouted for help in full view of German soldiers, nothing was done to save them, and permission was refused for the lifeboat to put out. All four were drowned.

(German discipline, however, was just as rigid for their own troops. Once some German soldiers, cut off by the tide when visiting the Seymour Tower, were drowned because a German sentry said that going out in boats was forbidden, and orders had to be obeyed. The Germans were heard shouting for help for nearly an hour before the tide finally came over and drowned them.)

Although the whole period of the escapes—altogether they helped about eight boatloads—was a nerve-wracking time for the Bertrams, and they knew they were under suspicion, they all got some amusement from the Germans. On one occasion the *Geheimefeldpolizei* arrived at Bill Bertram's house with two armed men. A German soldier had deserted and they must search—*immediately*! Bill Bertram stood aside while they rushed in. He hoped that the wireless they had recently been listening to was properly hidden, and watched them tramp ponderously about the inoffensive house with guns at the ready and every sign of bristling efficiency.

In the end, though they completely overlooked one entire room, they started rummaging in the drawers of a cabinet in the sitting-room. Bertram said innocently: "He must be very small for a German."

The *Geheimefeldpolizei* looked blankly at his straight face, and marched out of the house still crackling with military virtue.

CHAPTER XXXVI

A MESSAGE BY PARACHUTE

Alexander Coutanche, Bailiff of Jersey, once remarked that if any future grandchildren ever asked him what *he* had done during the war, his short answer would be "I protested". Never did he protest more effectively than in the struggle to save the islands from starvation during the last winter of the war Occupation. He had not only to convince the Germans in Berlin of the seriousness of the situation, but also to convince the Government in Whitehall. Up till now, Churchill had always insisted on the principle that the Germans were solely responsible for the food supplies of countries they occupied.

Soon after D-Day, in fact, Churchill urged upon the

Admiralty more strenuous efforts to see that no Germans escaped out of the Channel Islands, and that no food supplies got in.

Coutanche was shrewd enough not to count on an early end to the war, and able enough to see how serious the position would be. It was before the end of August that he drew up a lengthy memorandum to the *Platzkommandantur*. This impressive document, written in Coutanche's best style, gave detailed figures and reached the conclusion that "the stocks of most essential goods will be exhausted by the middle of November, 1944." It ended with a striking appeal implying that if the Germans could not ensure food supplies the time had come for them to go.

"Sooner or later," he said, "the clash of arms will cease. . . . May the Insular Government be spared the duty of adding to the problems which will face the Powers an allegation that, by an unjustified prolongation of the Siege of Jersey, the Military Representatives of the German Government unnecessarily endangered the health, and indeed the lives of the People of Jersey."

This memorandum had a wide circulation. One copy went to Guernsey, where most people praised it, but some called it "window-dressing". Other copies reached the War Cabinet in London, taken by men escaping to France. Coutanche also had it roneoed, with a copy sent to every member of the States in Jersey. Some months earlier a German had twitted Coutanche on not managing his public relations better. "You're always being criticised by your own people," he told Coutanche, "because you don't let them know what you're doing for them." Coutanche could not point out one reason was that often he did not want the Germans to realise it either. After his memorandum, however, the same German told Coutanche: "Your public relations policy isn't as bad as I thought."

Coutanche followed up his memorandum by a dramatic suggestion that he should be allowed to sail up the Channel on a yacht, get to London, explain the seriousness of the position at first hand, and then return under safe conduct.

Baron von Aufsess welcomed the idea, and so did Colonel von Helldorf, Schmettow's Chief of Staff. But General von Schmettow rejected it out of hand, as altogether too irregular by all rules of war.

Next, Eisenhower tried to contact von Schmettow from France, hoping to persuade him to surrender. On September 9 a plane flew over Guernsey, and dropped flares by the light of which a parachute could be seen coming down. It carried a cylinder, marked "Not Explosive", inside which were a series of envelopes—the last one, of oiled silk, addressed to Count von Schmettow personally. Enclosed was a message asking him to reconnect the cable between Guernsey and France, so that he could talk on the telephone with one of Eisenhower's staff.

This request von Schmettow ignored: merely remarking to one of his officers that, if it was technically possible, "I would like to re-connect the cable and send a high-voltage electric shock down it."

Ten days later, the island papers published a message from Schmettow to Dr. Goebbels: "The three Island Fortresses, conscious of their strength, and following the example of other fortresses, will faithfully hold out to the last. With this in mind we salute our Führer and our Fatherland."

Nevertheless, the Americans tried again. On the afternoon of Friday, September 22, a boat approached Guernsey, flying a white flag of parley. A German officer was sent out to meet a Major from Eisenhower's Headquarters. This naturally engendered a crop of excited rumours: but the upshot was rather an anticlimax. Eisenhower's envoy asked whether Count von Schmettow was aware of the latest developments in the war, and asked if he could have discussions on the position with the Count. The German officer went back to St. Peter Port, and a reply was signalled by morse that Count von Schmettow was fully informed about the war situation, and did not want to discuss it with anyone.

An unfortunate *contretemps* nearly followed. The batteries on Sark were warned not to fire on the boat as it went back to France, but by some mistake no such message went to Alderney. It was a gusty day with bad visibility, and the white parley flag was wound round a mast by the wind so that it was not noticed. To the horror of von Schmettow, always punctilious about military codes of honour, two batteries on Alderney opened fire. Luckily they missed.

Next day, when Leale asked Helldorf what had happened in the parley, he was told that the German officer had been asked "some silly questions." The Germans, Helldorf added, did not intend to discuss their position with the Americans. It would be different, he said, with the British. (This, apparently was simply a routine attempt to play off one Ally against another.)

The Americans still kept trying, another letter being dropped by parachute, but again with no success. One day von Aufsess in Jersey telephoned Helldorf in Guernsey to ask what was going on. Helldorf replied a little wearily, "The usual—the Americans want us to surrender."

Finally, on September 25, 1944, Count von Schmettow sent back a reply of some spirit to Coutanche's lengthy memorandum. The Germans, he said, were not to blame for any food shortages. "It must not be overlooked that the islands could not free themselves of the idea of profitable exports, such as tomatoes"—a criticism of Guernsey. Next came a hit at Jersey: "It would have been possible for the Island Administration, by greater discernment, social understanding, and precautions, to make provision for the poorer part of the population in Jersey . . . They could have been spared many hardships."

Schmettow then went further:

"People in the Islands do not know what war is, nor what war means. They can have no idea of what every German town, the whole of France, London, and the

South of England are experiencing daily, in the way of sacrifices and sufferings...

"Compared with this, the Islands have not felt the breath of war."

And Schmettow warned that in future it might be necessary to draw indiscriminately on cattle, flour, potatoes and other island supplies:

"The German Forces do not build Fortresses of such strength without holding them with the greatest bitterness until the final exhaustion of the Defending Forces...

"By reason of the cutting off of the Islands I can no longer supply the population...It now remains solely a matter for the British Government whether it considers assistance necessary for its subjects in the Channel Islands.... I am convinced that the British Government is aware of the exact position."

Among those who had their doubts on this last point was Alfred Sarre, the Guernsey representative in Jersey. With the aid of an unsuspecting official in the *Platzkommandantur*, who had the official Guernsey statistics about essential commodities, Sarre drew up a statement which was taken out by three young men who escaped to France on the night of October 9, 1944.

Although Coutanche and the other islanders could not know it at the time, Count von Schmettow's refusal as a soldier to think of surrender did not prevent him from being an unsuspected ally—at any rate with regard to resisting the more extreme proposals he received.

On September 18, 1944, a directive about the Channel Islands had been issued from OKW (Supreme Headquarters) in Berlin, signed by General Keitel. Civilian rations, it said, had to be reduced to the "barest survival level". If supplies of food were still insufficient, then the entire civilian population, except for able-bodied men, had to be *zum Feinde abgeschoben*—"pushed over to the enemy". The directive ended ominously:

"An Order will follow for the complete stopping of rations to the civilian population, and for measures to inform the British Government that this has been done."

One can only guess about the meaning of the phrase *zum Feinde abgeschoben*. Apparently the idea was to segregate the civilians in one corner of each island, and give Britain the choice of removing them, sending food for them, or letting them starve.

On the following day came a directive from Hitler himself. He said that an approach should be made, through a neutral power, to Britain and America. If they would not supply the civilians, everybody except able-bodied men should be removed from the islands. Hitler ordered the Commander-in-Chief in the West to discuss evacuation plans with the Navy. Where the civilians could be evacuated to, Hitler did not explain, and apparently did not care.

Count von Schmettow protested that about 70 or 75 per cent of the civilians were working for the Germans, either directly or indirectly—in agriculture, by keeping public utilities going, and so on. Removing the remaining 25 to 30 per cent would only give the garrison an extra month's supplies.

Meanwhile, from the opposite direction, von Schmettow was being subject to continual pressure from John Leale and Victor Carey, as well as Coutanche in Jersey. They protested that the rights and responsibilities of an Occupying Power were indivisible. "The only way you can divest yourself of your responsibilities is by giving up the rights, that is, by ceasing to be an Occupying Force ..." To them, von Schmettow gave the same reply as to Coutanche's memorandum. He said that German sailors had lost their lives in the past bringing food to the Channel Islands, but responsibility now rested with "the Besiegers"—that is, the Allied Powers.

Finally Schmettow repeated, even more emphatically, that the Germans meant to hold on to the limit: "Even if, in the long run, a calamitous situation should arise for the population."

This, at any rate, was certainly frank.

CHAPTER XXXVII

"CONDITIONS RAPIDLY DETERIORATING"

It seemed that everything depended on getting the facts to London. British Intelligence methods had depended, for the most part, on such rough-and-ready methods as counting the number of cows in photographs by reconnaissance planes, working out that there had been no large-scale killing of cattle, and deducing that things were not yet desperate.

Alfred Sarre had sent out one set of figures about Guernsey; and he sent out another early in November through Norman Rumball, a Westminster bank official, who reached France in a dramatic escape after the engine of his boat had failed for a time, and he had drifted back within two miles of Jersey. But obviously it would need a great deal of first-hand confirmation direct from Guernsey to convince Churchill that the blockade had to be relaxed.

Captain Fred Noyon at St. Sampson's, a retired sea captain who was now a fisherman, was asked if he knew anyone who would get the facts and risk trying to escape with them to England. Noyon, after thinking it over, said he would go himself. He had no dependants for the Germans to punish after he had gone, as his wife had died just before the Occupation.

Noyon went to see his Deputy (or M.P.)—C. H. Cross, Manager of the North Cinema. And Cross went to see Sir Abraham Lainé of the Essential Commodities Committee, saying he wanted to ask some questions about detailed economic statistics when the States met two days later. Sir Abraham protested that it was impossible to get the figures in time, but he was delighted and soon changed his mind when he heard that a fisherman was ready to take the information to England.

On the night of November 2, Noyon collected from Cross the statistics for every States Department, and he was also provided with copies of the recent correspondence with von Schmettow.

For his boat, the *Littlewood*, Noyon had go a stock of eight cans of petrol, acquired by barter for fish. His nephew Steve wanted to go with him, but Fred Noyon refused, for Steve's parents might suffer. It was decided that Fred would only take with him his other mate, Bill Enticott.

The next day, November 3, was a Friday: and on Friday mornings, reserved for German artillery practise, no boat could go out. After lunch, with his sealed papers in a fisherman's bag, carried casually over his shoulder, Noyon went down to get his fishing permit. In those days a German Customs Officer was supposed to go out with every boat, and they had discussed beforehand what to do about him.

"If he behaves himself," Noyon told Enticott, "he'll be all right; but if he tries to be funny I'll deal with him and dump him overboard."

Noyon reckoned on having a good weapon in his hand so long as he was steering the boat: a tiller can do a lot of damage.

He hoped, however, that if they waited for all the other fishing boats to go first, there would be no German left to go with them.

But a German Customs Officer arrived nevertheless, throwing his bag down in the *Littlewood*. Noyon, pointing to the net down in the bottom of the boat, said that he was just putting it out in the next bay; then he had to go to St. Peter Port to get his engine pump mended. It would probably take too long to get it done that day, so he would not be coming back to St. Sampson's till the day after. The German, not liking the prospect of walking home that night from St. Peter Port to St. Sampson's, picked up his bag and went ashore again.

In the next bay, Noyon and Enticott put out the net—an old one specially selected to be jettisoned—and then carried out towards Lancresse, pretending to be looking for longnose. They threw small pieces of wood in the water, but no longnose jumped over them. They met other fishermen who were genuinely on the job, and were glad when their boats drifted apart. At half past four a convenient drizzle sprang up, almost cutting them off from sight of the shore, and they made for the Channel. As soon as it was dark they put up a sail.

Helped by a fresh breeze from the West, Noyon made for Poole, which he knew well. It was after ten that night that he saw what looked like "a big black lump" to windward. The next moment a searchlight was trained on them; they pulled down the sail, and something came alongside them. They had no idea what to expect; it might have been a German E-boat, or anything else. Then a voice shouted, "Come aboard!" and Noyon turned to Enticott and said: "That's English, at any rate!"

It turned out to be an American submarine chaser. They were taken to Cherbourg: Noyon handed over his packet of papers and Bill Enticott, who had driven a lorry for nine months for the Germans, was able to give details of their guns and defences. The only thing that worried Noyon was that he had promised to get the B.B.C. to broadcast a pre-arranged message—"Personal message to George. The answer is Yes"—to tell Guernsey that he had arrived safely. It was not till over a fortnight later, after he had reached England, that he was able to ask for the message to be sent.

Noyon's papers proved to contain by far the fullest information yet received in London. Moreover, they confirmed the authenticity of messages which, passing through German hands, might otherwise have been suspect.

On November 5, Victor Carey was told that he could contact the International Red Cross over the German radio transmitter. Permission had been asked for this many times before, but had always been refused. The following succinct message was now prepared:

To the Secretary General,   Guernsey,
International Red Cross,   5th November, 1944
Geneva.

Conditions rapidly deteriorating here. Will soon become impossible . . . We urge immediate visit of Red Cross representative.

All rations drastically reduced.

Bread finishes 15th December.

Sugar finishes 6th January.

Ration of separated milk will be reduced to one third pint per head by end of year.

Soap and other cleansers—Stocks completely exhausted.

Vegetables generally inadequate to supply civilian population through winter. German consumption heavy . . .

Clothing and footwear stocks almost exhausted.

Fuel—Gas and electricity finish at the end of year.

Coal stocks exhausted. Wood fuel quite inadequate.

Many essential medical supplies already finished.

VICTOR G. CAREY,
Bailiff of Guernsey.

A few days later in Jersey, Coutanche handed a similar message to the *Platzkommandant*, for transmission to the Protecting Power: —

Sufficient anaesthetics until middle of January but only for really urgent operations. Many most essential drugs now exhausted . . .

Butter stocks will be exhausted end December. No margarine . . .

Soap exhausted except for hospitals.

No gas since September. Electricity will fail middle January . . . No matches.

Supplies of footwear and textiles practically exhausted.

General state of Public Health causing increasing anxiety to Insular Government.

Favour of reply requested.

A. M. COUTANCHE,
Bailiff of Jersey.

Carey wrote to Coutanche on November 11 that "starvation begins to stare us in the face, and I can see no way out of it."

Except for a few well-fed farmers and Black Market patrons, there was scarcely anyone now in Guernsey who was not going hungry. Life became completely primitive. In many poorer homes people went to bed soon after midday because there was nothing left to eat, and no more energy to go on working; and there, since hunger can make sleep difficult, they would lie and wonder if the next day would bring a few turnips and parsnips from some source or other.

Apart from the poorest people, those who were worst off were those in official positions who felt they could not use the Black Market. The once portly Victor Carey lost five stone, and his coat hung about him like a tent.

In Jersey, the Coutanches were almost unique among the wealthiest of the islanders in also being among the hungriest. By the end of the Occupation Mrs. Coutanche, normally a tall and slim ten stone, had dropped to six and a half: and she told the Chief of the St. John Ambulance Brigade: "You could use me as a skeleton in anatomy lessons." Coutanche himself, a frank *bon viveur*, lost more than two stone. Then a farmer, rather surprised to realise that there was anybody on the island who was taking the Black Market regulations seriously, discovered their plight: and from then on he asked them to lunch regularly once a month, promising that the meal would contain no illicit pork or other meat. All through the month the Coutanches would look forward to this day, and the farmer and his wife would kill their plumpest chickens or a couple of rabbits.

With petrol rationed even more severely than food, Coutanche could only go to his office five days a week. If anything unexpected arose which called for a sixth visit, he would have to walk or cycle the nine miles there and back, ending with the steep climb up the hill at St. Aubins to his house.

His lunch packet would usually consist of three cooked potatoes, a bottle of tomato juice, and some fruit. When possible there would be added a flask of hot soup, brought in from the communal kitchens which had been set up in the town. In the winter he worked in his fireless office, clothed in sweaters and overcoat, with his feet in a foot-muff containing a hot water bottle. Outside sat his interpreter swathed in blankets, with a dewdrop which seemed to attach itself permanently to the end of his nose from September until May.

Whenever the Bailiff wanted him, he would shuffle in bent half double, clutching his blankets round him; and then, like a duck returning to its nest, waddle back to the haven of his own chair and desk.

In Guernsey the shortage of fuel brought with it a shortage of water, because of lack of power for the pumping stations. There were a number of economy measures, and the Germans even demanded that the use of water for flushing lavatories should be banned, saying that people could use outdoor sanitation.

This was too much for old Dr. Symons, the Health Officer, who wrote a characteristic forthright protest. He told the Germans that nearly everyone now had a lowered resistance to infection, and that it was hardly humane "to expect the old and young to go into their gardens in winter, perhaps at night, like cats and dogs. . . ."

Moreover, continued Dr. Symons, "If the use of buckets is suggested, where are the buckets? Who is going to cleanse them, especially without water? . . . Many houses in St. Peter Port and St. Sampson's have no gardens. Are these people to go into the roads? . . ."

The tone of this letter, following that of some equally outspoken remarks, was too much for the Germans. Peremptory orders were given that Dr. Symons was to be dismissed. John Leale replied that there was no one else who could do the job: and he suggested, with typical tact, that perhaps the translation of Symons' letter might have seemed more offensive than the original. The Germans, in return, said that their original letter had also been misinterpreted; the matter was smoothed over, and Dr. Symons stayed at his post.

During this time there was a growing difference of opinion working up between Count von Schmettow and Admiral Krancke, who had been made responsible for the Channel Islands on October 25. Krancke said that relations between Schmettow and the island authorities were *too* good—"an embarrassment". He insisted that rations were still too high, and urged confiscation of all civilian stocks, to help the garrison hold out longer. And on November 4 Admiral Krancke went to Berlin to see Admiral Doenitz about it. Doenitz put Krancke's case to the German Supreme Command, which agreed to the confiscation. Count von Schmettow pointed out that this would break early promises—for instance, in the original Richthofen ultimatum to Jersey—to respect property: but he was told that the Supreme Command knew nothing of any such promises. If they had been given, they were "no longer valid".

There seems little doubt that the position of the islanders would soon have become even more desperate, but for the agreement reached soon afterwards between the German and British Governments to allow Red Cross supplies into the islands. On November 19 Schmettow learned that Churchill had given up his objections; and on December 6 Victor Carey was told that a Red Cross ship was leaving Lisbon the next day with 750 tons of food parcels like those provided for prisoners of war.

So sceptical had the islanders become, that it was not until the B.B.C. confirmed that relief was on the way that they believed it. Rumours about the contents and numbers of the parcels ran rife, and people did little but talk, think and dream of food. But the days passed and no Red Cross ship arrived. The next rumour was that the ship would arrive at Christmas, and spirits lifted. Once again there was disappointment.

Christmas Day came, and it was the barest within memory. One Guernsey housewife, combing through her almost empty store cupboard on Christmas Eve for something for her four children, found by chance four lumps of hard French sugar which she had overlooked. She brought them out, carefully coloured them with cochineal, wrapped them up in wisps of gay paper left over from previous Christmases, and laid one on each breakfast plate the next morning, as the children's sole Christmas treat. Many others were even less fortunate. Mrs. Champion, with her nine children, could only give her family two slices of bread each.

At last, on Wednesday, December 27, the Red Cross ship—an old Swedish vessel named the *Vega*—reached Guernsey. Joy, and apprehension lest further official difficulties and arguments arose, passed through the island. Happy crowds gathered round the harbour as the Red Cross representatives stepped ashore, and next day they held a meeting with the German authorities, and the Bailiffs of both islands—Alexander Coutanche coming over specially, with Baron von Aufsess, from Jersey. (As they climbed on the boat at St. Helier, some of the German guards were scandalised to notice that von Aufsess was

253

carrying Coutanche's bag.*) It was the first time that Carey and Coutanche had been together since the Occupation began: and while Carey did his best to cope with his duties as host, Coutanche was soon dominating the situation and making the conversation.

The two Bailiffs stated their islands' needs, particularly the acute shortage of flour. Dr. Symons said that the rations in Guernsey, plus a small amount of vegetables, came to only 1,137 calories a day.*

Later, the *Vega* went on to Jersey; and in both islands and in Sark there began the wondrous distribution of one food parcel per person, provided by the New Zealand and Canadian Red Cross Societies. The islanders opened them like children opening presents, and gazed enraptured at forgotten delicacies—real tea, real coffee, real biscuits, chocolate and marmalade, cheese and tinned meat. Some people carried their parcels with them everywhere, and would not be parted from them; some planned elaborate schedules for spreading their contents over a whole month; one man ate so much at one sitting that he was violently ill and had to be saved by a stomach pump. But everyone talked of little else for days except the marvellous parcels and the marvellous taste of the things in them.

The habitual grumblers, however, could not be deprived of their grouse. Some of those who had New Zealand parcels complained that they had not as much variety as the Canadian; and some with Canadian said they had not so much food value as the New Zealand.

* Aufsess explained afterwards that Coutanche was an older man, and it was a difficult boat to board.

** In England, calories per day averaged 2,010 in 1944 and 2,930 in 1945, according to Ministry of Food estimates.

CHAPTER XXXVIII

STARVATION AND STEALING

One candid comment by Admiral Krancke, still responsible for the Channel Islands as Commander of the German Naval Group West, shows that Churchill's opposition to Red Cross supplies was not altogether unreasonable. "Now that we have succeeded," wrote Krancke, "in getting the Red Cross to supply the civilians ... we can consider it certain that our Forces will be able to hold out in the islands beyond the year 1945." Yet there is no doubt that only the Red Cross parcels—the *Vega* came back with a fresh supply about every month—saved the islanders from actual starvation in the grim New Year which started. Few had thoughts, by now, of anything much beside food: thefts became more and more common as hunger brought desperation.

There were several robberies with violence and more than one with murder, though usually it was possible to frighten away the intruders by some show of force. At night all householders took up with them to their bedrooms whatever food they had, and sometimes even rabbits and hens in crates. Mrs. Coutanche in Jersey was among those who had her meat safe moved to the bedroom landing, after its contents had been rifled from the pantry. A strange collection of implements and knives and sticks were laid beside beds as emergency weapons, ranging from jugs of water for emptying on to the heads of prowlers, to such formidable things as the two knobkerries which the white-haired Dr. and Mrs. Symons of Guernsey took upstairs with them every night. Almost every house had its booby traps and burglar alarms, which sometimes prematurely misfired during innocent visits from neighbours.

Perhaps because of the Germans' traditionally large appetites, or because they had not had the same gradual conditioning to hunger as the islanders, it was they who seemed most hungry when the near-starvation period came. Some of them, like the more desperate islanders, went out ravenously foraging for food every night, breaking into barns and glasshouses and private homes for anything they could find. In Sark, Mrs. Hathaway was moved to tell the German Commandant that "you haven't got an Army, you've only got a pack of thieves and beggars. They're either coming round to one door begging for potato peelings to eat, or else breaking in another door trying to steal something."

Sometimes there was room for comedy. M. Lambert, who was not only French consular agent in St. Peter Port but an electrical engineer by profession, was surreptitiously listening to the B.B.C. one night on a wireless set which he was mending for the Germans. He heard stealthy footsteps in his garden, outside his workshop. Switching off the set and the light, he dodged down behind a bench. He could dimly discern two Germans outside, and felt almost certain they must have overheard him listening to the B.B.C. They still went on creeping round the shed, as though about to pounce; Lambert kept creeping round under cover of the bench. The dodging went on for several minutes before Lambert realised that the Germans were just as anxious to avoid being caught by him as the other way about; they were after the pears on a pear tree in his garden, and had got away with them before Lambert emerged in fury.

But on the whole the German discipline was remarkable. There was one shocking case when an elderly man and his wife were murdered for their Red Cross parcels; but there was only one other reported case of a parcel being stolen, and no attempt was ever made to divert them from the civilians to the troops. When the *Vega* first came to Jersey, in fact, an anonymous letter went to the *Platzkomman-dantur* urging that nobody but German soldiers should be

256

allowed to handle the parcels, because nobody else could be trusted.

One housewife in Guernsey, for whom an obliging German soldier had done a job in the garden, offered him a present afterwards of a few cigarettes. He refused to take them, because they had been brought by the *Vega*, and General von Schmettow had given the strictest orders that everything brought by the *Vega* was for civilians only.

To get extra supplies for his own troops, Schmettow asked for a U-boat to be sent from Germany. He suggested that it should be loaded with $10\frac{1}{2}$ tons of sugar, 11 tons of fats, $3\frac{1}{2}$ tons of soap, and $\frac{1}{2}$ ton of razor blades—Schmettow had a true soldier's belief in trying to keep up the appearance of his men.

The plan, however, was never carried out: and once the *Vega* started coming regularly, the civilians were almost certainly better off than the German soldiers—which is something of a tribute both to the "correct" policy always followed by the island authorities, and to that of the German Commandant. To those who remembered the cock-a-hoop German conquerors of 1940, it was ironic to see men in the same uniform, five years later, rummaging in dustbins, or being lined up on parade to search for limpets, or combing the hedgerows for berries and nettles to boil and eat. Some of them even died, in Socratic fashion, by eating the poisonous roots known to the Greeks as hemlock.

One unforgettable memory: the young German who suddenly caught sight of a raw turnip so small that it had been tossed aside on a manure heap. In a moment he had seized it, scraped it perfunctorily with a knife and started eating it.

Hunger had a way of wiping out any merely nationalistic distinctions between the Germans and their enemies. It reduced some Germans and some islanders alike to a common denominator of thieving; and it fostered the Black Market in which a few farmers grew fat. But, at the opposite extreme, the common hardship brought much kindness and fellow feeling, even self-sacrifice.

There was the occasion when Mrs. May Sherwill, left

alone with her two younger boys after her husband was deported to Laufen, had to go to hospital suddenly for an operation. While she was away, it was the German Army cook billeted in her house who looked after the boys for her, and always made sure they had good meals.

Then there was Mrs. Winifred Green, the same Mrs. Green who had been sent to Caen Prison for saying "*Heil Churchill*". Afterwards, at a time when she was expecting a baby, she had to pass a German barracks on her way home from work. Sometimes a soldier, noticing her condition, would quietly slip a loaf of bread or a small bag of flour into her arms. She would think of her husband, who had not had a proper meal for weeks, and gratefully accept.

Then, in the days when the Germans themselves were starving, Mrs. Green would be so moved by the pinched cheeks and protruding shoulder blades of the young soldiers that she sometimes gave them crusts which she could well have eaten herself.

The food shortage brought only one compensation. All Guernseymen imprisoned locally for having wireless sets were released because it was impossible to feed them. One man who had just been sentenced to four months was let out after serving only four days.

To those who have never known real hunger, it is hard to describe how food can become an obsession; how the theft of a turnip can be a tragedy, and the sudden appearance of some long-forgotten item on the dinner table can be a matter for almost hysterical rejoicing. During January and February, flour stocks were exhausted, and the islands were left completely without bread. Then flour was brought by the *Vega* on its third trip, and rushed to the bakers. As people hurried down to claim their loaves, they saw that many of those coming back, carrying their booty, had tears in their eyes. The flour brought by the *Vega* was made from hard Manitoba wheat; and, as the bakers were used to softer wheat, the loaves ballooned out to the size of gigantic footballs, made of purest white bread. One family could not help laughing at the mere sight of the huge loaf on the table, and went on laughing throughout the meal.

Lack of food was not the only deprivation. With no coal from the Continent, gas and electricity finally ran out almost completely. Cooking could only be done over a few sticks; any lighting depended on rare candles or paraffin lamps.

There was no singing of psalms in churches with stained glass windows, because there was not enough light for the congregation to read the words. Clergymen would conduct services with a candle in one hand and a prayer book in the other.

Jersey was lucky in that supplies of firewood never ran out completely, though at a grievous cost to the fine trees on the island. In Guernsey the available trees had soon gone. A party of Germans arrived to cut down twenty in Dr. Symons' beautiful garden overlooking the Russel. He and his wife watched the destruction. At the end, when the men had gone off, their officer came up and saw plainly enough what they were thinking. He said quietly: "At home I have just such a beautiful house and gardens as you have. When the war is over *for God's sake kill every Nazi that is left.*"

One of the most remarkable things was the skill and devotion with which, under all the circumstances, the hospital and medical services were kept going. At one time hospital nurses in Guernsey were doing a full day's work on a cup of acorn coffee for breakfast, turnip stew for lunch, and no supper whatever. On night duty, after the electricity supplies ended, they would sit in the dark until a patient called for attention. Then they would light up some improvised lamp, and carefully blow it out again, to save fuel, when finished. The usual lamp was a "nicky light", made out of a jam jar of diesel oil, with a hole pierced in the cap through which a piece of tape or bootlace would be threaded to act as a wick. For blood transfusions, or a serious operation, they would bring out one of their carefully hoarded candles.

The staff at the Guernsey Emergency Hospital still remember one occasion when a difficult instrumental birth was taking place by candlelight. Just when the doctor was applying the forceps the candle blew out, and nobody had a match on them.

There were no anaesthetics for childbirth. But, in spite of all the difficulties, out of 1,413 mothers, only one died—in a twin birth with complications. It was a record that any hospital could have been proud of under the best of conditions.

Perhaps some of the nurses did not take too kindly to looking after the "Jerrybags" who were having babies by German fathers. But they had the same scrupulous attention as the rest, and one Quaker nurse in Jersey took these girls, sometimes desperately unhappy, into her special care.

When bandages gave out the nurses tore up curtains, and instead of dressings and cotton wool they got hold of paper used for packing tomatoes. When, in Guernsey, water was cut off completely except for three hours a day, it naturally added to the difficulty of sterilising and cleaning bed pans. With the shortage of antiseptics, Out Patients were told to wash their dressings in the sea.

No one can dogmatise about how many deaths were caused by the Occupation; a man may die of more causes than one. A typical enough story was that of Tommy Mansell Simon, in whose Guernsey farmhouse nearly ten years later, a large part of this book was written.

Of young Simon—pronounced as a French name—it could be said that he lived his life with *panache*. He was good-looking, gay, and a fine horseman. He came of an old island family. At twenty-three he married a beautiful English girl whom he met at a ball at St. Peter Port, proposing to her during their third dance. When war came, Simon and his young wife were still building up their farm. He wanted to follow his family tradition and go into the army, but he decided he had to stand by his old parents, his wife and children and, above all, their land. There was no one else.

In the hard years that followed he tried to keep a guard on his temper and his tongue. He was a man used to giving orders, not taking them—especially from enemy soldiers who clambered about his fields planting mines, erecting pill-boxes and barbed-wire barricades, and stealing his roots and his animals.

His nearest neighbours, two aunts of his, had German troops billeted on them. They were moved into a small back bedroom while the Germans slept in their exquisite four-poster beds—before finally chopping the beds up for firewood.

Simon's English wife said: "I'll never have Germans in *our* house." She collected together all the hats and coats she could find, and told their three children that whenever Germans came to the door they were to keep changing their clothes, and run about making as much noise as they could. The high-spirited young Simons entered into the plot, with the result that when their mother told enquiring German billeting officers "There's no room here. I've seven children. You'd never be comfortable..." they retired only too abashed.

Simon himself was forced by the Germans, when petrol grew scarce, to drive them about in his horse-drawn van. Sometimes he would take soldiers down to the quay when they were being drafted abroad, and on these occasions he would accept his summonses to the German barracks with grim satisfaction. A few minutes later the townsfolk would be chuckling as, with a dash of his old spirit, he would whip his horses through the streets, nod contemptuously towards the jolting soldiers sitting unhappily behind him, and give a shout of: "Here they come—more cannon-fodder for the British!"

But it could not go on. Sometimes Simon's remarks were understood by the Germans, and there were ugly incidents. His own unhappiness went deep, and his family noticed the change in him as his pride fought with his concern for their safety. Added to this was the strain of hunger; for, as in most families, what food there was went first to his children and to the old people. One day when he returned from the German barracks his wife saw that his face was ashen and his body badly bruised. There had, she gathered, been some sort of fracas to do with Churchill and the war. All Simon said was: "There comes a limit to what you can take."

The next day he developed pneumonia. The doctor attributed it to shock and physical weakness. He was taken to hospital, but the supplies of drugs and oxygen which could have saved him were exhausted. Ten days later, at the age of thirty-six, Tommy Mansell Simon died.

CHAPTER XXXIX

ESCAPE

The grim last winter was still relieved, from time to time, by tales of escapes which inspired envy and admiration; with Bill Bertram still showing the way from Fauvic.

Among those who owed their freedom to him were two American Army officers, who got away from their Prisoner of War Camp in Jersey and arrived, after four days' hiding behind hedges and in empty houses, at Bertram's door. They were exhausted, dirty and starving.

On that very day the following notice had appeared in the *Jersey Evening Post*:

"On January 8, 1945, the American Prisoners of War, Captain Clark and Lt. Haas, escaped. . . . They will attempt to obtain shelter and help from the English civilian population. It is expressly announced that anyone who takes in or extends help in any way to Captain Clark or Lt. Haas will be punished by death."

Bill Bertram invited Clark and Haas inside, and sheltered them while the chase continued. Nobody else knew they were there except Bertram's brother and his young nephew John.

One evening, as someone was heard approaching, the airmen slipped quickly out of the sitting-room. There came in a self-important neighbour who sat down heavily in a chair still warm from one of the Americans. "Those airmen now," he began, and the Bertrams looked up apprehensively. "Those airmen. *I know where they are.* Only a mile or so from this very spot. But best not to say where, don't you think?" Bill Bertram agreed gravely, "Best not to say"; while his brother and nephew turned away to hide their smiles.

After a week, during which the Bertrams gave the airmen their own food to help build up their strength, they were able to steal a boat and get to France.

Another escape helped by the Bertrams which aroused particular admiration was that of Frank le Sueur. Trying to get away before, he had been caught and sentenced to fifteen months' imprisonment. In prison, he made a point of chatting to his German guards, and spread the news that he had some fishing tackle. By this time there was a great shortage of nets and fishing gear—in fact the Germans had even requisitioned wire netting around tennis courts, and tried to use it for fish traps. So it was not long before a German officer became interested enough to visit le Sueur in prison.

Mr. le Sueur was most forthcoming, but explained with regret that the tackle was hidden in a secret place, that he was the only person who could find it, and of course it would be out of the question for him to be let out of prison for an hour for this purpose. The officer grandly explained that this was something which it was within his power to arrange. So that afternoon they set off by car, and Mr. le

Sueur took the officer to an outhouse where he said the fishing tackle was kept. He showed the officer in politely, slammed the door behind him, fastened the latch and jumped over the fence.

For over four months he remained at large sheltered by different friends, until the Bertrams finally arranged for him to get away from Fauvic with four other young men.

Escaping to France from Guernsey was much more difficult than from Jersey—not only was there farther to go, but Sark, with its German observation posts, stood in the way. Nevertheless, one escape was made which brought out valuable documents and information. It was done by two fishermen, the le Page brothers; and it was inspired by M. Lambert, the French Consular Agent.

M. Lambert had been indefatigable in looking after a group of French prisoners of war on the island. One day he found that there had been sent down to their prison, for punishment, some of the Georgians serving in the German Army. They told Lambert that they were planning a mutiny, and asked him to get news of their plans to the Allies.

As well, Lambert wanted to send word to the authorities in Paris that his French prisoners of war needed Red Cross parcels.

Lambert had also got to know a mechanic named Golivet, a French worker in Guernsey, who was trying to escape; and Lambert agreed to help him get away. In return, Golivet could give Lambert detailed information on German naval constructions, minefields, etc., for he had been doing work for the Navy at St. Peter Port.

One Sunday morning, M. Lambert was riding past the Longstore on his bicycle when he saw John le Page crossing the road, and asked to speak to him. Would the le Pages be willing to try escaping to France in their boat, taking with them military information which would mean they might be shot if caught? John le Page talked it over that night with his brother Tom, and Lambert came round too. They told him they would go. There was little fear of reprisals against relatives, for the brothers were living on their own.

With his wife helping him to copy the plans supplied by Golivet, Lambert filled a strong sealed box with papers. He gave it to the le Pages. It was weighted so that, if the boat was intercepted, the box could be dropped overboard and would sink immediately.

In those days, whenever a fishing boat went out, the Germans would decide who went in it. Lambert's plan was to get Golivet, armed with a dossier of documents, sent out in the le Pages' boat; so Golivet had to pretend to be a fisherman.

He went to the Germans and said he was good at fishing; if the Germans would allow him to exercise his skill in his spare time he would give them some of the fish he caught. The Germans agreed. So from time to time, Golivet would go out in a boat, with fishermen who had been warned not to be too critical of his performance. Needless to say, he frequently caught nothing; and to keep up his reputation, Lambert had to *buy* fish for him to give the Germans.

The le Page brothers knew it was hopeless trying to get to France from Guernsey on a spring tide; they had to wait for the neap tide. And it would need some mist to escape attention. John le Page told his brother: "The day that we can't see Herm and Jethou, we'll go."

For eight successive nights, Lambert went round to the brothers. Then one evening, John told him, "There should be enough mist tomorrow." Next morning, the le Pages were up early. They looked out across the Russel, and they could not see Herm and Jethou.

Everything went to plan. Shortly before eleven that morning, Golivet arrived at the Albert Pier, and went in first to the guard room where the Germans were assigning different men to different boats. The le Pages, arriving a few seconds later, were asked to take Golivet with them. John le Page professed some unwillingness—"I can't speak French," he said, "so he'll have no one to talk to all day" —but he was overruled. At the last moment, just before the boat set out, Golivet excused himself and went in from the quay to the men's lavatory on the Albert Pier. Inside, Lambert was waiting—having gone in from the side of the Esplanade. He handed Golivet some more documents with last-minute news of German operational plans.

Golivet strolled back with them in a fisherman's bag slung over his shoulder, and the boat set off into the mist.

It was the custom for a patrol boat to go out each evening to round up the fishing boats. To make sure that, when they were missed, the search would begin in the wrong place, le Page told the patrol that he was going east to pick up lobster pots, and then turning south. Actually they sailed east, and then turned north between Herm and Sark.

About two o'clock in the afternoon, to their dismay, the mist cleared and it turned into a nice sunny day. But by then they were ten miles north of Sark, and passed undetected. At eleven next morning, Lambert saw a plane fly across to Guernsey, circle the island, and fly back again to France—the signal he had asked to be given if the boat arrived safely.

There had been some doubts in London about whether the Germans were seizing food parcels from the *Vega* for themselves. At their interrogation, the le Page brothers confirmed that the parcels were going intact to the islanders: and so the *Vega's* visits continued.

Meanwhile, in Jersey, the deportation of Crawford-Morrison had not stopped Major L'Amy carrying on the work of collecting information about German defences, and continually bringing it up to date. He now entrusted papers giving the latest facts to a party of five young men who were planning to escape.

An Englishman living in St. Martin's, William Gladden, was a seventy-year-old builder who occupied his time quietly in sheltering escaped Russian prisoners, collecting military information for Major L'Amy, and illicit boat-making. By good luck he just had a boat ready. Some of the necessary petrol was found by Dr. McKinstry. The next problem was to move the boat the four miles from St. Martin's to the sea. The young men found an old furniture van, but there was no horse to go with it. So the five of them took hold of the shafts and pulled the van to St. Martin's, loaded the boat in it, and pulled it to Bill Bertram's beach at Fauvic. Strangely enough, no German asked them what they were doing.

They left Fauvic at 8.30 p.m. on the night of February 23, 1945; having arranged that, if they reached France, there would be six flashes of light from the French coast at 8 p.m. The following evening L'Amy saw the flashes of a gun firing six times.

L'Amy wanted, however, a way of sending out information without depending on occasional escapes. This called for a wireless transmitter and a secret cipher. The perilous assignment of getting a transmitter into working order was undertaken by P. G. Warder, the chief Post Office Engineer, and Dr. McKinstry arranged for it to be installed, when the time came, in a room at Les Vaux Convalescent Home. This was selected because the Germans were always afraid of tuberculosis and kept well away from it; and because it was a building raised on tall foundations, so that Warder could get in and out of the room unseen from underneath.

Major L'Amy had invented his own cipher earlier; it now only remained to get the key to the cipher, and a pre-arranged call sign, to England. Escapes were more and more difficult now for lack of boats: but, during April, Gladden finished building one more. The instructions for using the cipher were divided into two parts, put into small copper tubes, and given to two members of the escaping party. The weather, however, turned against them, and the attempt had to be abandoned.

CHAPTER XL

THE FERVENT ADMIRAL

As mentioned earlier, Vice-Admiral Hüffmeier had arrived in the Channel Islands in the middle of 1944. A fervent Nazi supporter, as early as September 1944 he was complaining to Admiral Krancke, of Navy Group West, that Schmettow was being "too magnanimous" over civilian rations. When Schmettow estimated that about 70 per cent of the population were working for the Germans, Hüffmeier told Krancke that, on the contrary, only 20 per cent were really necessary, and that the rest should be removed from the islands.

Somebody in the German Admiralty scribbled in pencil, on the margin of one of Hüffmeier's despatches about Schmettow which is still preserved: *Sie sprechen da gar nicht miteinander*—"Evidently they are not on speaking terms."

Hüffmeier told Krancke that Schmettow and the Army leaders had been in the islands too long, and had got too many ties with the civilians. The solution, suggested Hüffmeier, was gradually to bring the islands under the command of the Navy—that is, of Hüffmeier. Even Krancke thought this was going a bit too far at the time, for the German forces on the islands then totalled about 35,000 men, of whom only 3,500 were sailors.

But in October 1944, when the Channel Islands were put under Admiral Krancke, Hüffmeier was made Schmettow's Chief of Staff. In this position Hüffmeier still did not hesitate to send reports to Krancke without showing them to Schmettow.

Hüffmeier's Nazi zeal soon came to Hitler's attention, and increased his favour in the highest quarters. According to the Minutes of Hitler's naval conference on November 1, 1944, Admiral Doenitz referred approvingly to "the proposals of Rear-Admiral Hüffmeier . . . who suggests prolonging the Occupation of the Channel Islands until the end of 1945 by means of drastic confiscation and by severely reducing consumption." Doenitz added that Hüffmeier's appointment as Chief of Staff to Schmettow was "a happy choice, and the proper way to give this energetic personality a voice in the overall command of the Channel Islands."

The inevitable *dénouement* came before the end of February 1945. Hüffmeier cheerfully informed Count von Schmettow that he had received a message from Germany, whereby Schmettow was recalled on grounds of ill health —although, as Schmettow pointed out, he had not seen a doctor for fifteen months. His position as Commander-in-Chief of the Channel Islands was to be taken by Hüffmeier. The Order from Berlin emphasised that Schmettow was to return to Germany immediately, without even waiting for the arrival of his successor as Commander of the 319 Infantry Division.

It was nearly a fortnight, however, before Schmettow could be flown back on one of the few planes now risking the night flight over Allied-occupied territory. He was summoned to report to Admiral Krancke, who accused him of being too "soft" in his treatment of the islands, and generally deficient in Nazi zeal. Schmettow half expected to disappear soon afterwards in a Hitler purge. But he was backed by his uncle, General von Rundstedt, and saved by the general confusion in Germany as defeat grew nearer.

Meanwhile, Hüffmeier announced to his soldiers in the islands:

At 12 noon, on February, 1945, I took over the Command of the Channel Islands and of the Fortress of Guernsey from General Graf von Schmettow, who has been called home, for reasons of health.

I have only one aim: to hold out until final victory.
I believe in the mission of our Führer and of our
people.
I shall serve them with immutable loyalty.
Heil our beloved Führer.

HUFFMEIER.
Vice-Admiral and Commander of the
Channel Islands.

Schmettow's other position, as Commander of the 319th
Infantry Division, went to Major General Wolfe, who
moved the Divisional Headquarters from Guernsey to
Jersey, where he became Commandant. The previous
Commandant in Jersey, Colonel Heine, was promoted
Major-General and went to Guernsey as Hüffmeier's Mili-
tary Adviser.

Colonel von Helldorf, von Schmettow's friend and
second-in-command, was deposed with him. Hüffmeier
gave the key positions to the Navy, Korvetten Kapitän
Reich being put in charge at the *Platzkommandantur* in
Guernsey, and Korvetten Kapitän von Cleve in Jersey.

Hüffmeier left no doubt of his determination to go on
fighting: had not Hitler declared, on the very day of Hüffmeier's appointment, that "no country in the world will
ever bring us down"? And it is hard not to admire the
audacity of one final German exploit planned by Schmettow, and carried out just after his supercession, but before
his return to Germany.

Towards the end of 1944, five German prisoners of war
had escaped from Granville, stolen a small boat, and eventually reached Jersey. They brought exact details about the
American troop locations at Granville. Count von Schmettow called for volunteers for the Germans to stage a Commando raid of their own on the port. A sand model was
built of it to brief the selected troops, and a firm in Guernsey made some scaling ladders. These preparations came
to the knowledge of M. Lambert in St. Peter Port, and he
sent out a warning among the papers he gave Golivet in-

side the lavatory on the Albert Pier. But the first attempt at the raid, on February 7, 1945, ran into bad weather. The landing boats got out of formation, their escorts were scattered, and the raid was called off; though one boat got close enough to shore to hear the jazz music from the American-occupied Hôtel des Bains, one of the objectives.

When nothing happened following Lambert's warning, the troops in Granville relaxed their precautions again. They were taken badly by surprise when the Germans came again next time the tide was right—on the night of March 8, 1945. At precisely 1 a.m., two German minesweepers sailed straight through the port entrance, followed by a tug. The signal station flashed a challenge: the Germans replied by the simple device of signalling back the same Morse letter. This apparently disarmed any suspicion: before the alarm was given, the two minesweepers had made fast at the piers, disgorging soldiers who held the port against sporadic counter-attacks while docks and shipping were destroyed.

As a diversion, a second party landed and surrounded the Hôtel des Bains, caught some assorted officers in bed, and carried them away as prisoners. ("But," said Schmettow afterwards in recounting the story, "they left the girls behind.") The Germans described their bag as one Colonel, one Captain, four other officers, an UNRRA official, and about twenty other prisoners, most of them escorted back to Jersey in their pyjamas.

They also claimed to have destroyed three ships (totalling 5,000 tons), eight cranes, a railway engine, and a petrol store; all for fewer than twenty German casualties. But some of the stories told of the exploit may have been exaggerated; not only by the Germans, but also by the French. It seems that some people of Granville had found that their American Occupation, so far as drink and women were concerned, contrasted unfavourably with the German Occupation; and they got some glee out of the way the Americans had been caught unawares.

There was one disappointment about the raid from the German point of view. It had been hoped to help out food or fuel supplies on the islands by capturing a ship complete with cargo. But the tide was going out, and most of the ships were aground and could only be scuttled, after exploding charges in the engine rooms. One 1,200-ton British collier, the *Eskwood*, was towed out of port by the tug, but the holds were nearly empty.

It seems that the French were not the only people to appreciate the daring of the raid; for one German account says that the crew of the *Eskwood* took a "sportsman-like view of the proceedings".

The arrival of the American prisoners of war in Jersey gave Hüffmeier particular pleasure. At his one previous meeting with Coutanche, Coutanche had ruffled him by remarking, "The truth is, we're both of us prisoners of the British Navy." There was an arrangement whereby the Germans always notified the island authorities how many prisoners of war they were holding, so that welfare organisations could arrange gift parcels. Hüffmeier sent a message to Coutanche: "Beg to report, there are now thirty more of us who are prisoners of the British Navy."

Some of the American prisoners of war, without the remotest idea of the privations and hardships being endured in the Channel Islands—or, for that matter, anywhere else —unwittingly caused some irritation by their reception of gift parcels, provided by the islanders at the price of real sacrifice. One, presented with a set of underwear, sent back a message that he never wore anything except silk; another, given a rare present of Virginia cigarettes, asked for blended next time. . . .

The Granville raiding party also released some thirty or forty German prisoners of war there, bringing them back to Jersey. Their grievance, perhaps, was even greater than that of the Americans; being transferred in a day from a life of good food and good treatment to a grim prospect of near starvation.

Although the raid had been planned, and neatly carried out, while Count von Schmettow was still Commander-in-Chief, Admiral Doenitz was quick to impress on Hitler that Hüffmeier had been "the heart and soul of this vigorous action". In reply to Doenitz's congratulations, Hüffmeier signalled that he hoped to hold on in the Channel Islands for another year.

Apart from the Granville raid, there was little enough to cheer the Germans, with the Allies crossing the Rhine and advancing into Germany. The Army newspapers in the Channel Islands, however, still remained valiant for victory. The *Deutsche Guernsey Zeitung* described the effects of the V2 under the headline *"Nichts als Trümmer"* (nothing but ruins) in England; and when all else failed on every front, the main news story would be of a U-boat exploit: "U-Boats sink 7 ships round England," "New Record for our U-Boats." It seems that, however grim the outlook might be, the *Deutsche Guernsey Zeitung* could always cheer itself up with a U-Boat exploit as a streamer on the front page, and a joke for the *Lach mit, Kamerad!* column at the back:

CHILD: Mummy, has our maid got wings?
MOTHER: Why?
CHILD: I heard Daddy calling her his lovely angel.
MOTHER: I'll soon send her flying!

And however bad the news, Admiral Hüffmeier's speeches to his troops still remained undaunted. According to a typical report of one of them in the *Deutsche Guernsey Zeitung* for March 19, 1945:

Vice-Admiral Hüffmeier left no doubt in the minds of his audience that, with firm, unshakable faith in the victory of our just cause, he is determined to hold as a pledge, to the very end, the Channel Islands which have been entrusted to him by the Führer.

A settlement of accounts with the Anglo-Americans, arms in hand, is quite possible, and perhaps not far ahead. . . .

Those who kept within their hearts the ideal of National Socialism, in its original purity, would have the upper hand.

It was the Channel Islanders on the Continent, in prisons and Nazi concentration camps, who were the first to be saved by the Allied victories. In Naumburg prison, on the

273

night of April 13, Frank Falla of G.U.N.S. heard the rumble of Paton's tanks. Next morning American soldiers came into the prison, and were heard shouting, "Any Americans or British here?" The frightened guards said *"Nein"*. Falla waited until an American Sergeant passed his cell, and then yelled with all his strength. His door was opened, and he stumbled out, mouth wide open, but no words would come. "Sit down and take it easy," said the Sergeant; and in a few minutes Falla was able to talk, and tell about his fellow British prisoners.

For others, release did not come so easily. As the Allies advanced, the Germans desperately brought back the concentration camp prisoners in nightmare journeys which could take their place in any annals of horror.

Harold le Druillenec was among those moved from Wilhelmshaven. For five days and five nights over a hundred men were crowded in one closed railway wagon, without sanitation, food or even water. Many were suffering from dysentery and hunger œdema, that terrible swelling of fluid in the legs and body which may follow semi-starvation. One man died whose blown-up body had turned quite black, and when le Druillenec and two helpers tried to drag it clear of the wagon it burst in their hands. All the time some men were dying, and others were losing their reason and shrieking as they trod down the sick in an effort to reach the air vents. An old French professor, as he lay dying in one corner, pleaded with them desperately: "Your only hope of life is to keep still. If you fight each other you use up air. Remember, gentlemen, you are civilised beings, whatever those swine may have done to degrade you."

His words brought quiet; and when he himself died, not long after, someone said a prayer over his body.

Le Druillenec, and two others who were still relatively sound mentally and physically, tried to bring about some order. Bodies were stacked at one end of the wagon; anyone who lost control of himself was knocked unconscious.

And so the prisoners reached—Belsen.

By now Belsen was crammed with thousands of men

sent on from other camps, and food supplies had almost ceased. The prisoners were eating grass or leaves, and were dying everywhere from starvation. Le Druillenec, through a blockhouse door, caught a glimpse of corpses stacked neatly in rows, score upon score of them, the crown of each head resting under the chin of another.

In another part of the camp le Druillenec, as he shuffled about, saw children playing among uncollected corpses.

The Crematorium stopped working because there was no fuel left, and the prisoners were told they had to dispose of the dead. Le Druillenec and the others dug great pits, dragging along the corpses by strips of blanket tied round their ankles. The half-dead buried the dead in thousands, driven on by the S.S. with guns and whips.

Once le Druillenec found, among the bodies, a Frenchman who was still just breathing. Quickly he dragged the man clear, hoping to return and help him later. But while he was away, working at the burial pits, the guards came on the Frenchman and threw him back in the mortuary. Here, next day, le Druillenec went searching for him again; but this time found him dead. Amid all the overwhelming and stupefying horror which surrounded him, le Druillenec found he could still feel pity for this one man he had failed to save.

Then suddenly the prisoners heard distant rifle shots, followed by the rumble of tanks.

The guards disappeared. Le Druillenec staggered into the compound and there he saw a British Army truck. He crawled towards it, crying: "Wait! Wait! I am British." The officer in charge stopped the truck and pulled him gently on to the bonnet, for he was too covered with lice to be put inside.

When he was taken to hospital, and given a mirror to shave himself, he looked round to see who the face belonged to: he did not recognise himself. He was later found to weigh seven stone, less than half his normal weight.

CHAPTER XLI

ASSASSINATION OR LIBERATION

In the Channel Islands, the rejoicing at the news of Allied advances, heard on hundreds and thousands of little crystal sets, was tempered by fear and foreboding of what Nazi fanaticism might yet have in store for them. As late as March 25 Hüffmeier, in the Forum cinema in St. Helier, was telling his troops that "I mean to hold out with you here until the Fatherland has won back its lost territory and the final victory is won." Rumours went round of gas chambers being built so that civilians could be killed off to save food: and the fact that the rumours later proved untrue did not make them any the less frightening at the time, to those who knew that Nazism had no limits. And one rumour began to be heard which *was* true. This was that Hüffmeier, realising at last that Germany was beaten, had nevertheless decided to hold out even after the war had ended. His idea was to keep the islands as a bargaining counter for Germany's representatives at the Peace Conference. This would mean the death of thousands of islanders, either under the bombardment of an Allied assault, or by starvation in a prolonged siege. And starvation now seemed to be very few weeks ahead, for the islanders and the German troops alike. It needed little imagination to think of the desperate acts of murder or mutiny to which men might be driven by hunger.

But Hüffmeier seemed determined to keep to his course and to crush any opposition.

On April 12, 1945, the *Platzkommandantur* in Jersey was ordered to draw up a list of a hundred civilians, considered dangerous to the Occupation, to be sent to a punishment camp on Alderney. With some difficulty, owing to the continued absence of any hint of a resistance movement, a list was compiled of fifty. But nothing further happened, the idea apparently being abandoned soon afterwards; and, fortunately for the peace of mind of the chosen, they never learnt of the fate for which they were being considered.

To Alderney, however, were sent a number of the Georgian soldiers whose plans for a mutiny, taken out by the le Page brothers, were suspected by Hüffmeier. Colonel von Helldorf, Schmettow's deposed Chief of Staff, was put under house arrest for a time; his hatred of Hüffmeier was only exceeded by Hüffmeier's suspicion of him. The Germans on the island, as in Germany itself, were split more and more by secret intrigues and secret fears.

Among those whose fears were greatest was Baron von Aufsess, who had heard no news of his wife since her arrest by the Gestapo for speaking her mind about Hitler. Aufsess felt it inevitable that Nazi suspicion would soon fall on him too, and he made plans to escape. He provided himself with a set of false papers, describing himself as a French worker, and authenticated by a *Platzkommandantur* stamp of his own manufacture. He got to know two Jerseymen who were also planning to escape, and who had a boat ready in Gorey harbour. Aufsess got some petrol, and enough food for eight days. He knew the German Army Captain in command of an area near there, and who would see that the sentries were looking the other way. He had another friend in the wireless office, who had agreed to give an advance warning if any signal came from Berlin ordering Aufsess to be arrested.

Then Aufsess was disconcerted instead by a sudden order to report to Hüffmeier in Guernsey. His first thought was that this was a summons to be shot. But at the time it was low tide, and escaping would have meant dragging the boat a mile out to sea before it could be launched. Aufsess had a talk with von Cleve at the *Platzkommandantur*, who said—as proved to be the case—that the posting to Guernsey was only part of a general interchange ordered by Hüffmeier, on the ground that German officials had got too friendly with local inhabitants where they were stationed.

Before he left Aufsess asked Duret Aubin to see him secretly at Langford, the German Officers' Club. Aufsess took him down to the lawn, to sit on two deck chairs where they could talk without being overheard.

"The Admiral has gone mad," began Aufsess. "He is giving the wildest orders."

Aufsess told how he had planned to escape from Jersey, but was now being transferred to Guernsey. If he had the chance there, he would not stop short of trying to get rid of Hüffmeier, should Hüffmeier carry out his plan to hold on to the islands even after the war ended. Aufsess would have no hesitation now in removing a man whom he believed to be set on useless carnage. For all he knew, his wife might already have been shot by the Nazis.

As for Duret Aubin, his liberty and perhaps his life were in danger; for Hüffmeier's main complaint against the previous German administration was that it had been too friendly and made too many concessions to men like Duret Aubin. Aufsess warned him to watch von Cleve. So long as von Cleve was there, he would refuse to carry out Hüffmeier's worst orders. If he went, that would be Duret Aubin's final warning.

Arriving in St. Peter Port, Aufsess was given a subordinate position at the Guernsey branch of the *Platzkommandantur*, under Korvettenkapitän Reich. Aufsess was just in time to hear Hüffmeier's speech for Hitler's birthday on April 20. A mass parade was called in the Regal (Odeon) Cinema. Hüffmeier strode on to the stage, which was draped with a swastika. He stood erect under the spotlights, and gave the Nazi salute. Then—always a master orator—he paused dramatically in complete silence before beginning to speak. He called on them to fight for the Führer to the end; he told them to think of their wives and children in Germany. . . . His speech was so skilful that even anti-Nazi officers found that, in spite of themselves, they were half believing it. But Hüffmeier seemed to make little impression on most of the rank-and-file. Their chief topic of conversation afterwards, as they filed out, was that they were now to lose their last miserable comfort, the issue of three cigarettes a day.

On April 23, 1945, two men met in Guernsey to plot the removal of Hüffmeier. By now, he had not only made plain his intention to hold on even after the war ended. It was believed that, if finally overcome, he would believe it to be his duty to blow up all the ammunition stores—which might have destroyed half the islands.

The two plotters were Baron von Helldorf, Schmettow's deposed Chief of Staff, and the Baron von Aufsess. They agreed that, to stop a crime being committed in the name of Germany, it might be necessary to kill Hüffmeier, and for Helldorf to take his place. Helldorf and Aufsess talked till late in the night, almost in whispers, going to the door from time to time to make sure no one was listening outside. As they talked, they drank port. "What with the port wine and the plans"—von Aufsess wrote afterwards—"we became quite jolly. I never realised that serious matters could be discussed in such an atmosphere."

At the time there was an Officers' Club at Castle Carey. Baron von Aufsess now passed on to von Helldorf the information that Hüffmeier always went to this Club at nine o'clock every morning to drink a glass of milk. Hüffmeier could be surprised there alone. That was all that Helldorf needed to know.

But Hüffmeier, having suspected Helldorf for some time, abruptly banished him on April 28 to the island of Herm, with only a fisherman and his wife to look after him. This placed von Aufsess in a difficulty: although by now both he and von Helldorf had enlisted supporters in the plot, they had agreed not to tell each other who their supporters were; and von Aufsess did not know what men had pledged themselves to back Helldorf. He was left wondering if fate would call upon him to take Hüffmeier's life himself, should Hüffmeier prove as obdurate as expected.

No one can say how many people, all plotting and planning in secret, were ready to encompass the death or downfall of Hüffmeier. Another of them—as might be guessed—

was the ebullient M. Lambert, the French consular agent in St. Peter Port. Early every morning, M. Lambert noticed, Hüffmeier walked a hundred yards or so through a garden which provided a short cut between the house where he was living and his headquarters. Lambert's plan was to use an attractive woman—Hüffmeier had an eye for attractive women—to decoy him to a place where he could be captured by Alsatians serving in the German Army, chloroformed, and taken on a boat to England.

There were more ambitious plans for a general mutiny by the German soldiers, inspired by anti-Nazis among them. Early in March, ammunition stores in the Palace Hotel in St. Helier, used as a German training centre, were blown up with over thirty casualties—though it was never definitely established whether it was sabotage or an accident. Typed manifestos were circulated among the Germans, with such repeated slogans as *Death to the Nazis! Long live a free Germany!* Another began:

Comrades!

In Germany to-day the breaking up of the Hitler regime is nearly completed. The German people have seen through the swindle, and now the Nazi clique must defend their own lives after sending millions to their deaths for the obstinate ideas of the man called Hitler.

When the signal is given for rebellion, tie a white towel or handkerchief round your left arm. . . .

One mutiny was planned for May 1—May Day. On the firing of a gun on Fort Elizabeth, soldiers were to kill any Nazis among their officers.

It is doubtful whether any of these mutinies planned on paper would have materialised, even if the plans had not been overtaken by the march of events. The beginning of May brought no mere rebellion against Hitler's officers, but celebrations of the death of Hitler himself. Yet even the rejoicing at this event, and the imminent end of 'the war, was heavily clouded by anxiety about what might come next so far as the islands were concerned. Hüffmeier showed no sign of mitigating his truculence. When the *Vega* arrived at St. Peter Port soon after, on another of her regular visits. Hüffmeier demanded that she should fly a flag at half-mast for Hitler; on the captain refusing, Hüffmeier grandly retaliated by not inviting him to the ceremonial obsequies which he was holding. An Allied ship appeared off Alderney, and signalled (by Morse flash-lamp) proposals for the German surrender of the islands. Hüffmeier replied: *Ihr Angebot ist überflüssig*. (Literally, "Your offer is superfluous," or "You're wasting your time.")

Hüffmeier was beginning to show, however, something of the nervous strain of a man who knows his life is threatened. When he crossed to Sark to address the garrison there, he was so afraid of assassination that he began by making his audience pile their arms on one side. He then harangued them about the horrible treatment which the British gave to any Germans who allowed themselves to be taken prisoner.

Hüffmeier went to Jersey on Sunday, May 6. Von Cleve, at the *Platzkommandantur*, told Coutanche of his relief that Hitler had been succeeded by Admiral Doenitz, and not by Himmler. Von Cleve thought Hüffmeier might obey an order to surrender from Doenitz.

As a matter of fact, though Coutanche could not know it, Hüffmeier had gone to Jersey because he had arranged another raid on Granville for the following day. This was only stopped at the last moment by a strict order from Doenitz on the Sunday afternoon.

By the following day, Monday, May 7, the whole world knew that the war was virtually over. But, when John Leale was summoned to a meeting at the *Platzkommandantur* in Guernsey, he found no sign of any disposition to give up. The only formal business was a German protest because some Union Jacks had been seen flying in the town. This provocative behaviour, Leale was told, must cease.

That same night the Germans doubled all their guards. Liberation might be at hand, but it appeared likely that it would be liberation with bloodshed. It seemed that hundreds and perhaps thousands of men and women, for whose survival Leale had worked and struggled and planned and been patient for all these years, were doomed to die beneath a bombardment from their own countrymen.

Next morning, Tuesday, May 8, they went to the offices of the Controlling Committee, and still there was no news. Louis Guillemette, in his direct way, could not stand the suspense. "I'm going up to Grange Lodge to find out." He came back to say that Leale and the Bailiff were wanted at the Royal Court House at 10.30.

Victor Carey, Leale and Guillemette waited in the Bailiff's room. Punctually at the time stated, there entered Baron von Aufsess and Korvettekapitän Reich. The first words Leale heard were: *"Der Krieg ist zu Ende, und in den Kanalinseln auch."* He knew enough German to understand without waiting for the translation: "The war is ended, and in the Channel Islands too."

Leale thought he felt his heart turn over.

Nothing else mattered now, not even the reason for Hüffmeier's last minute capitulation. Perhaps Hüffmeier felt he could not disobey an order to surrender from his immediate superior, Admiral Doenitz; perhaps he realised that his officers would have refused to stand by him if he did. Leale scarcely heard what happened at the rest of the interview. The Bailiff was saying that he thought he should call a meeting of the State at midday to give them the news formally, and the Germans agreed. Someone remembered to ask for an assurance that the Germans would not carry out any sabotage or demolition before the British forces came. No, said the Germans, they would not blow anything up.

The Germans told them that Churchill was broadcasting that afternoon at three, and they asked that no Union Jacks should be flown till afterwards. Then they offered politely to lend a wireless set for hearing the speech.

"You needn't worry," said Guillemette. "We've had our own sets for months."

In Jersey, Churchill's speech was relayed over loud-speakers in Royal Square. Then Coutanche appeared on the balcony. "It is nearly five years since I have spoken to you from this place," he said. "On that occasion I prayed that the blessing of God might rest upon you in your days of trial. To-day my first words must still be a prayer, and I would ask you to join me in offering thanks to Almighty God for the deliverance of this dear island of ours."

Then Coutanche made a typically dramatic gesture. For five years the invaders had stood between him and his people; and he knew that criticism of himself had mounted without his having a chance to reply. He knew that, in the crowd, there was a spirit of vengeance as well as joy. Soon "Jerrybags" were to be shouted at in the streets and threatened with head-shaving. Soon the cry would go up: "Punish the collaborators and informers!" Coutanche knew that there might be those who did not know the full facts, and would include his name among the first.

He called out: "Wait a moment until I can come among you." He left the balcony and went down to the Square. Standing on a chair on the pavement, surrounded by his fellow Jerseymen, he finished his speech and finally led them in singing "God Save the King". Then there came such a tumult of cheering, so many hands outstretched in thanks and friendliness, that Coutanche knew his work for five years had not been for nothing. . . .

At Laufen, Major Sherwill had spent a busy morning, helping the camp staff to shovel portraits of Adolf Hitler on to a fire. He was asked if there was anything the internees wanted. "Yes," said Sherwill, "a wireless set in good working order." It was only just fixed in time: the familiar voice was already speaking when they switched on:

". . . Hostilities end officially at one minute after midnight on Tuesday, the eighth of May, but in the interests of saving life the 'Cease fire' began yesterday to be sounded all along the front, *and our dear Channel Islands are also to be freed to-day.*"

At these words, Sherwill was not the only one who was not ashamed to show tears.

Addressing the States in Guernsey, Victor Carey had most prudently suggested that, though flags might be hoisted after Churchill had spoken at three o'clock, there should be no further celebration until the arrival of British soldiers, apart from Thanksgiving Services in the churches. One such service was held that evening in St. Sampson's Church; and following it the German padre asked and received permission for the Germans to hold their own service too, their own thanksgiving for the end of the war. When it was over the padre wrote in the Church Service Register:

"*Ich danke für alle Leibe Christus, die wir während unserer Zeit auf Guernsey in diesem Gotteshause erfahren haben . . .*"

"I give my thanks for all the love of Christ which has come to us in this house of God during our stay in Guernsey. I pray that the Lord may lead the world towards the Eternal goal of His Heavenly Kingdom and establish a Peace higher than all human understanding."

Hüffmeier addressed a mass parade—his last—in the Regal Cinema. He was defiant to the end. When the British officers arrived, he told his soldiers, they should be saluted in the streets—with Nazi salutes. His audience trooped out of the cinema into an island transformed, with Union Jacks flying everywhere.

Tuesday night passed in a state of expectancy: some Germans, however, felt something more was called for. The neighbours saw an odd spectacle at one house in Queen's Road which was used as a soldiers' club. A line of Germans could be seen winding about through the grounds, each with a blazing torch in one hand and a bottle of champagne in the other, and singing as they went. One of them explained: "If the British won't celebrate their victory, we thought we'd better celebrate it for them."

CHAPTER XLII

"OPERATION NEST EGG"

Though Tuesday night was something of an anti-climax
in both Guernsey and Jersey, with no sign of the relieving
British forces which were expected at any moment, the fault
did not lie with the British Government. Back in England,
Naval Force 135 had spent many months preparing
"Operation Nest Egg"—the liberation of the Channel
Islands. Apparently it had always been understood that
this would never be attempted by force: in September
1944, the Outline Plan laid down that "The operation will
take place after the surrender of the German Garrison."
But the possibility of sporadic resistance, demolitions and
booby traps could not be overlooked. The inhabitants of
Brixham Harbour, chosen for rehearsals because it was like
St. Peter Port, had grown used to the spectacle of soldiers
practising coming ashore, and picking their way carefully
up the streets to avoid objects meant to represent mines.
One of these occasions even ended with an embarrassed
officer mounting a box and gesticulating with a piece of
paper held in front of him: that was a rehearsal of the
reading of a proclamation to the liberated islanders.

It was 10 a.m. on the Tuesday morning, May 8, that the
destroyer *Bulldog*, with the destroyer *Beagle* as escort, left
Plymouth for a rendezvous with the Germans four miles
off Guernsey. The German surrender ship, arriving precisely at 2 p.m., was a dirty minesweeper, red with rust,
and flying a swastika. From it there was launched a rubber
dinghy, with three German soldiers paddling in front, and
a slim young naval officer, carrying an attaché case and
getting very wet from spray, sitting in the stern. The young

officer was piped aboard the *Bulldog* to the click of saluting rifles. He gave a Nazi salute, and was escorted to the wardroom.

He was Lieutenant Commander Zimmermann, sent with a paper authorising him to receive armistice terms and take them to Admiral Hüffmeier.

Brigadier Snow, in command of "Operation Nest Egg", said that it was not a matter of an armistice. Zimmermann would be sent back with a copy of an instrument of surrender—immediate surrender—and instructions to keep another rendezvous. Zimmermann agreed, but then he stood up and declared: "I am instructed to inform you that your ships must move away from these shores. Otherwise Admiral Hüffmeier will regard their presence as a breach of faith and a provocative act."

His face broke into a sweat as he said it, as though rather taken aback himself at this bravado. The British officers were equally astonished when they realised the implication of the threat. Brigadier Snow is reported to have growled: "Tell Admiral Hüffmeier that if he opens fire on us we will hang him to-morrow." Nevertheless, not taking any chances, *Bulldog* and *Beagle* withdrew on patrol till the time for the next rendezvous—at midnight.

Zimmermann now came back from St. Peter Port in an armed trawler with Hüffmeier's military adviser, Major-General Heine, an ornate figure in a light-blue great-coat with huge red lapels. Hüffmeier himself was afraid to come out for fear of his own troops. He sent a rather plaintive message to Brigadier Snow: "I allowed the English population to fly flags and hold religious services, and therefore had to foresee that a certain agitation might be created among my soldiers. This has happened. I was and am, therefore, not in a position to meet you personally."

Heine, however, brought with him Hüffmeier's authority to sign an unconditional surrender. For two hours they went into detailed arrangements: then Heine was escorted to a cabin. After dawn, 7.45 a.m. on Wednesday, May 9, 1945, he signed eight copies of the surrender documents, and the Channel Islands were free again.

A German soldier climbed to the top of a quayside crane in St. Peter Port, and flew a Union Jack from it.

Soon afterwards the first British soldiers, led by Colonels Power and Stoneman, came ashore to a delirious welcome. It was not long before Colonel Power's cap had been knocked off his bald head, and his head itself covered with lipstick marks from all the girls who planted him with kisses.

For years, John Leale had dreamt of the day when British troops would step ashore on the island again, and he would be the first to greet them. During the night when Heine had gone out to surrender, for the first time during the Occupation, Leale did not sleep at all. But he was still in his bed next morning when Power and Stoneman arrived at his house. And so, with all the fine speeches and ceremonies which were to have marked the great occasion forgotten, John Leale came down to greet the Liberation forces in his pyjamas and an old dressing-gown.

Meanwhile, in Jersey, the Bailiff was still sitting in the Royal Court House waiting for something to happen. It was his birthday, and he was impatient for his birthday celebration to begin. The British authorities, knowing something of the traditional rivalry between Jersey and Guernsey, would doubtless have tactfully preferred to arrange their Liberation simultaneously: but the fact that Hüffmeier was in Guernsey inevitably meant that it should come first.

All that happened for Coutanche so far was a call from Colonel Power, speaking from Guernsey, to say that the destroyer *Beagle* was on the way.

The Bailiff went on pacing up and down for what seemed an interminable time.

The phone rang again

Would the Bailiff call at the Pomme d'Or Hotel at 12 o'clock, and take out General Wolfe to the *Beagle* to surrender?

"I have never received an order," said Coutanche, "which it gives me more pleasure to obey."

At the Pomme d'Or, Coutanche found that Wolfe, the

Military Commandant in Jersey, was proposing to take two of his staff officers out to the *Beagle*. "Very well," said Coutanche, "if you're taking your staff officers I must have mine." And he insisted on holding up the proceedings while he sent for Duret Aubin, the Attorney-General, and Cecil Harrison, the Solicitor-General. Then they all went out together to the *Beagle* in a launch, Coutanche waving gaily to the crowds.

Aboard, the formal surrender was soon signed, and Coutanche was asked to stay to lunch.

He and his party were offered pink gins—their first for years—and Coutanche lit his pipe. After a while one of the officers wrinkled his nose and remarked, "There's a rather peculiar smell about." Soon they were all sniffing, but it was some time before Coutanche realised that they were referring to his home-grown Occupation tobacco. . . When they understood the situation, the Navy responded with typical hospitality: "Steward, a tin of tobacco for the gentleman. Tins for all the gentlemen." They went into the wash-room, and Coutanche remarked how strange it was to see real soap again. "Steward, a cake of soap all round." And by the way, how were they off for shaving soap? "Steward, sticks of shaving soap." Soon their pockets were all bulging.

Was there anything else the Navy could do for Coutanche? Yes, he would like to send off two official signals.

One to the King, rejoicing "that we can once more take our place and play our part within Your Majesty's Empire."

One to the Prime Minister: ". . . On this day of liberation I address to you in the name of the States and People of Jersey our undying gratitude to you for your inspired leadership. . . ."

Anything else? Yes, said Coutanche, but it was a personal thing, which he had really no right to ask for. He had had no news of his son in the Navy for over a year. He did not even know whether he was still alive. They sent for a Navy List, and found his son's name in it. Yes, said Coutanche, but the list was eight months old . . . In the meanwhile? . . . Would they mind? And so a third signal followed the other two, asking the Admiralty for the latest news of Midshipman Coutanche.

They were having lunch when a slip of paper was handed to Coutanche. It was a reply to his first signal, and a similar one from Guernsey:

From Admiral Stuart . . . H.M. The KING has received your messages and . . . they gave him great pleasure and satisfaction.
Type of code: P-L.   -102358.

Then came a second message:

To Bailiff of Jersey from C. in C. Plymouth. Following received begins. From the Prime Minister to the Bailiff of Jersey. You should have heard the House of Commons cheer at the news of your liberation. Every good wish. Ends.
Code: Light via Crosby.   2231.

For a third time there was a message for Coutanche. Everyone knew what it would be about.

He took it and read:

Sub-Lieutenant J. A. G. Coutanche granted leave of absence to-day.

Next came the turn of Sark to be liberated. The Liberation Force felt some concern about what was going on there, which they would have been spared if they had known the Dame of Sark better.

On Tuesday night a huge fire had been seen burning there by the *Beagle* and the *Bulldog*, and it was feared that the Germans were indulging in an orgy of destruction. In fact it was a liberation bonfire, long prepared and energetically organised by Mrs. Hathaway. At eleven o'clock that morning, in advance of the official surrender, she had defiantly hoisted the Union Jack and the Stars and Stripes at the Seigneurie; at three o'clock the whole island had assembled at the village hall to hear Churchill.

After the British troops had landed in Guernsey on the Wednesday, they tried to get through to Sark on the telephone, but the Germans on the other end were not answering. Next day a naval tug took over a small detachment, under Colonel Allen, to find out what was happening.

There was not a German to be seen when they landed, but Mrs. Hathaway promptly took charge of the situation, leading the party to German Headquarters. They found the Germans had locked themselves in, and they had to hammer on the door till one of them came out fearfully. Mrs. Hathaway then proceeded to arrange the surrender, with herself acting as interpreter.

Colonel Allen explained apologetically that he could not put any men on the island for the moment; would Mrs. Hathaway mind being left on her own? She replied that Colonel Allen need only authorise her to give the Germans what orders she wanted, and she would be only too delighted. So she enjoyed herself hugely for the next few days while the Germans, under her supervision, began clearing up the island by removing posts put up in the fields against glider landings, and disposing of the land mines.

The people of Sark came upon one final piece of evidence of the astonishing discipline of the Germans. Towards the end the soldiers had been so weak from lack of food that they could be seen collapsing when walking up the hill from the harbour. But, stored in the Girls' School, there was found three months' food supplies, untouched, which they had been ordered by Hüffmeier to keep intact for any final last ditch stand.

Last of all came the liberation of Alderney. By now only a handful of Britishers remained with the German garrison, the remnants of those who had worked on the farms or buildings, and had stayed on when Alderney was partially evacuated. There was also Frank Oselton, the wiry farmer who had stayed with his cattle the whole time, and George Pope the mystery man.

Oselton, with matted hair and the unkempt looks of a man whose wife had been away five years, was waiting on the quay with a huge milk pail when the British troops arrived, and offered them all glasses of milk as they came ashore. Pope was waiting with tales of German atrocities to feed eager journalists.

Little evidence remained at Alderney, by now, of what

had gone before: nothing but squalid desolation. Everywhere were concrete fortifications and gun posts, many of them already beginning to get water-logged. Barbed wire abounded. As the liberating force went in, they saw flames from the Germans burning the wooden concentration camp buildings, so that nothing was left but the concrete foundations and the barbed wire. The Alsatian dogs were now roaming loose. Lying in the bottom of Judge French's garden was found a swagger cane reinforced with steel wire, some relic of the methods of the S.S.

CHAPTER XLIII

THE MEN WHO CAME BACK

And now it was all over. The Germans went out, and the British came in.

There went out Admiral Hüffmeier, marched down to the quayside, watched by mostly silent crowds. He had been seen so little by ordinary people in Guernsey that some of them, thinking his uniform was that of the British Navy, cheered him in mistake for a British admiral. He was eventually to arrive at Waterloo Station, where few people paid any attention to him as he travelled (by Metropolitan Line) to his interrogation.

There went out the German soldiers, twenty-thousand within a fortnight, to prisoner of war camps in England. Sometimes their departure was not without sympathy: some people in Sark complained that they were herded in a field all day without food while waiting to be taken off from the harbour.

In time, the German prisoners of war went on from England to Germany, with one interesting exception. Phyllis Baker of Sark went to England to see Werner Rang, whom she had first met when Rang had been sent round, as a German Medical Orderly, with some pills for her. They got permission to marry a few days before he was due to be repatriated; and so both could return to live on Sark.

There came in to the islands more and more detachments of British Tommies, receiving a rapturous welcome. The islanders were amused to notice, lining the quays to pick them up, some of the very same girls who had been free with the Germans. ... Helped by some German prisoners kept behind for the purpose, the soldiers tackled the huge task of clearing up the mess in the islands—beginning with half a dead horse, partly prepared for the cookhouse, found in the reception hall of the Pomme d'Or Hotel, the German Naval Headquarters.

May Sherwill, who had been living in the basement of her home with seventy German soldiers above, had grown used to formal Germans knocking punctiliously, standing to attention, and saluting before making the simplest request. Now she had Tommies clattering down the steps, with some such cheery request as "Got any milk, Ma?"

There came in to the islands Mr. Herbert Morrison, the Home Secretary. In Guernsey, Victor Carey was somewhat taken aback to find a cheerful Cockney like Morrison introducing himself as the Secretary of State for the Home Department. Carey had not realised that Britain had a Coalition Government, with Socialists in it. In Jersey, Morrison stayed with Alexander Coutanche, and they were talking most of the night. In a speech next day Morrison expressed full appreciation of Coutanche's "sterling work, courage and integrity," adding jokingly: "If anything he has done requires whitewashing, I will take care of it for him."

There came in innumerable officials from Whitehall, armed with bowler hats and brief cases. The careful accounts of the cost of the evacuees in England were scrapped; any nominal debts owing by the islands were written off, and a free gift of £7,000,000 was made to them by the British Exchequer, to help pay off the indebtedness to the banks.

There came in Home Office medical experts, who decided that the health of the islanders was much better than expected. (But a number of people were to die in the next few years from delayed effects. Coutanche himself had a breakdown which lasted many months. Duret Aubin had to resign as Attorney-General in Jersey, owing to illness brought on by nervous strain.)

There came back to the islands the children who had left five years before: and there were heartaches as well as happiness. For often they were different children with a new outlook, even a new language, with "Ba Gooms" from Lancashire or a Scots accent picked up in Glasgow; and their mothers and fathers realised that the five years had turned their own children into strangers, and made a gulf which might never be bridged.

Just after the Liberation, Coutanche had an important conference in the Bailiff's Chambers in Jersey, with senior servicemen, to discuss security arrangements for a coming visit of the King and Queen. He was surprised to be interrupted by a young naval officer, who saluted and stood stiffly to attention in the doorway. Coutanche looked up irritably.

"What do you want?"

"Don't you know me?"

"No—who are you?"

The young officer kept to attention for a moment longer. Then he stepped forward and said "Dad! "

After five years, Sub-Lieutenant J. A. G. Coutanche was home on leave. . . .

The evacuees of 1940 did not always come back to a happy welcome. There was an undercurrent of feeling between the "Occ-occs" and the "anti-Occ-occs", between those who stayed during the Occupation and those who had gone. The latter would be told "You ran away." They would retort: "While you were getting on all right here with the Germans, *we* were helping to win the war for you." It took some years for these multiple wounds to be healed; and they were not helped by the presence of those island farmers and shopkeepers who had not appeared too prosperous in 1940, but now seemed to have money to burn. . . . Both Jersey and Guernsey introduced retrospective taxation of war profits: but, as always, the smartest profiteers found ways of escaping the net.

Who else came back? There was cheery Sergeant Ferbrache, awarded the D.C.M. for landing in Guernsey to look for Martel and Mulholland, the two forerunners of the 1940 Commando Raid. He returned to his job as a foreman with Wheadons. Philip Martel himself came back to St. Peter Port to manage his family jewellery business. Rogers in the Arcade. Desmond Mulholland, after surviving his adventures as a spy and nearly five years in a prison camp, went to Brighton for a holiday. He was overcome in a bath by fumes from a gas heater, and found dead.

There came back, after long years of imprisonment, Nicolle and Symes, the other two officers whose landing on Guernsey had caused such an upheaval. Each got the Military Cross. It would be true to sentiment if they had married the sweethearts who came into the dranatic events of 1940; but real life rarely has story-book endings. Jessie Marriette and Mary Bird married other men and left the island after the war. Symes and Nicolle both married other girls. Symes stayed in the Regular Army; Nicolle became a life insurance agent in Guernsey.

There came back Captain Fred Noyon, who had taken such chances escaping with papers to England. He called on the member of Controlling Committee who had been most grateful to him at the time for volunteering to go. "I'm sorry I can't see you now," said this man. "I'm very busy."

Some Channel Islanders were never to return. Over two hundred Guernseymen had died fighting with the British Forces.* As for the Commando visitors to the islands, not only Geoffrey Appleyard and Anders Lassen, but all three

* The exact figures were Guernsey 221, Alderney 18, Sark 1. We were surprised to find no figures for Jersey available.

other officers in the 1942 Commando raid on Sark, had failed to survive the war. Each of the five had gone back into action again and again until he had been killed; for that is the kind of men they were, and that is the rule of war, which will kill the best so that the rest may live.

There came into the islands young George Dawson, quickly off the mark, sent out with the blessing of Whitehall to buy up the steel in the German fortifications for scrap. Dawson arrived in Guernsey with a wad of notes in his wallet, calling everybody "Sir", and in no mood to waste any time. "So much a ton?—Done!" According to a subsequent account of his rise to fortune, "the start was in the Channel Islands". He swiftly bought plenty of scrap which he swiftly re-sold for more than he paid for it, and departed on the road to further riches through buying and selling the debris of war.

To Alderney there came back Brigadier French, who had led his fellow islanders away five years before, and now gave up a big job in the War Office to lead them back. They found an island of rusty barbed wire and waterlogged bunkers, farms gone to ruin and overrun by rats, weeds growing in the streets of St. Anne's, and houses stripped of doors and staircases and any other woodwork that could be ripped down by Todt workers for fires to cook their meals.

A W.V.S. team, doing valiant work, helped in the herculean task of recovery. Farming was re-started on a communal basis. Land was re-seeded with pasture grasses. And an attempt was made to re-distribute the remains of people's furniture on different stores, giving rise to the legend now known as "The Battle of the Butes". According to this, surviving furniture was placed in different occasions upon the Butes, where Judge French had made his speech before the evacuation; and at a given signal the islanders went forward to claim their own possessions. The story has it that as many as six women might be seen sitting on the same bed, or fighting over the same sofa; and the bitterness was to survive for years. The present authors, innocently enquiring about someone's whereabouts, were told tartly by one woman: "I wouldn't know and I wouldn't care; she's still got a chest of drawers of mine from the Butes, for she says it was her grandmother's."

Gradually life was got going again in Alderney, but with something of a personal tragedy. French and his wife were not always popular: a duodenal ulcer, the legacy of his heavy responsibilities at the War Office, sometimes added to the peremptoriness of his manner. He found an undercurrent of criticism, too, from some of the very men who had clamoured five years ago for him to get them away from the Germans. The Occupation, these now said to themselves, hadn't been half so bad after all; but for French they might have all stayed put on their farms and done nicely selling food to the German Army, instead of coming back to find everything they possessed in ruins . . .

Less than two years after his return, Brigadier French had resigned. He retired, not without some bitterness, into private life, keeping very much to himself, and spending his time writing Elementary English text books, sold in big numbers in the colonies by the Oxford University Press.

To Sark there came back Bob Hathaway and Mrs. Pittard, Miss Duckett and Miss Page, from internment in Germany. The Dixcart Hotel was by now wrecked and verminous, with most of the furniture broken or stolen, and £500 worth of wines and spirits missing—the entire stock. Miss Duckett and Miss Page got no compensation at all, then or thereafter, but proceeded undaunted to build up their business again.

Miss Page made a point of re-visiting Paris as soon as possible, dressed in her best clothes, to eradicate the memory of how she had been marched through the streets there on the way to Biberach.

To Guernsey there came back Bill Symes, after the grim journey through prison camps and Buchenwald which had begun when he was caught sending out messages to a British Intelligence Agent. He found himself with a wife and four children to support on their return from evacuation in England, and with no home, no job and no money.

There came back Frank Falla of G.U.N.S., from Naumburg prison. On the way he stayed with his sister-in-law in Manchester, where a newspaper was putting on a "Belsen Exhibition". Falla went to it but soon came out again—"I overheard people saying it was all propaganda and couldn't be true, and I felt sick at their stupidity."

When Falla got home to Guernsey he found, like others, that there was no compensation or recognition for losses suffered through patriotism, whoever else might have made money. He had to go back to work again while still a sick man, and sometimes he found the struggle hard. But on the last Saturday of each April he always had a reunion dinner with Legg, Duquemin, and one or two other Guernseymen who had survived imprisonment on the Continent. "We eat what we like," explained Falla. "We drink what we like. We have as many cigarettes as we want. Our toast is 'Absent Friends', and we think about the chaps who died, like Canon Cohu—a fine and brave man."

There came back Stanley Green, to his little printing business and his old job at West's cinema in St. Helier; where few laughing holiday-makers knew that the man in the projection-box behind them had suffered in Buchenwald.

There came back Harold le Druillenec from Belsen, after a long, critical illness with a mental breakdown. His mind sought relief from the memories of the past in fantasy—he told his nurses that he was a rich man and owned a yacht, and had to take Churchill away on it for a holiday; and he was immensely cheerful. Then his robust physique and mental resilience carried him back to his usual self: the only thing that showed the past was that he no longer cared for solitary reading or writing. He was now always on the go, always active.

There came back Herbert Gallichan, who had protested against the confiscation of wireless sets. Even after Wolfenbüttel concentration camp he kept a spirit of Christian charity towards his enemies, and he afterwards became a missionary.

There were some who came back but who never recovered. One gay and attractive young girl had been deported by the Germans and kept in solitary confinement. Her mind was affected, and though she often seemed normal and her old self, she would then act queerly and become aggressive, complaining that everyone was against her. She was kept quietly by her family at home.

There were some islanders, like Mrs. Gould and the Painters, who were never to return at all. It was not till December 1945 that Mrs. Cohu had any definite news of Canon Cohu of St. Saviour's. Then a letter from a fellow prisoner reached the Jersey authorities.

It seemed that, some time in September 1944, Canon Cohu had been sent to the concentration camp at Spergau. Already he was a sick man, and picked out for special malice and brutalities as an Englishman. When his group of prisoners arrived, a sadistic German guard called out *"Welcher is der Engländer?"* and then told Cohu *"Du wirst da krepieren"*. Cohu, bullied and beaten, was sent out to work every day, although he was so weak that he could hardly lift his shovel. At night he would return to sleep in a squalid little tent, on a palliasse laid on the earth. He had not been at Spergau long before he had a violent attack of dysentery. There was no medical attention. A few days later, lying in filth on a dirty palliasse, Canon Cohu died.

Prisoners in concentration camps were forbidden to have books. But after Cohu's death there was found on his breast, hidden under his shirt, a little Bible.

CHAPTER XLIV

HONOURS AND INFAMY

What of the informers responsible for fellow islanders suffering and dying in concentration camps? What of the tiny few who became notorious for favouring the enemy? One woman in Jersey, a creature with a particularly evil reputation, was so frightened of revenge that she fled to the prison and asked to be locked up; after sheltering in a cell there for some days, she went to England. So did others. But some who had informed, and some who had been over-helpful to the Germans, still stayed on, apparently unaffected by what their neighbours said and thought. Often it was their children who suffered most, through the jeers and torments of schoolmates. Sometimes there were miscarriages of the rough justice of public opinion. After the Occupation there was published, in an official report in Guernsey, a strong criticism of the activities of Timmer Ltd., which had grown food for the German soldiers. But there was more than one Timmer on the island, and there could be confusion between them

The "Jersey Loyalists", formed by Major Manley and Major L'Amy, demanded a Court of Inquiry to investigate charges of any disloyal conduct during the Occupation. But their efforts were completely unsuccessful, and a bland legalistic blanket came down to protect the guilty. It was explained that being an informer was not an indictable offence. Could not legislation be introduced to make it indictable? No, said the lawyers properly, changes in the criminal law could not be retrospective. What about proceedings under the Defence of the Realm Act? No, said the lawyers, this had been made inapplicable to the Channel Islands during the Occupation. The Jersey Loyalists had to admit that officialdom had an answer to everything; and most people were glad enough to get back to the slow-moving ways of British justice, which even discouraged informing on informers, after their experience of the Nazi variety.

There had been unbridled talk, during the war, of taking private revenge after it on "Jerrybags". In Guernsey, anonymous letters had been sent by people calling themselves the G.U.B. or Guernsey Underground Barbers, threatening head-shaving or worse. Nothing came of such threats, though in Jersey there was one ugly incident when a girl was chased by hooligans in St. Helier, and some others lost jobs as waitresses or shop assistants after anonymous phone calls had told their employers that otherwise the premises would be wrecked.

It was in Jersey that the demand was strongest, though completely frustrated, for an official action against disloyal conduct. In Guernsey, the influence of John Leale was thrown strongly against any recriminations over the past. When the British Liberation Force arrived, its Security Officers soon tired of listening to people who accused everyone but themselves of collaboration, and were glad enough when they could give up their investigations.

There were, of course, tongues ready enough to say that any investigation into collaboration should begin at the top. Perhaps the strongest criticism of the authorities came from returning islanders and servicemen who had missed the Occupation. ("Guernsey people," wrote one soldier from the island, "acted disgustingly.") There was a different opinion from Frank Falla of G.U.N.S., whose record also gave him a right to speak:

"My own feeling is that ninety-eight per cent here were loyal to Britain and their neighbours. The two per cent who weren't did damage beyond all proportion to their number. But a lot of those who came back didn't

300

know what they were talking about, when blaming some of those who remained for 'collaboration'.

"You only know what they went through if you have been through something like it yourself. No one else has any right to judge.

"I do not blame Victor Carey for signing the much-criticised £25 reward notice. He was an elderly, extremely worried man; he had no choice; if he had not signed, the Germans would have put their own signature or anybody else's."

Frank Falla's tolerant attitude was shared by those who knew Carey best. They knew there was no question whatever of his loyalty to Britain; and they were certain that, in some of his actions, he had not realised the full implications of what he was doing. He had stuck to a thankless task for many years after the normal retiring age of a Bailiff, becoming the focus for the bitter criticism aroused by policies for which others were responsible. (At one time he was receiving an average of four anonymous letters of abuse every day.) In addition to all his other worries, he was without news of his two sons in the Forces. But to refrain from blame was one thing; to bestow Honours was more open to controversy.

We believe the main reason why there was no action against disloyal conduct was the feeling that it would be bad for British prestige to admit that, in the only British territory to be occupied, everybody had not behaved perfectly: and this is rather borne out by the fact that, immediately after the Liberation, Churchill demanded that a list of Honours for the islanders should be prepared as quickly as possible.

He lost office soon after: but the new Labour Government was ready to carry on the traditions of the British ruling class. Carey's acceptance of a Knighthood, in the Occupation Honours announced in December 1945, had the unfortunate result of reviving bitterness against him which he deserved to be spared, and which might well have been forgotten while his many lovable qualities and fine services to Guernsey were remembered.*

Many names on the Occupation Honours List** (led by knighthoods for Coutanche, Leale and Carey) won general approval. There was particular pleasure at the British Empire Medals for Bill Bertram, of the Fauvic escape beach, and for Harry Bichard, a stocky quarryman who had volunteered to unload foodships during the worst of the R.A.F. raids on St. Peter Port. But it seemed unfortunate that, for the most part, the Honours were only given to those in high places and official positions, and included few who had risked their lives doing anything which might offend the enemy. There was nothing for Captain Noyon, who had taken vital documents to England; nothing for the le Page brothers, who would have been shot if they had been caught taking out German naval blueprints for M. Lambert; nothing for those who had charted German defences in Jersey, or for Stanley Green who had photographed a schedule of them; nothing for Frank Falla of G.U.N.S.; no recognition for any of those who had suffered and sometimes died in exile for hearing and repeating B.B.C. news, or helping escaped Russian prisoners.

It is understandable that the island authorities, fearing anything that might bring reprisals on their people, should have felt—rightly or wrongly—that they could not countenance anything like sabotage or resistance. But it seemed strange for this attitude to be carried over, by the Home Office, to the bestowal of awards after the war was over***, and it struck the present authors as even more strange, when they began their work, that no attempt had

* We would like to add a tribute we heard paid to him in 1954: "He never baulked at meeting the Germans and backing the rest of us when necessary, and that trait has always endeared him to us. We always looked upon him as a good boss, and he never forgot to be kind to those who worked for him."

** Given in full in Appendix III.

*** Sir John Leale has commented to us on this passage: "It might be difficult for a Government which is a signatory to the Hague Convention to recommend Honours for those who broke the Convention."

been made to compile a Roll of Honour of those who, like Canon Cohu, had died for their courage. We found it hard even to get a complete list of islanders who had ended their lives in gaols and concentration camps, and to separate out the patriots from the thieves and Back Marketeers.

For the general desire seemed to be to forget anything to do with the Occupation as quickly as possible—except as a useful adjunct for the tourist trade, which was to resume its former importance. Jersey, with business acumen, was soon charging 6d. a head to see the underground German hospital; and 25,000 people a year paid to visit the Museum of Occupation relics, including whips found at "Gestapo Headquarters". Guernsey tried to grow mushrooms in its underground hospital, failed, boarded it up and then followed Jersey's example in opening it for tourists. Mrs. Green, of *"Heil Churchill"* fame, could show her summer lodgers in St. Peter Port the piece of a sheet she had embroidered in Caen Prison. Listening to tales of the Occupation became a recognised tourist attraction for wet days, with the Celtic Jerseymen leading the way in gay stories of how they had led the Germans a merry dance and generally defied them. In Alderney, tourists were shown a sea wall with marks on it, and told that they were bullet marks made when the Germans lined up and shot Russian prisoners who had become too feeble to work.

One curious thing was the refusal to take any warning from the Occupation for the future. It had been shown how precarious, in war or even in depression, was an economy based on external trade, tomatoes, and tourists. But there was little attempt to become more self-sufficient. More and more agricultural land was taken in Guernsey by the spreading glasshouses; fewer and fewer young men in Sark would learn farming or fishing, when there were tourists to be driven round the island at £2 a trip.

CHAPTER XLV

"YOU MUST SPEAK AS YOU FIND"

Can any good thing come out of an Occupation? Sir John Leale talked about this in a speech soon after the Liberation. He pointed out that thousands of Germans, perhaps hundreds of thousands, had passed through the islands, and he went on:

"What did those men think of us? What kind of reports did they take back with them about the British people?

"I like to feel that those who came here with a respect for the nation to which we belong, found no reason to lose that respect, and that those who came with their hearts full of hatred for us had cause to think again.

"If I am right, I say that if Guernsey was able to do but little in winning the war, she may by her behaviour towards the foes of her country have made a real contribution to the future peace of the world."

Here again there was a characteristic difference between Guernsey and Jersey. "I never held the opinion," said Leale, "that it didn't matter a scrap what the Germans felt about us." Most people in Jersey, following the lead of Sir Alexander Coutanche, would have retorted that they did not care in the slightest what the Germans thought of them, and that they did not want any future friendship.

Up to the time of writing, it has been rare indeed for a German soldier to revisit Jersey; nor would any German be likely to get a Labour Permit there, except under very special circumstances. But in Guernsey, as with Werner Rang and Phyllis Baker in Sark, it is possible for an ex-enemy to return and settle down with a local girl. Sergeant Hesse, of the German billeting office—a job which might have been expected to make him universally unpopular—married the Guernsey girl whom he had met when he went swimming during the Occupation, and he became manager of the Berthelot Restaurant in St. Peter Port.

Sir Victor Carey, who said he never wanted to see a German again, was unusual among Guernseymen. Others, led by Leale and Sherwill, were eager for *rapprochements*; and Leale's hopes that the Occupation might help world peace and understanding found some support in the friendships between the islanders and their invaders which were to survive the war.

Obermeyer, the Harbour Master at St. Peter Port, was so much respected by the fishermen that they signed a petition asking for his early release as a prisoner-of-war. He and his opposite number, Captain Franklin, the Guernsey Harbour Master, would regularly exchange Christmas cards: and Franklin's son married a German girl after the war. The Hathaways went to Bavaria to re-visit their friend Prince von Oettingen. The Sherwills made a tour of Germany, calling on Baron von Aufsess and Major Bandelow.

By then the Baron was re-united with his wife in their *Schloss* at Oberaufsess—after two tormenting years when, as a prisoner of war in England, he had no news of her and could not even find out whether she had survived imprisonment by the Gestapo. After dinner one night, Sherwill brought up the puzzling matter of how his wife and children had not been deported from Guernsey. Von Aufsess explained how he had disobeyed General Müller's order. Sherwill asked, "If Müller had discovered—what would have happened to you?" Von Aufsess smiled and drew a finger across his throat.

When they went away, May Sherwill wrote in the Visitors Book: "May God bless the House of Aufsess. Now the war ends we'll always be friends."

For most of the German soldiers, times were bad just

305

after the war. Major Bandelow, the Sherwills found, had taken a job as a groundsman; and Sherwill, believing that he had helped to save those arrested over the Symes-Nicolle affair, saw that money was sent to him. Count von Schmettow, to whom many more islanders had reason to be grateful, had a particularly harsh time. His home was lost behind the Iron Curtain, and he was overtaken by illness from his old lung wound of the First World War. Even when released from internment in 1947 he could only live on charity until, in 1951, his pension was restored.

Many other Germans also faced desperate conditions for several years, and some food parcels and clothes were sent them from the islands. Harrison of the *Jersey Evening Post* heard that one of the Germans who had censored his paper was in need of food, with his wife ill and expecting a baby. He sent a parcel.

During the last Christmas of the Occupation, when supplies for Germans and civilians alike had been at their lowest, Miss Nowlan of Steiner's Language School in St. Helier, had sometimes been offered ill-spared gifts of food by German soldiers who were taking English lessons. After the war she found herself in Germany, where food was just as short, and she was glad to give some help in return to the families of the same men.

While some Channel Islanders bore the marks of Belsen and Buchenwald on their bodies and their minds, others remembered kindness at Biberach and Laufen. Charles Roche of Jersey Airport, on his way to Oberammergau in 1951, visited the man who had run the internment camp at Biberach. "But why have you come to see me?" asked the German. "I wanted to thank you," said Roche, "for having been lenient when you might have been strict." Sherwill, similarly, had grateful recollections of the Commandant at Laufen: and perhaps we can best leave it to Sherwill to sum up what can be said on the enigma of the German character, in some words actually written during his internment, scribbled in pencil in a little blue notebook which he had with him:

"From Jews and Poles in this camp I have heard tales of horrible German cruelties, and I have little if any doubt that they are substantially true. Brought up in the English tradition, I detest many things which I know to exist in this country, and I have not failed to detect traits in the German character which to me are obnoxious. But I have not failed to observe much that is admirable in that character, and, strange as it may seem, almost without exception I have experienced courtesy and consideration from Germans, often genuine kindness, and in one instance chivalry of a very high order."

As the underground German leaflet had put it, *Death to the Nazis! Long Live a Free Germany!* . . . "I suppose it's the same in every nation," said John le Page, the Guernsey fisherman, to the present authors. "There's good and there's bad." And Mrs. le Page, who lived under the Occupation for five years, nodded her head and said "You must speak as you find."

Above all nations is humanity . . . And above all other human compulsions, perhaps, is that of earning a living somehow or other. So far as many people on the islands were concerned, it seemed they had long since stopped giving any thought to the Germans at all, one way or another. Total war might have given place to imperfect peace; the world might be arguing over German rearmament, the statesmen might be wrangling, the scientists inventing ever more terrible weapons; the Channel Islanders did not bother much about such things in 1939, and they did not seem to bother much about them now. The new glasshouses were going up and up in Guernsey, and the growers were watching the price of tomatoes at Covent Garden. There was an argument about whether the official tourist brochure should have a bathing belle on the front cover, or have something more distinctive. Guernsey abolished all super tax, first introduced during the war, and thus brought itself more into line with Jersey in offering attractions to the sorely taxed. The Channel Islands were themselves again . . . And let it be said that, after all, they are as pleasant islands

307

as you can find anywhere for a retreat from the world, when the breeze blows fresh up the Russel and the sun warms the narrow lanes; so that one almost feels sorry for these Germans who, alone among their visitors, cannot count on a glad welcome if they return. And if, to the casual tourist, all the fear and dreariness of the Occupation seems forgotten for ever in the summer sunshine, the secret stories of those five years still live on in the memories with which each man is rewarded or tormented, and which each man keeps to himself. Memories which cannot be explained, in a few words, to outsiders who could never imagine what an Occupation is like; memories of heroes and cowards and true friends and informers; memories of humiliation and memories with half a smile; memories sour and memories proud.

THE END

APPENDIX I. THE GERMAN DIRECTIVES FOR THE OCCUPATION OF THE CHANNEL ISLANDS

A wireless signal, "The capture of the British Channel Islands is necessary and urgent," was sent from Berlin at 15.00 hours on Thursday, June 20, 1940. It was followed the same day by a more detailed directive from Admiral Schniewind, Chief of the Naval Operations Staff, the salient points of which were as follows:.

Berlin, 20th June, 1940.

From: Naval High Command,

Naval War Staff.

To:　　Flag Officer Commanding Northern France.
　　　　and other Operational Commands.

Reference: Occupation of the Large Channel Islands and the Island Ushant.

The expeditious occupation of the three large British Channel Islands, Alderney, Guernsey and Jersey, and the French island of Ushant (near Brest) is essential.

The British Channel Islands in enemy hands constitute a forward enemy observation position right in our own flank, to the detriment of our own naval and air operations in the centre and west of the Channel. The island of Ushant is highly important as a navigational point for shipping and for aircraft.

As far as is known the old defence installations on the Channel Islands have not been extended.

On the island of Jersey there is an old casemate fort for the defence of the harbour of St. Helier, and this is alleged to have 7 guns of questionable value all pointing towards the south.

Little is known of the defences of the harbour of St. Peter Port on Guernsey. But their value is questionable.

Nothing is known about the defence installations on Alderney, but in 1939 mention was made of the importance of the island as a base for anti-submarine vessels and motor-boats. Should the Alderney harbour of St. Anne have been used for this purpose then auxiliary defences can be expected.

On all three islands there are airfields which were used in peace time. On Alderney the airfield is supposed to have been taken over by the R.A.F. and extended . . .

The occupation of the Channel Islands and Ushant should, from a practical point of view, be carried out simultaneously by units of naval assault parties already in northern France. Army and air support will be arranged in co-operation with the local commanders of these armed services. The troops should be transported to the islands on coastal vessels or tugs seized in the area in question. Light weapons appear to be necessary in order to facilitate the formation of a bridge-head and for defence against attacks by enemy aircraft. In any case, Luftwaffe support for the landing appears essential. . . .

Should Naval Group Command West consider it necessary, additional staff can be recruited for the preparation and execution of the operation.

Note: This directive gives further confirmation of the complete ignorance of the Germans about the islands—for instance, the Alderney airfield had never been taken over by the R.A.F., nor the harbour used as an anti-submarine base. The latest source of information available to German Intelligence was a pre-war visitor to the islands.

APPENDIX II. BRITISH COMMANDO RAIDS DURING THE OCCUPATION

Code Name

"AMBASSADOR"	13-14	July	1940	Guernsey	(p. 68 ff.)
"DRYAD"	2-3	September	1942	Casquets	(p. 176)
"BRANFORD"	7	September	1942	Burnou	(p. 176)
"BASALT"	3-4	October	1942	Sark	(p. 177 ff.)
"HUCKABACK"	27-8	February	1943	Herm	(p. 216)
"HARDTACK 28"	25-6	December	1943	Jersey	(p. 194)
"HARDTACK 7"	25-6 27-8	December	1943	Sark	(p. 184)

APPENDIX III. THE OCCUPATION HONOURS

(From *The Times*, December 12, 1945)

The following Channel Islanders are being honoured by the King in recognition of their services during the enemy occupation of the islands:

KNIGHTS

Victor Gosselin CAREY, Bailiff of Guernsey.

Alexander Moncrieff COUTANCHE, Bailiff of Jersey.

The Rev. John LEALE, Jurat of the Royal Court and President of the Controlling Committee, States of Guernsey.

C.B.E.

Charles W. DURET AUBIN, Attorney-General, Jersey.

Jurat E. A. DOREY, President, Dept. of Finance and Economics, Member of the Supreme Council, Jersey.

A. J. SHERWILL, H.M. Procureur, Guernsey.*

O.B.E.

Jurat T. J. BREE, President, Dept. of Agriculture, Member of Supreme Council, Jersey.

C. J. CUMING, Constable (Mayor) and Chief of Police of the parish of St. Helier, Jersey.

R. H. JOHNS, Deputy, Member of the Controlling Committee, Guernsey.

R. N. McKINSTRY, M.O.H. Jersey.

H. E. MARQUAND, States Supervisor and Treasurer, Guernsey.

* Sir Ambrose Sherwill was knighted in 1949, after succeeding Sir Victor Carey as Bailiff of Guernsey in 1946.

M.B.E.

A. N. Symons, Health Officer, Guernsey.

Miss K. J. Bond, Member of Queen's Institute of District Nursing, Jersey.

H. F. Ereaut, Secretary, Dept. of Finance and Treasurer, Jersey.

L. A. Guillemette, Secretary to the President of the Controlling Committee, Guernsey.

Miss E. Hall, A.R.R.C., Matron, Guernsey Emergency Hospital.

G. Heggs, Assistant States' Engineer, Engineer in Charge of States' Water Board, Guernsey.

J. H. Loveridge, Secretary of the Essential Commodities Committee, Guernsey.

Miss E. J. Young, Member, Queen's Institute of District Nursing, Guernsey.

BRITISH EMPIRE MEDAL

W. J. Bertram, Farmer and Deputy, Fauvic, Jersey.

H. T. Bichard, labourer, St. Sampson's Guernsey.

T. Camp, postman, Gorey, Jersey.

T. G. Cross, Senior Sergt. of Police, Jersey.

Miss J. Fraser, manager, Communal Restaurant, St. Helier, Jersey.

A. P. Lamy, Inspr., Guernsey Police Force.

Mrs. E. E. Langmead, cook, Commnnal Kitchen, St. Peter Port, Guernsey.

Miss M. M. Messervy, lady supt., St. John's Nursing Division, Jersey.

J. Remphry, chief officer, Fire Brigade, Jersey.

APPENDIX IV. STATISTICS FOR ILLEGITIMATE BIRTHS DURING THE OCCUPATION

(See pp. 89-90)

JERSEY

	Total Births	Total Illegitimate	Percentage Illegitimate
1939	862	51	5.1
1940	723	35	4.8
1941	458	28	6.1
1942	404	29	7.2
1943	444	35	7.9
1944	527	58	11.0
1945	475	34	7.2

GUERNSEY

	Total Births	Total Illegitimate	Percentage Illegitimate
1938	834	45	5.4
1939	744	40	5.4
1940	568	35	6.2
1941	243	15	6.2
1942	261	49	18.8*
1943	337	55	16.3*
1944	395	86	21.8
1945	393	80	20.3

SARK

1939	7	1
1940	7	1
1941	3	1
1942	6	Nil
1943	3	Nil
1944	3	1
1944	3	1
1945	4	Nil

* During the Occupation these figures were circulated by Dr. Symons, the Health Officer, to the members of the Controlling Committee of the States of Guernsey. His memorandum ended: "The only possible comment seems to be *C'est la Guerre.*" To which Raymond Falla, the Agricultural Officer, added the marginal annotation *"C'est la Femme!"*

A DOCTOR'S OCCUPATION

The dramatic true story of life in Nazi-occupied Jersey

John Lewis

In 1939 Dr John Lewis was building up a successful general practice in Jersey.

In 1940, as the Germans were poised to invade the Channel Islands, he managed to get his pregnant wife across to England. He then returned to Jersey to look after his patients.

In 1945 the German garrison surrendered to the British. Five years of occupation were at an end.

This is the story of Dr Lewis's experiences during those years: a first-hand account of life in the only British territory to be controlled by Nazi Germany during World War II.

NEW ENGLISH LIBRARY

HITLER'S FORTRESS ISLANDS

Germany's occupation of the Channel Islands

Carel Toms

Throughout the Second World War the Nazi jackboot was only planted once on British soil: in the Channel Islands. And within months these beautiful islands were turned into a massively organised and impregnable fortress.

Today all that remains of Hitler's stronghold are overgrown gun emplacements, decaying bunkers and a scattering of gaunt towers. But they are a legacy of half a decade of despair and subversion which the Islanders suffered at the hands of the Germans.

The men of the Islands were forced to work at insane speed to finish the immense programme born of a fanatical desire to surround the territory with walls of steel. It proved to be one of Hitler's greatest follies, for the gigantic installations against invasion were never used; the vast and brilliantly designed coastal defences were never attacked.

The grim story of the building of Hitler's futile fortress is told in revealing text and by contemporary photographs, most of them never previously published. They were taken by the Islanders themselves at great personal risk of imprisonment, punishment and even death.

NEW ENGLISH LIBRARY

JAMES ROUCH

Tiger

They were behind enemy lines as the battle for Normandy raged around them; their radio was useless; and between them and their base lay the deadliest weapon of the entire German army – a lone Tiger tank.

The Tiger Mark 1 – the pride of the mighty Panzer divisions; the scourge of the Allied forces. To fight against one was a nightmare; to fight against one and survive was close to a miracle.

Each man in Sergeant Ellis's patrol had his own reason for hating them. Now they had their chance for revenge. Six men against a monstrous machine of death, and all the exits were blocked . . .

The War Machines

"In the machines those boffins keep bodging up it's more like bloody suicide. And as if it's not bad enough going to war in their death-traps, in this god-forsaken hell-hole of a desert, we have to have Hoskins the only sergeant in the war who actually enjoys being shot at – and takes a sadistic pleasure in sharing the experience with his less heroic subordinates. That crazy bastard's antics are more terrifying than the entire German army . . ."

How Frank Davies and his mates coped with everything the enemy and their superiors threw at them, and how they hit back, makes an explosive novel of World War 2.

Gateway to Hell

Monte Cassino, impregnable core of the German defences, looming over the most savage battlefield in Italy, stands between the advancing Allies and their goal. Lieutenant Saville's Assault Engineers and their escort from the crack New Zealand 2nd Division are ordered to destroy a key position in the shadow of the Monastery. None of them can foresee the ferocity of the enemy's attempt to obstruct them. Cut off, forced to shelter behind the corpses of their comrades, they face the fanatical paratroops of the Hermann Goering Division. With the Paras, pitting his wits against Saville and staking his life on success, is Hauptmann Wolff, the engineer who designed the strongpoint. It is a struggle neither can afford to lose, because whoever holds the Fuehrer Emplacement controls the road to Rome – and the armies are poised for battle.

NEW ENGLISH LIBRARY

Book Tokens

**Give them
the pleasure of choosing**

Book Tokens can be bought
and exchanged at most
bookshops.

NEL BESTSELLERS